Colin Wilson was born in Leicester in 1931 and was educated at the Gateway School, Leicester. He left school at sixteen, and for eight years worked at a series of labouring jobs. Since the publication of his first book, *The Outsider*, in 1956, he has been a full-time writer. He has lectured widely in Germany, Scandinavia and America, and has been a visiting professor in America in 1966, 1967, and 1974. His many books include: *Religion and the Rebel, The Age of Defeat, Origins of the Sexual Impulse, Poetry and Mysticism, An Encyclopaedia of Murder, A Casebook of Murder, Voyage to a Beginning, Order of Assassins, New Pathways in Psychology, The Craft of the Novel, The Occult* and *Strange Powers*. He is also the author of many novels including *Ritual in the Dark, Adrift in Soho, The Glass Case, The Black Room* and *The Philosopher's Stone.*

Also by Colin Wilson and available in Abacus

STRANGE POWERS

Colin Wilson

THE STRENGTH TO DREAM

Literature and the Imagination

ABACUS edition published in 1976
by Sphere Books Ltd
30/32 Gray's Inn Road, London WC1X 8JL

First published in Great Britain
by Victor Gollancz Ltd 1963

Reprinted 1979

To Dan and Jeanette Danziger
With Affection

Set in VIP Times

*Printed in Great Britain by Hazell Watson & Viney Ltd
Aylesbury, Bucks*

Contents

Acknowledgments

The selection on pages 59–60 from 'Musée de Beaux Arts' by W. H. Auden is reprinted from *The Collected Poetry of W. H. Auden* by permission of Random House, Inc., and Faber and Faber Ltd. Copyright 1940 by W. H. Auden.

The poem 'On Some South African Novelists' on page 60 is from *Selected Poems* by Roy Campbell, published by Henry Regency Company.

The Selections on pages 64 and 82 from 'Portrait of a Lady' and 'The Waste Land' are reprinted from *Complete Poems and Plays* by T. S. Eliot by permission of Harcourt, Brace, and World, Inc., and Faber and Faber Ltd.

The quotation from 'Soles Occidere et Redire Possunt' on page 201 is taken from *Leda* by Aldous Huxley. Reprinted by permission of Harper and Row, Publishers, and Chatto and Windus Ltd.

The various selections from *Collected Poems* by W. B. Yeats on pages xv, 12, 13, 14 and 15 are reprinted by permission of the publishers, The Macmillan Company, and A. P. Watt and Son. Copyright 1928, 1933 by The Macmillan Company. Copyright 1940, 1956, 1961, by Bertha Georgie Yeats.

The quotations from 'Land of Heart's Desire' on page 11 are reprinted from Yeats's *Collected Plays* by permission of The Macmillan Company and A. P. Watt and Son.

Preface

When the idea of this book first came to me, its aim was simple; to examine the question, What is imagination, and how does it work? I had tried to gain some enlightenment from Sartre's book *L'Imaginaire*, but found it baffling; all I could gather, peering through Sartre's prickly hedge of abstract language, was that imagination means forming an *image* of something or someone not actually present.

This seemed to provide an obvious and simple picture of the imagination as an aid to experience, a kind of catalyst. Let me suggest an example. I find my headmaster a terrifyingly dignified man, and I cannot avoid blushing and stammering when I speak to him. One day, I see him being chased out of someone's front garden by a large dog, divested of his dignity. From that day onward I lose my fear of him, since I am now more deeply aware of him as a human being like myself. On the other hand, I may never be so fortunate as to see him being chased by a dog, but by an effort of imagination, I can create the scene in my mind. The effect is not as powerful as if I had actually seen it, but it still helps to make me less afraid of him. The imagination in this case aims at being a carbon copy of possible reality.

This might be called the 'social realist' definition of imagination, the kind of thing that some Soviet commissar might have in mind if he said, 'A good engineer makes use of his imagination', or what an American business magnate would mean if he said, 'The man I need for the job must have vitality and imagination'. It is a useful and practical faculty, whose aims can be defined as easily as those of any other gadget. But plainly, this definition would be useless in writing of the imagination of Poe or Dostoevsky.

With certain nineteenth-century romantics, one suspects, the imagination is a kind of psychological balancing pole whose purpose is to keep the writer sane in a world that horrifies him. Here, the relation of imagination to the practical world seems to be nebulous. For convenience, this type of imagination might be labelled 'compensative'.

Yet it might be objected that compensative imagination is only a special case of the 'social realist' imagination. Thurber's Walter Mitty uses his imagination to compensate for inadequacies in his practical life; a social realist would claim that Mitty is simply abusing his imaginative faculty. Extending the argument, it is easy to see that Poe and Dostoevsky might somehow be explained as special cases of abuse, with complicated roots.

Having considered the matter this far, I saw that my attempt at a simple and practical definition was evading many of the issues in which I am most interested. It was ruthlessly pruning and lopping off complexities, and then pretending they had never existed.

The problem presented itself to me in a new light one day. I happened to pick up a volume of ghost stories by a writer whom I had never read – H. P. Lovecraft – and browsed through it. The first story, *In the Vault*, was about a lazy and inefficient undertaker who makes a coffin too short to house the body of a tall man, and who therefore chops off the feet of the corpse. This happens in an icy winter, when the ground is too hard to bury anyone, so the coffins are stored in a shed on the edge of the graveyard. One day the undertaker accidentally locks himself in the shed. He piles coffins on top of one another in order to reach a high window. Uppermost is the coffin of the man without feet. As the undertaker is halfway through the window, he feels his ankles being grasped and bitten. He kicks out wildly and manages to excape. And Lovecraft has saved for the last line the disclosure about the cutting off of the corpse's feet, to give the reader a final thrill of horror.

Clearly, Lovecraft hoped to give his readers nightmares. But he succeeded only in amusing me. It struck me that, treated in a slightly different way – by Petronius or Apuleius, for example – the story could be extremely funny. What was the difference between my state of mind and Lovecraft's?

The next day, I read more Lovecraft, and started to talk to my wife about the problems of imagination that are raised by his work. She mentioned that Wells's novel *Men Like Gods* has a kind of imprecision that is somehow related to Lovecraft's. The use of the word 'imprecision' pulled me up. It implies a goal that has been missed. But does all imagination have the same goal? According to the social-realist definition, each act of imagination has a different goal, and the goals have in common only some movement towards an ideal society. While I would like to see an 'ideal society', I do not feel that its achievement would be the end of human evolution; on the contrary, it might only leave men free to concentrate on the real problems of evolution. All this was implicit in the problem of imagination.

I am interested in goals and values. Whether or not the question is meaningless, I cannot stop myself wondering about human life and society: what's it all in aid of? Every time someone uses the word 'ought', I want to probe and find to what system of ultimate values he is relating it.

Every time I found a writer intriguing – either because he seemed to be saying something important, or because he seemed to be an interesting kind of crank – I found myself returning to the problem of his imagination. In writers as different as Graham Greene and Kazantzakis, Lovecraft and Aldous Huxley, Andreyev and Dürrenmatt, I tried to discern the thread connecting them. Only one arbitrary statement could be made: in every writer who possesses intensity of imagination, *the imagination is closely bound up with his sense of values* – that is to say, ultimately with his notion of the meaning and purpose of human existence.

The ideal aim of such a survey would be to establish certain standards of value for art and literature – standards that might have a wider application than the makeshift values of fashionable 'literary criticism'. While I was engaged on this book, the BBC perpetrated a musical hoax; two or three men in a studio banged tin cans and made strange noises; the result was announced as a new composition by a Czech serial composer Pyotr Zak. The 'piece' was criticised seriously by many music critics. The point was well made. No one doubts the sincerity of Webern and his younger followers, or the 'logic' of serial composing; but a logical argument can be pursued to a point where it loses all contact with commonly appreciated standards of values. It would have been equally easy to read aloud a 'newly discovered' fragment of James Joyce, or a new Canto by Ezra Pound, and to improvise nonsense. It would certainly be easy enough to improvise a new epic poem by an American Beat poet, filling in with grunts, groans and perhaps even cruder noises. Each new school of incomprehensible music, painting or literature argues in its own jargon, remote from ordinary usage, but somehow developed 'logically' from the standards of Mozart or Rubens or Shaw.

If certain general laws could be discerned from attempting to grapple with the eccentricities and imprecisions of different imaginations, then the attempt would be worth making. This was the attitude with which I approached this book.

Introduction

The Crisis in Modern Literature

Most published writers receive their share of manuscripts in the post. Some months ago two parcels arrived at about the same time, one sent to me by a schoolteacher friend who was living abroad, the other from a young writer I had known for many years in London. The manuscripts were first novels. On glancing through them, I was struck by the similarity of theme and treatment. Both dealt with dissatisfied young men living in dingy rooms in London, drifting from café to café, getting involved in casual sexual relations, discussing religion and politics with a sense of futility rather than enthusiasm.

It is not so surprising that two young writers should produce strikingly similar novels. In *Crome Yellow*, Aldous Huxley makes Mr Scogan describe the plot of a novel written by the hero:

> 'Little Percy . . . was never good at games, but he was always clever. He passes through the usual public school and the usual university and comes to London, where he lives among the artists. He is bowed down with melancholy thought; he carries the whole weight of the universe upon his shoulders. He writes a novel of dazzling brilliance; he dabbles delicately in Amour, and disappears, at the end of the book, into the luminous Future.'

In fact, Mr Scogan's description will loosely fit any number of novels written in the first twenty years of this century, from Joyce's *Portrait of the Artist* to Compton Mackenzie's *Sinister Street* and Scott Fitzgerald's *This Side of Paradise*. Heroes tend to run in types. Dozens of nineteenth-century heroes are carbon copies of Young Werther; dozens of Russian heroes after Turgeniev are vague revolutionists and indefatigable talkers. This, I am inclined to believe, is not necessarily imitation. Put young authors in glass cages and forbid them to read any contemporary fiction, and they would probably still produce novels with interchangeable plots and heroes. Any author who sets out to write honestly of his time will find that there are a limited number of attitudes to draw upon.

The author of one of the manuscripts I have mentioned produced a parody of Sartre some years before, and won a magazine competition with it. I cannot quote it accurately, but it went something like this: 'I look at my lumpish football boots, caked with mud. Suddenly I am overtaken by a sense of absurdity. What am I doing here? Why am I dressed like this? Why does that man keep on blowing a whistle? The turf seems to take on a grisly quality, like uncooked meat. They are shouting to me to stop the ball. The rules of the game define a necessity; for them, victory is a meaningful crescendo preceded by a muddy overture. Salauds! They preserve their complacency by submitting to the tyranny of arbitrary rules. With deliberation, I kick the ball towards my own goal.' But parody is not rejection; for in due course, I find the hero of my friend's own novel staring at his reflection in a pool of tea on a café tabletop, and brooding on his sense of boredom and purposelessness.

Moreover, the situation has a ring of familiarity. My mind is carried back to my own attempts at a first novel, to the dissatisfied hero making himself cups of tea and trying to dam the stream of consciousness with chunks of metaphysics. My journals for that period are filled with entries about the problem of form in the novel, and frequently refer to Eliot's comment on *Ulysses*: '[Joyce's method] is simply a way of controlling, of ordering, of giving a shape and a significance to the immense panorama of futility and anarchy which is contemporary history.' The first novel of any writer who takes himself seriously is a personal statement; it says, in effect: 'This is what I see, this is *how* I see the world.' It ought, ideally, to begin from a total perception grasped by the novelist at the moment he takes his pen to the first blank sheet of paper. But there can be no 'total perception' of anarchy; so he must build with hundreds of unconnected fragments and impressions. Even a plot implies direction, a way of connecting up these impressions. So there can be no plot, only an unselective description of the day-to-day life of an isolated individual.

W. B. Yeats has a three-line poem that goes to the heart of the matter:

> Shakespearean fish swam the sea, far away from land;
> Romantic fish swam in nets coming to the hand;
> What are all those fish that lie gasping on the strand?

The Shakespearean imagination was detached, impersonal. He told stories as Homer did and the old ballad singers. Innumerable critics have remarked that it is possible to guess very little about Shakespeare's life from his plays.

The Romantics felt the need to speak about *themselves*. Wordsworth was at his worst when telling a story, and at his best in philosophical and personal passages. The Romantic poet often conceived himself as a teacher of society. Goethe invented the 'novel of education'. Fielding and Swift had taken care to sugar-coat the pill of social criticism, but Zola and Ibsen delighted in the scandal they caused: Zola declared, in effect, that people *ought* to like novels about conditions. With the decay of the church, writers scrambled for the pulpit. They also thought of themselves as scientists and social historians, and priests. Balzac was the 'chronicler' of his age; Zola's novels expounded a theory of heredity; Flaubert preached art as a form of salvation.

From this development in the nineteenth century, one might almost have expected the artist to go on to claim political power, to announce himself as the philosopher-king. But by the beginning of the twentieth century, the messianic artist had virtually disappeared (Shaw was an exception, but he was never taken seriously anyway). In the church, the burden of thought, the guardianship of society had been spread among many men. But writers like Ibsen and Tolstoy tried to be everything in one.

Only one school continued to flourish – the party of the 'priests', with its source in Flaubert. It is this school that created the most important literary tradition of the twentieth century. Its creed was 'art for art's sake' (which is to say, of course, for the pleasure it gives – i.e., for entertainment), but it had nothing in common with the attitude of the 'Shakespearean fish'. The new 'absolute artist' was still very much the priest. In a passage in *A Portrait of the Artist*, Joyce declares that the artist should have no opinions, and *Ulysses* is apparently a demonstration of the principle. But this is only on the surface. In fact, the writer is saying continuously: 'This is the way I see reality, and it is superior to all other ways of seeing reality.' This comes out most clearly in the 'Nausicaa' and 'Oxen of the Sun' chapters. In 'Nausicaa', a sentimental Irish girl sits on the beach and dreams about the 'dark, handsome man' who is watching her. The chapter opens in the language of the sentimental novelette of 1900; Gerty thinks of romance and weddings and of her own ineffable superiority. Then it switches to the dark, handsome stranger, who is Leopold Bloom; the language becomes flat, realistic, and we realise that Bloom's feeling about Gerty is purely libidinous. The chapter culminates in the scene of auto-eroticism that got the novel banned when it appeared as a magazine serial.

Joyce's attitude is even clearer in 'The Oxen of the Sun'. The scene is the waiting room of a hospital; in a nearby ward, a woman is in labour. The chapter begins by parodying the style of the Anglo-Saxon Chronicle, then parodies Malory, Pepys, Mrs Radcliffe, Dickens and modern journalism. A critic has pointed out that Joyce seems to be saying: 'See how these previous writers would have described this scene, erecting a screen of words and conventions between the reader and the subject. Then compare it with my own method . . .'

It is the whole concept of the *content* of art that has changed. It would be absurd to ask what Homer 'expresses'. He tells a story. In the course of telling the story, he may express various human qualities – heroism, wickedness, etc. But the content of Homer is, first and foremost, the story. Joyce is expressing his own vision of reality. Homer would never have said, as Joyce did: 'I expect nothing from the reader except that he should devote his life to studying my works.'

But a 'vision' is an instantaneous thing, and a work of literature depends on a story – or a form of some kind. So the 'problem of form' begins to worry the writer; and when he has found a 'form', it is a kind of string on which he can thread his incidents. The 'form' of a novel such as Mann's *Magic Mountain* is hardly important: the story of Hans Castorp in the sanatorium is not a story at all, but a series of intellectual discussions and observations of character, connected by the presence of the young hero. Hermann Hesse's characters take to the road and undergo a series of 'educating' experiences. The simplest 'thread' of all is autobiographical; this was favoured by Proust, Lawrence and Joyce.

The problem can be simply stated. The novel is an impersonal form, developed by men who wanted to entertain. The twentieth-century writer usually has an intensely personal viewpoint to express. The struggle lies in uniting the two. Certain writers without the true novelist's vocation – such as Gide or Aldous Huxley – got around the problem by incorporating chunks of their journals into their novels. This is a poor compromise. The idea is to lure the reader into studying their ideas by getting him interested in the story; but most sensible readers skip the journals of Edouard or Anthony Beavis and get back to the story.

One might say that certain modern novelists are trying to catch an intensely personal form of reality, to make a personal comment on existence, in a manner that is closely akin to music – and to the intimate form of chamber music rather than to symphonic composition. The quartets of Beethoven, or of Bartok or Bloch or Schönberg, are 'personal' comments and attempts at summaries. It is not difficult for a musician, or even a poet, to make a completely personal statement. (Eliot's *Quartets* and Rilke's *Elegies* are also 'summaries'.) But such a statement, by its very nature, tends towards the static. It is the inner content of the experience that counts. This will be noticed in most accounts of 'mystical experience'; the place where the experience took place is described in a few lines, but a great deal of space is taken in trying to express the experience and its meaning. It is no accident that Joyce's theory of art was bound up with his idea of 'epiphanies' – moments observed by an artist that seem to symbolise whole areas of experience. 'Epiphanies' are sudden snapshots which are 'a revelation of the whatness of a thing', the moment in which 'the soul of the commonest object seems to us radiant'. Such a moment might occur in a glimpse of a servant girl saying goodbye to her lover on a doorstep at dusk. Stephen Dedalus describes another in the 'Aeolus' chapter of *Ulysses* – the two old ladies spitting out plumstones and throwing them off the top of Nelson's Pillar.[1]

The modern novelist, then, wants to 'say something' more often than to tell a story, and the result is not always communicative. The worst results can be found in many literary magazines published in the past thirty years; there are slabs of 'experimental prose' that show clearly that the writer wanted to 'say something' in the form of fiction, and had no desire to compromise by telling a story; unfortunately, he was usually uncertain about what he wanted to say. (In many cases, the solution would be to write music instead of prose.) The 'story' still remains the writer's chief excuse for expressing his views in life. And many writers feel instinctively the need to produce a 'big work' that will give them leisure to express their finest shades of perception of reality. But the old problem remains: what form will it take?

In a sense, Joyce and Proust were highly misleading examples. Both are widely read (or at least widely quoted) because they have reputation. Both flouted the convention that a novel must tell a story in an interesting manner. Proust swelled out a hundred pages of story with two thousand pages of essay and commentary, and called the result a novel – although less 'happens' in it than in the fifty pages of Gide's brief masterpiece *Theseus* (it might also be contended that Gide 'says' as much in those fifty pages as Proust in two thousand). But although Proust and Joyce may be beacons of hope to modern writers who are struggling to say something but who don't want to tell a story, it is nonsense to pretend that they have established a new form, the 'experimental novel'. No matter what their rewards may be, *Ulysses* and *A la Recherche du Temps Perdu* are about as readable as a telephone directory. They are not a new form of literature; they are fortunate exceptions to the rule that a novel must tell a story to be interesting to the general reader. And they are widely read for reasons of reputation rather than because they are 'successful' solutions of the problem of 'the experimental novel'.

All this is said not in disparagement of two great works but only to clear away a fallacy. When the casual reader opens a book by Samuel Beckett or Alain Robbe-Grillet, he is usually baffled. He explains his bewilderment by reasoning something like this: 'There have been great changes in twentieth-century literature. These changes are analogous to the change in the scientific outlook brought about by relativity and quantum theory. I find these novels incomprehensible for the same reason that a nineteenth-century physicist would find the work of Dirac incomprehensible.' But in fact, Einstein and Planck effected a *real* revolution in science, while Joyce and Proust remain exceptions who have by no means produced a justification for the experimental novel.

No one can pretend that hundreds of fishes 'gasping on the strand' amount to a satisfactory state of literature. In fact, critics have been predicting the end of the novel for the past thirty years. But the novel has not come to an end, just as philosophy did not come to an end with the great unsolved problems of the nineteenth century: it has simply gone backwards, or tackled easier problems. Twentieth-century pragmatism (and I including under this head philosophies as wide apart as those of G. E. Moore and the Vienna Group) simply declared that philosophy is not supposed to be concerned with the problem of the human condition, and so allowed philosophers to breathe again. In the same way, the English novel has regained a certain vitality in the 1950's by becoming a vehicle of social observation and social comment. But this state is not very satisfactory either. The 'serious' and Joycean school of novelists are as intent as ever on 'saying' something, on finding a way of writing that will finally tell the whole truth about the human condition. (I am thinking now of, for example, Nathalie Sarraute, Robbe-Grillet, Beckett.) And they become steadily less readable, while the social realists potter along with happy philistinism, producing good minor work.

The problem is to find a way of producing 'serious work' that doesn't eventually get bogged down in its own problems. Philosophy and literature have shown the same unfortunate tendency to pursue a line of thought until they end up in a cul-de-sac. It might almost be called a nineteenth-century habit, since it is so typical of nineteenth-century thought. Schopenhauer sets out to analyse the human estate, and ends by declaring that men must learn to reject life and its inevitable torments. Andreyev has a story about the return of Lazarus from the dead; Lazarus has 'faced reality', and all he can do now is to stare gloomily into space and look forward to dying again. Hawthorne's Ethan Brand sets out to find the 'unforgivable sin' (i.e., the knowledge of good and evil), and ends by discovering it 'in his own heart'; he commits suicide. Even

Goethe's Faust declares that, after years of searching for truth, he has come to the conclusion that 'we can know nothing'.

There is a tendency to believe that if you pursue truth too far, you will regret it. But literary pessimism should be scrutinised with a certain cynicism. If Schopenhauer and Andreyev had been honest about their conclusions, they would have committed suicide. In fact they both enjoyed comfortable living. Artzybasheff actually argued that the only logical response to the meaninglessness of life is suicide. Yet for a man who had faced the futility of life, he showed a lamentably peevish spirit towards the Russian revolution, and spent his last years in exile, writing bad-tempered books about Russia's new rulers.

It is to be suspected that literary pessimism is usually an expression of intellectual laziness. It can be used as a convenient cover for any amount of loose thinking. Like the subject of deaths at the end of many a tragedy, it produces an impression of conclusiveness. Like positivism, it preserves its virginity by declining to consider anything outside its own narrow bounds. And examined on its own territory it is almost impossible to refute.

The literary premises of experimental writing are closely analogous to those of pessimism. Pessimism discounts human effort. The extreme experimentalism associated with *Finnegans Wake* and Pound's *Cantos* discounts time and space and all that most people understand by 'meaning' (the kind of meaning that one finds in, for example, Shaw's plays). There are many critics who are still afraid to pronounce on the *Wake* and the *Cantos*, suspecting that the surface difficulty of these works hides an immense Hegelian structure, some complex message that will emerge only after years of study. But the premises of Pound and Joyce are opposed to such a meaning. The books are constructed on the theory that literature should be analogous to music. (Pound compared the *Cantos* to a Bach fugue.) When reading them, one is often reminded of Scriabin's attempts to 'expand' music – his 'colour organ' that would accompany music with bands of changing colour on a screen. One suspects that both Joyce and Pound often wished for a new art form that would somehow utilise music and painting to express their meanings.

It is easy to understand the state of mind of artists like

Joyce, Pound, Scriabin. When they looked back on the nineteenth century, they saw a series of gigantic structures that had all been abandoned, or that had been subsequently discredited. Balzac's *Human Comedy*, Wagner's *Ring*, Zola's Rougon-Macquart Cycle, Hegel's 'System', Marx's Workers' Utopia – all looked in retrospect like the work of an insane builder with a *folie de grandeur*. So the 'artist saviour' had to be dismissed, and Mr Eliot symbolised his dismissal by donning the uniform of the artist-bourgeois – the bowler hat and pinstriped trousers. A new set of literary forerunners had to be chosen. Instead of Ibsen and T. H. Huxley, it was now Baudelaire and Flaubert and Laforgue. Instead of humanism and optimism, the new basis was authoritarianism and tragedy.

All of this has led to the impasse of today, when it seems that literature and philosophy are in a state of crisis. A literature that is not in touch with its own traditions cannot make any significant advances; it is as bound up with the past as science and mathematics. But the literature of the twentieth century has been a series of rejections – down to the latest rejection of Joyce and Eliot by the Beat Generation and the Angry Young Men.

As a practising writer, I am personally concerned to discover how literature can become again purposeful and exuberant. That is why it seems to me worthwhile to keep holding post-mortems on the literary and philosophical failures of the past hundred years. There is no point in accepting pessimistic conclusions until you are convinced that they are inevitable. There are times when a slightly different approach to the facts produces completely different conclusions. This strikes me most clearly when reading the work of the generation that grew up during the first world war. The critical writings of Sir Richard Rees, for example, possess clear vision of our position today, based on a profound knowledge of the cultural history of Europe. He understands that great art can flourish only where a strong religious or cultural tradition exists, and can also understand how the rise of scientific scepticism has undermined religion and left nothing in its place. The forces that our knowledge sets in motion sweep us towards spiritual bankruptcy and destroy all possibility of a return to a fruitful tradition.

I can read Rees with sympathy, because he has a

xxi

profound sense of what religion means (a rare thing among humanist critics), and therefore of the impossibility of modern man being saved by a religious revival. Yet although his reasoning seems to me completely accurate, I cannot identify myself with his acceptance of our cultural exhaustion. It certainly *looks* as though the forces of history were preparing to dispense with Western civilisation, since Western man has failed to gain the conscious control of his political destiny that would make further progress possible. But is there ever a time when there is no point in trying to gain further conscious control? It is true that we know more of psychology and history than any previous civilisation, but what we know is still absurdly limited, and a thousand times smaller than what the medieval churchman *claimed* to know about man and the universe. The scientific method has discredited the churchman's eschatology without even beginning to supply an eschatology of its own. Only Marxism claims to replace the old vision of man, which it destroyed, with a new eschatology; and there are signs in Russia that its claims are becoming less dogmatic. Most of the other new 'ologies' make no claim to replace theology; they all admit modestly that their purpose is practical and limited. Darwinian biology and Freudian psychology may seem to discredit religion; but they make no claim to be religions in themselves.

The situation can be made clear by a metaphor. For the medieval church, the map of the universe contained no *terra incognita*. It claimed to cover all questions of human destiny, divine grace, human psychology, philosophy, astronomy and biology. The great cartographers worked busily to aid the church; Aquinas sketched in new areas; even Descartes tried to do his small share by demonstrating that science agreed with the church about the divine plan. (The church suppressed his book.) But when the disagreements between science and theology became too great, the scientists declared that the church's map would have to be scrapped completely. In its place was a great blank, marked from end to end 'terra incognita'. On this map, the scientists proceeded to fill in whatever small areas of certainty they had gained. They allayed any panic that their supporters might feel by explaining that, in due course, the scientific method would cover the whole universe just as thoroughly as the old map, and that, what is more, the new map would be guaranteed to be absolutely accurate.

But for many years now, the scientists have ceased to make any such claim. Some of them, such as Jeans and Eddington, admitted that they needed religion to complete their map of the universe. Another philosophical school, of which Bertrand Russell was a representative, has declared, in effect, that it doesn't know how to complete the map, but that it prefers the discomforts of scepticism to wild guesses and assertions that seem to be born of wishful thinking. So now, after a hundred years of scepticism, the map is still labelled 'terra incognita'. Unfortunately, most creative artists and thinkers cannot live happily in Lord Russell's state of stoical agnosticism. Rees is right to point out that we must either fill in the map or become enfeebled by a creative anaemia.

This enables me to define the cause of my own optimism. I would define my viewpoint as 'religious' only in the sense that, like anybody else, I would prefer as little *terra incognita* as possible. My disagreement with Freudian psychology and logical positivism is not directed against their positive aspects (i.e., their heuristic aspects); it is more often an irritation with the positivist who declares confidently that it is all right with him if the map never gets filled in, and who feels that he is thereby defending the scientific attitude.

It seems to me that we may be closer to a solution than we realise. The nineteenth-century attempt to create a new map may have failed; but it had its moments when it looked as if it might succeed. It is impossible to read many writers of the late nineteenth and early twentieth centuries and not feel how nearly it succeeded; the works of Zola, Wells, Tchekhov (who, strangely enough, was a great scientific optimist) are full of premonitions of the new 'authorised' map.

This brings me to the subject of the present book. As I said in my Preface, it struck me one day that many writers of fiction about the supernatural are making their own halfhearted attempts to supply themselves with a new map of the universe. They may or may not try to create a consistent 'system', but you can often see, from a mere phrase, an image, a symbol, what kind of 'map' a writer has in mind.

At this point, one always asks the same question: *If this writer's vision were true, what kind of universe would it presuppose?*

In short, the serious writer, no matter how feeble his talent, must always sketch in some kind of meaning over the *terra incognita* before he can create in comfort.

This, it seemed to me, is a new way of approaching the whole problem in our 'predicament'. The workings of the imagination might provide the clue – for it is the imagination that goes to work on 'familiarising' the *terra incognita*.

Philosophy begins from the assumption that the map *can* exist. Otherwise, the whole discussion would be pointless. Wittgenstein declared that such a map cannot exist because all the important things are unsayable, but his opinion is not general. Russell defined philosophy briefly as 'the attempt to understand the universe'. The Russell view is the traditional basis of philosophy.

If this view is accepted, then the 'plan' is possible, even if it has to admit that certain things fall outside its range. We might say that it already 'exists', in the sense that the answers to all mathematical problems 'exist' even if we do not happen to know them. And one method of finding the answer to a problem is to try out various solutions to see if they 'fit'. Even solutions that fail hopelessly can give an inkling of the nature of the correct solution.

To put it another way: the creative imagination attempts to produce a reality that is consistent with the 'facts' it sees around it. A study of the imaginations of different writers reveals something about the way these facts can be interpreted and, indirectly, something about the nature and implications of the facts.

Imaginative writers are like philosophers in one important respect: generally speaking, the more they attempt to be universal, the more they are likely to be inaccurate in detail. And sometimes this inaccuracy is so consistent that it can be regarded as a kind of astigmatism. The present book is a study of the inaccuracies of the imagination, because the inaccuracies of different imaginations tend to cancel one another out, and what is left is a perception of the general laws of imagination. These inaccuracies are sometimes so compulsive as to qualify as diseases. But the 'sick imagination' is only a starting point. The moment one uses the word 'sickness', one has admitted to having an idea of the meaning of health, of normality. And normality suggests the idea of an underlying order, a basic pattern. This pattern is, I suppose, what Plato would have called 'reality'. Hence this book could be called an attempt at a classification of unrealities, with a view to defining the concept of reality.

NOTE

1. This chapter, incidentally, contains another example of Joyce's belief in his own 'vision of reality'. After the 'older generation' of Irishmen have each told stories illustrating their idea of the noble or enterprising side of Irish character, Stephen tells his minutely realistic, apparently pointless story of the two old women. Joyce's criticism of 'false realities' is again implicit.

One

The Assault on Rationality

H. P. LOVECRAFT

'Life is a hideous thing, and from the background behind what we know of it peer demoniacal hints of truth which make it sometimes a thousandfold more hideous. Science, always oppressive with its shocking revelations, will perhaps be the ultimate exterminator of our human species . . . for its reserves of unguessed horrors could never be borne by mortal brains.'

Thus wrote that man of dubious genius, Howard Phillips Lovecraft, who died in 1937 at the age of forty-seven. Lovecraft has often been compared with the man who influenced him most, Poe. But in spite of superficial resemblances, the two have little in common. Poe's grave-yard romanticism sprang from weariness and a longing for peace. The spirit of Poe is epitomised in the lines 'For Annie', where the poet says from the grave:

> The sickness – the nausea—
>   The pitiless pain—
> Have ceased, with the fever
>   That maddened my brain—
> With the fever called 'Living'
>   That burned in my brain.

and goes on to speak of the ineffable peace he now feels, as he 'drinks of a water that quenches all thirst'. Lovecraft carried on a lifelong guerrilla warfare against civilisation and materialism, albeit he was a somewhat hysterical and neurotic combatant.

In some ways, Lovecraft is a horrifying figure. In his 'war with rationality', he brings to mind W. B. Yeats. But, unlike Yeats, he is sick, and his closest relation is with Peter Kürten, the Düsseldorf murderer, who admitted that his days in solitary confinement were spent conjuring up sexual-sadistic fantasies. Lovecraft is totally withdrawn; he

1

has rejected 'reality'; he seems to have lost all sense of health that would make a normal man turn back halfway.

H. P. Lovecraft lived most of his life in his native city, Providence, Rhode Island. He was born in 1890, son of a psycho-neurotic mother and a paretic father who died insane eight years after Howard's birth.[1] He was a tall, delicate child, and was a seni-invalid throughout his adolescence. He liked to spend whole days in his grandfather's library. In adulthood, he continued to live like an invalid, preferring to go out at night. He became a gentle friendly man, who loved arguing all night; fundamentally lonely, he would write a twenty-page letter on the slightest provocation. He was interested in archaeology, and spent much time in antiquarian exploration in New Orleans, Natchez and other 'old cities' of America.

He wrote his earliest stories for pulp magazines – particularly *Weird Tales*. He earned very little money by writing, and spent long periods of his life in semi-starvation. There was a brief marriage, with a woman several years his senior; but the need for loneliness was too strong in him, and they separated after two years, in 1926. Finally, after years of poverty and obscurity, he died in 1937 of an internal cancer and Bright's disease. Almost immediately, a 'Lovecraft cult' sprang up, to whose deflation Edmund Wilson devoted a scathing essay in *Classics and Commercials*. He began as one of the worst and most florid writers of the twentieth century, but finally developed a certain discipline and economy – although he always remained fond of words like 'eldritch' and 'grotesque', and such combinations as 'black clutching panic' and 'stark utter horror'. Two short novels, *The Shadow Out of Time*[2] and *The Case of Charles Dexter Ward*, are certainly minor classics of horror fiction; while at least a dozen stories deserve to survive.

What is so interesting about Lovecraft is the extraordinary consistency of his attempt to undermine materialism. His aim was 'to make the flesh creep': more than that, to implant doubts and horrors in the minds of his readers. If he had been told that one of his readers had died of horror, or been driven to an insane asylum, there can be no doubt that he would have been delighted. (If he had lived another year, he would have envied Orson Welles the nation-wide panic created by the War of the Worlds broadcast of 1938, when people fled the cities under the impression that the earth had been invaded by Martians.) In a tale called 'The Unnameable', the writer claims that one of his horror stories, published in 1922, had caused a magazine to be withdrawn from the bookstalls because it frightened the 'milksops'. Whether this is true or not, there can be no doubt that Lovecraft wished it to be true. Like Kürten, he wanted to horrify the world; fortunately, he chose a less direct means of doing it than the German mass-killer. To increase the illusion, he never set his stories in the remote past; in fact, he took care to date them close to the time they were written. He may have also taken a schoolboyish delight in trying to upset his friends. The hero of 'The Haunter of the Dark' is a writer who comes to a very nasty end; the writer's name is Robert Blake, and the story is dedicated to his fellow author, Robert Bloch. In the same story, Lovecraft mentions a treatise on magic by the Comte D'Erlette, in whom one cannot help suspecting a sly reference to August Derleth. But the stories of 'Robert Blake' mentioned in 'The Haunter of the Dark' have titles that might be by Lovecraft himself: 'The Burrower Beneath', 'The Stairs in the Crypt', 'Shaggai', 'In the Vale of Pnath'. It seems as if Lovecraft is saying: 'As a writer of horror stories, I am exposing myself to the same horrible forces that killed Blake' – as if, that is, he is also trying to frighten himself!

Lovecraft's early tales follow the usual pattern of ghost stories: man enters haunted house, leaves with his hair white. But he is very far from being satisfied with ordinary ghosts of the Shakespeare type (who can do nothing but walk the earth and utter warning of catastrophes). The horrors have to be tangible.[3] And in some of the stories, the effect is one of absurdity and pathos. A typical example is a tale called 'The Lurking Fear', leaning heavily on the style of Poe and Mrs Radcliffe. ('There was thunder in the air the night I went to the deserted mansion atop Tempest Mountain . . .') The story takes place in modern times, in a remote place in the Catskill Mountains, where Washington Irving set some of his weird tales. This is typical of Lovecraft; he is willing to make his setting modern, but it must be remote from civilisation, a kind of admission of defeat. A week before the story opens, a whole village has been destroyed by strange forces that are conjured up by a storm. There follows a characteristic episode; the narrator goes into a wooden hut to shelter from a storm, taking with him a newspaper reporter. The reporter looks out of the window, and stands there throughout the storm. When the narrator touches him on the shoulder he is found to be dead, his head 'chewed and gouged' by some monster.

Anyone who has seen a modern horror film will recognise the technique: there have to be a number of innocent 'fall guys' whose role is to be killed by the 'horror'. At the end of this story, the horror is revealed to be a horde of gorilla-like demons (of semi-human origin) who live underneath the 'deserted mansion'.

If it were not so atrociously written, this story would be funny. Lovecraft hurls in the adjectives ('monstrous', 'slithering', 'ghoulish', 'thunder-crazed') until he seems to be a kind of literary dervish who gibbers with hysteria as he spins.

But he must have realised that this kind of thing would terrify no one but a schoolboy, and soon he set out to build a complicated and erudite myth that would convince by its circumstantial detail and plausibility. Recognising that modern city dwellers are not likely to be impressed by ghosts and other such arbitrary exceptions to the laws of nature, he relies on the sense of disgust, and on a pseudo-historic or scientific framework. An early story, 'The Picture in the House' (1924), is a nearly convincing sketch of sadism. An old man who lives alone is so fascinated by a book about cannibals that he becomes a cannibal himself. The scene in which the old man drools over the picture of the cannibal butchers' shop, losing his caution as he gets carried away while speaking to the narrator, is an accurate piece of psychological observation, recalling the sketch of a different kind of pervert in Joyce's story 'An Encounter'. But Lovecraft's clumsiness comes out in the catastrophic end of the story – the house is struck by a thunderbolt as the narrator notices blood dripping through the ceiling.

Somewhat more skilful, though the ending is as clumsy as ever, is another story of the same period, 'The Rats in the Walls', in which a man restores his old family mansion and goes to live in it. At night he hears the sound of scurrying rats inside the walls. Investigation in the basement reveals a flight of steps that leads down to subterranean caves which contain much evidence of some old

4

witch cult. Lovecraft was here connecting his horrors with ancient cults – the worship of Cybele and Atys. (One wonders if he was influenced by Professor Margaret Murray, whose *Witch Cult in Western Europe* came out in 1921; Professor Murray believed witchcraft to be a survival of the worship of pre-Christian nature deities.)

But it was not until 1928 that Lovecraft finally developed the 'mythology' that gives his subsequent work a certain internal consistency. He produced a story called 'The Call of Cthulhu' (the unpronounceable name is typical), about which he wrote later: 'All my stories, unconnected as they may be, are based on the fundamental lore or legend that this world was inhabited at one time by another race who, in practising black magic, lost their foothold and were expelled, yet live on outside, ever ready to take possession of this earth again.'⁴ Like most of Lovecraft's stories, 'The Call of Cthulhu' is powerful and interesting in its first half, then tails off into vague horrors. He begins by quoting Algernon Blackwood to the effect that there may still be 'great powers' surviving from a remote period in earth's history, powers hinted at in legends of gods and monsters. But the story seems to owe more to Madame Blavatsky's *Secret Doctrine* with its myths of Atlantis and Lemuria. It opens with the typical Lovecraft statement: 'The most merciful thing in the world, I think, is the inability of the human mind to correlate all its contents.' This is the usual romantic pessimism, aimed against science. The subject of the story is the idea that at certain times, the 'dark powers' find conditions better for influencing the earth. A sensitive young artist has dreams of the early civilisation of Cthulhu. All over the world disturbing things happen: cranks and visionaries multiply, there are voodoo orgies in Africa and Haiti, a painter exhibits a 'blasphemous *Dream Landscape*' at the Paris Spring Salon of 1926, people commit suicide, etc. Then follows a narrative of a police inspector who arrested a gang of men engaged in black magic orgies in the swamps near New Orleans, and gathers more evidence about the 'Great Old Ones who lived ages before there were any men'. The third part of the story tells of the experience of a sailor who lands on a strange island that had risen out of the sea and finds a city of great stone blocks carved according to some 'non-terrestrial geometry'. (This is one of Lovecraft's favourite phrases; it occurs in many of the tales, and proves that Lovecraft was no mathematician, since he thought there could be a difference between geometry on the earth and elsewhere.) Then great Cthulhu himself – an indescribable gelatinous Thing – emerges. The evil odours from Cthulhu's tomb ascend into 'the shrunken and gibbous sky'. Finally, the island sinks back into the sea.

After 1928, Lovecraft frequently drew on his Cthulhu mythology to explain his 'horrors'. Many of his stories are set in New England (no doubt because it was the scene of the witch trials), and Lovecraft's New England is over-crowded with Cthulhu's friends and relations. A story called 'The Dunwich Horror' again exploits the theme that the 'Old Ones' would like to regain control of the earth. On a remote Massachusetts farm, a deformed albino woman gives birth to a hideous, hairy child. The child is a fully grown adult in six years, when he takes up the family heritage of witchcraft, and begins to rear a strange monster that feeds on cows. He also tries to borrow from various university libraries a 'blasphemous volume' called the *Necronomicon*. (This turns up in several of Lovecraft's stories.) Finally, he is killed by a dog when trying to steal the volume, and is found to be a semi-human creature with tentacles hanging from his belly, eyes in his hips, and a trunklike tail; his proportions 'seemed to follow the symmetries of some cosmic geometry unknown to earth'. How a mere house dog managed to kill him is not explained. Then the monster escapes and begins to destroy whole villages: it is also invisible. In the end, a group of occult students manage to destroy it by muttering spells.

There are several more stories in which Lovecraft uses his Cthulhu mythology as the basis of the plot. The theme is always the same – the strange beings from beyond space and time who want to take over the earth. In 'The Whisperer in Darkness', the beings are crablike creatures from a planet beyond Neptune. One of the most effective of these stories is 'The Thing on the Doorstep', which has some unusually horrible touches and which utilises Lovecraft's favourite idea of incubi who can steal a human body, expelling its rightful owner.

Nevertheless, it must be admitted that Lovecraft is a very bad writer. When he is at his best, his style might be mistaken for Poe's. (A tale called 'The Outsider', about a

6

monstrous-looking man who does not realise that he is monstrous until he finally sees himself in a mirror, owes something to 'William Wilson' and perhaps to Wilde's *Birthday of the Infanta*; it might easily pass for an unknown work by Poe.) But he makes few concessions to credibility, in spite of his desire to be convincing. His stories are full of horror-film conventions, the most irritating of which is the trustful stupidity of the hero, who ignores signs and portents until he is face to face with the actual horror. ('There was something about his voice which gave me a vague thrill of horror, but which I could not quite place . . .') All his stories have the same pattern.

But although Lovecraft is such a bad writer, he has something of the same kind of importance as Kafka. If his work fails as literature, it still holds an interest as a psychological case history. Here was a man who made no attempt whatever to come to terms with life. He hated modern civilisation, particularly its confident belief in progress and science. Greater artists have had the same feeling, from Dostoevsky to Kafka and Eliot. They have used different techniques to undermine man's complacency. Dostoevsky emphasised the human capacity for suffering and ecstasy; Eliot emphasised human stupidity and futility. Only Kafka's approach was as naïve as Lovecraft's. He also relied simply on presenting a picture of the world's mystery and the uncertainty of the life of man.

Possibly future generations will feel that Lovecraft is 'symbolically true'. A book I was given as a child illustrated the view of man held by modern psychology. In it was a picture one half of which showed a little man with a bowler hat and briefcase on his way to the office. Below the edge of the pavement, apelike creatures stare up at him. In the second half of the picture, the little man is asleep, now the apelike creatures are clambering over the pavement and invading his world. The area 'below the pavement' represented the subconscious mind. Thomas Lovell Beddoes expressed the same idea:

> . . . if man could see
> The perils and diseases that he elbows
> Each day he walks a mile.

This is a sentiment that Lovecraft never tires of expressing.

7

He finds an effective symbol for it in a story called 'Pickman's Model'. Pickman is an artist who lives in Boston, and who specialises in painting morbid subjects – 'Ghoul Feeding', for example.

Lovecraft's motivation appears with particular clarity in some of Pickman's speeches to the narrator. 'The place to live is in the North End. If an aesthete were sincere, he'd put up with the slums for the sake of the massed traditions . . . Generation after generation lived and felt and died there . . . in days when people weren't afraid to live and feel and die . . . Cotton Mather, damn him, was afraid somebody might succeed in kicking free of this accursed cage of monotony.' Oppressed by the ordinary, Lovecraft keeps declaring passionately that the extraordinary exists. There is nothing unusual about this; it is the pattern of all creative artists. Some write about heroism, some about sex, some about supernatural grace, some about 'outsiders' and rebels. But the great artist tries to *reveal* the extraordinary that is always present in the world; Lovecraft, a hypochondriac, creates 'other worlds' in a fever of spite.

Pickman takes the narrator to a cellar in the slum quarter which he uses as a studio; there, at the side of a boarded-up well, he paints horrible monsters. Later Pickman disappears under strange circumstances, and his friend finds a photograph of one of the horrible monsters in the cellar. It has evidently been taken from life, the inference being that these monsters really exist below Boston, and come up through the disused well.

Some interesting aspects of this 'hypochondriac' Lovecraft are revealed in certain of his letters and essays. In a rather vague way, he was an anti-Semite, but the anti-Semitism is so obviously the emotional response of a sick, introverted man that no one could regard it as dangerous. Like W. B. Yeats, he was something of a snob, and liked to assert that he was a 'gentleman' by birth (although his father was actually a commercial traveller); he was proud of being a 'light skinned, fair haired nordic', and speaks contemptuously of the 'loathsome Asiatic hordes who trail their dirty carcases over streets where white men once moved'. He writes in another letter of his 'mad physical loathing' of Semitic types, and says that he has often felt capable of murdering a score or two when jammed in a New York subway train. All this is strangely adolescent; it is not a carefully *thought-out* attitude, like Houston Stewart Chamberlain's anti-Semitism, but the emotional response of a fundamentally good-natured but weak and shrinking man. His only attempts to state his beliefs in intellectual terms are certain philosophical essays of no great merit. One of them, 'Nietzscheanism and Realism', declares: 'There is no such thing, and there never will be such a thing, as good and permanent government among the crawling and miserable vermin called human beings.' He exalts the 'urge to supremacy', but ends typically: 'It is good to be a cynic; better a contented cat; best not to exist at all.'

All this is simply a half-baked Schopenhauer pessimism, with echoes of Nietzsche and Hulme. (Although Lovecraft almost certainly never heard of Hulme: he was totally ignorant of twentieth-century literature, and some of his letters to Derleth reveal the usual adolescent intolerance about it.)

All the same, Lovecraft is not an isolated crank. He is working in a recognisable romantic tradition. If he is not a major writer, he is psychologically one of the most interesting men of his generation. And his work makes the best possible beginning to a study of the problems of imagination.

W. B. YEATS

Lovecraft is interesting mainly because he is a perfect example of the 'escapist imagination'. It is hard to agree with August Derleth that his death was 'a great loss to American letters' because he had not yet reached 'the fullest development of his powers'. It is doubtful whether Lovecraft had any more to say. As it is, he wrote far too much. Moreover, since he so determinedly created an unreal world in opposition to the real world, it seems that he willed his own death. His whole life is a spectacle of self-destruction; he strikes one as being like a chronic alcoholic or a drug addict.

For this reason, it is interesting to compare him with W. B. Yeats. We tend to think of Yeats as a combination of poet and politician: he has been compared to the older Goethe. And yet Yeats, like Lovecraft, created his own world of myths and symbols, and tried to force it upon the

9

'real world'. There was a great deal in Yeats of the nineteenth-century messiah-artist. In an essay on Shelley's poetry, he writes:

When I was a boy in Dublin, I was one of a group who rented a room in a mean street to discuss philosophy . . . I thought . . . that if a powerful and benevolent spirit has shaped the destiny of this world, we can better discover that destiny from the words that have gathered up the heart's desire of the world, than from historical records, or from speculation, wherein the heart withers.

Here can be seen the anti-science attitude at work. When one thinks of Arnold Toynbee's version of the purpose of history as a 'preparation for the Beatific Vision'[5] or of the philosophy of Hegel, it is hard to agree with Yeats.

Yeats goes on to state that he has studied *Prometheus Unbound* as a 'sacred book'. In the *Autobiographies*, he also admits the enormous influence on him of certain lines about the wandering Jew, from *Hellas*:

> Some feign that he is Enoch; others dream
> He was pre-adamite, and has survived
> Cycles of generation and of ruin.

This 'old Jew' lives:

> . . . in a sea-cavern
> 'Mid the Demonesi, less accessible
> Than thou or God . . .

and he is the receptacle of all wisdom – a prefiguring of Shaw's Ancients in *Back to Methuselah*. Yeats adds that he was attracted to the Theosophists (Madame Blavatsky's followers) because they affirmed the real existence of the Jew (or of his like, the 'Masters' of Tibet).

Yeats unites in himself all the late nineteenth-century revolt against the Age of Science that characterises figures as disparate as William Morris and Oscar Wilde. He dislikes London's miles of stone and brick, and dreams of some John the Baptist who will summon all the city dwellers into the wilderness. He recalls a remark of Ruskin: 'As I go to my work at the British Museum, I see the faces of the people become daily more corrupt.' His early poetry creates fairylands that will be a refuge from the materialistic world. His 'Man who dreamed of fairyland' is a successful bourgeois who believes that man's task is to make the best of this world, but who is shaken by sudden glimpses of the 'other world'. The fishes raise their heads and sing of a 'woven world-forgotten isle . . . where Time can never mar a lover's vows'. This is the 'Land of Heart's Desire', where 'even the old air fair/And even the wise are merry of tongue'. Fairies lure away a child, singing:

> Come away, O human child!
> To the waters and the wild
> With a fairy, hand in hand,
> For the world's more full of weeping than
>   you can understand.

This would seem to be harmless enough. But Yeats declared that his fairies existed. Chesterton quotes him, in his *Autobiography*: ' "Imagination," he would say with withering contempt, "there wasn't much imagination when Farmer Hogan was dragged out of bed and thrashed like a sack of potatoes – that they did, they had 'um out." ' Stephen Spender, describing the later Yeats, says that Yeats claimed that a carved wooden head of a baby at the bottom of some banisters had spouted Greek to him.

This is a slightly different type of self-assertion from that practised by Lovecraft. Lovecraft did his best to convince the reader of the reality of his unseen world, but he never asserted in print that he had *seen* Cthulhu. Yeats's extraordinary attack on the 'materialistic world' reached a climax in a strange book called *A Vision*. Like Blake, Yeats felt that he had to 'create his own system, or be enslaved by another man's'. It speaks for his good sense that he was not able to embrace any of the currently fashionable anti-materialistic systems, spiritualism or Christian Science or Theosophy. But his own system was a strange hotchpotch of Boehme, astrology, Blake and theories about the great artists of the past. It is aimed at systematising the human personality, somewhat after the manner of Jung's 'psychological types'. Two mental extremes are posited – total subjectivity and total objectivity – and these are compared to the full moon and the new moon. All types of human personality are then compared to the various phases of the moon.[6] *A Vision* is Yeats's counterblast against Freud, his own 'mystical psychology'.

But the chief interest of the book lies in Yeats's claim that it is of supernatural origin. He explains that Mrs Yeats

11

often went into trances and produced automatic writing. (This explanation was an afterthought; the book was first published privately in 1926 and the information about its origin in 1929.) Supernatural beings were trying to communicate with Yeats through his wife. They declared, admittedly, that they were not offering him a new philosophical system, but only 'metaphors for poetry'. There was also another race of supernatural beings who wanted to keep this knowledge secret, and who often 'frustrated' the dictating spirits.

It is worth noting that Yeats admits that he cannot be said literally to 'believe' everything he has written. Years later he wrote a poem, 'The Apparitions', that begins:

> Because there is safety in derision
> I talked about an apparition,
> I took no trouble to convince,
> Or seem plausible to a man of sense . . .
> *Fifteen apparitions have I seen;*
> *The worst a coat upon a coat-hanger.*

(Yeats's italics.)

So one is inclined to ask the plain question: was the whole story about automatic writing a hoax? The answer is almost certainly yes. An anecdote in the *Autobiographies* is revealing. Yeats carried on a running battle with an Irish nationalist orator, John F. Taylor, for many years. One day, at a party, Yeats declared that five out of every six people have seen a ghost. Taylor fell into the trap and proposed that they ask the people present. Yeats arranged that the first two people to be asked should be people who actually believed they had seen a ghost, and Taylor was so disgusted that he did not pursue the matter further. Yeats quite deliberately cheated, and makes no bones about admitting it. He felt that he was fundamentally right, and the 'practical politician' Taylor was wrong, and he obviously thought that the end justified the means.

It is instructive to compare Yeats with another modern founder of a 'system', George Gurdjieff. Yeats believed that the poet must wear a mask, his 'anti-self', as self-protection; Gurdjieff was also a man who 'acted' all the time. Gurdjieff's *All and Everything* tries to increase its effect of being sacred scripture by deliberate obscurity; so does Yeats's *Vision*. Gurdjieff also created a complicated theory of the human personality, tied up with the moon, planets, elements, etc. (which Ouspensky expounds in all seriousness in his books on Gurdjieff). And both tried to give their systems authenticity by creating legends about 'hidden masters'. But in Gurdjieff it is clear that he is trying to model his system on the religions of the past, trying to make it assimilable by all types of people. Basically, it is a penetrating and profound psychology, dressed up as a religion. One is reminded of Wagner's Machiavellian essay on the State and Religion, written for his patron, King Ludwig, in which he tells the king that the people must be kept happy with the lies of religion; only the king must stand apart from the deception, unhappy in his knowledge, yet godlike. Yeats also felt that certain deceptions are necessary if people are to hold the right attitude to truth. He was vaguely in favour of Catholicism because he felt that its legends, dogmas and hierarchies are such 'necessary deceptions'. And his own work reveals the same principle.

But a full understanding of Yeats cannot exist until one basic fact is understood; there was a certain pessimism at the bottom of his vision of the world. This pessimism is the usual nineteenth-century feeling that the 'world of matter' and the 'world of spirit' are ultimately irreconcilable. It emerges clearly in the short dialogue between heart and soul in *Vacillation*:

> *The Soul:* Seek out reality, leave things that seem.
> *The Heart:* What, be a singer born and lack a theme?
> *The Soul:* Isaiah's coal, what more can man desire?
> *The Heart:* Struck dumb in the simplicity of fire!
> *The Soul:* Look on that fire, salvation walks within.
> *The Heart:* What theme had Homer but original sin?

This is simply another form of the pessimistic assumption that truth can be of no use to man. Art is lies, but Yeats prefers to be an artist. In another poem he says of himself (speaking of the sexual instinct): 'But a coarse old man am I; I choose the second best.' This is not simply the resignation of the 'sinner' who intends to keep on sinning. It is based on an ultimately Manichaean position: the spirit is good, the world is evil. This emerges clearly in a late poem, 'The Circus Animals' Desertion', in which the poet considers all his early symbols and legends – Usheen, the

13

Countess Cathleen, Red Hanrahan, etc. – and admits that they were merely an attempt to 'evade reality'.

> Those masterful images because complete
> Grew in pure mind, but out of what began?
> A mound of refuse or the sweepings of a
>   street . . .
> . . . Now that my ladder's gone
> I must lie down where all the ladders start,
> In the foul rag-and-bone shop of the heart.

Art, Yeats is saying, is 'escapism'. The reality is the stupidity and ignobility of the world. And even if the world can be transformed by play-acting and ideals, we are still basically animals. Just as Swift seemed to be tormented by the fact that the most beautiful ladies have to go to the lavatory and wash themselves to keep from stinking, so Yeats turns away with a shudder from the 'nauseating' reality depicted by Zola and Joyce, yet has to admit finally that it is 'more real' than the pretty stories he prefers. Yeats is here very close to the Sartre of *La Nausée*.

So although Yeats prefers the 'Shakespearian fish' swimming far away from land, he has to admit that honesty leads us to recognise the superior reality of the fish that lie gasping on the strand.

It is true that Yeats is not entirely a pessimist. In his very late poem 'Under Ben Bulben' he propounds a Shavian notion that the purpose of art is to lead the human spirit upward, towards the godlike. Yet his own epitaph is the buddhistic: 'Cast a cold eye / On life, on death.'

Yeats is not very far from Socrates, who cheers up his disciples in the *Phaedo* by stating that, since the philosopher spends his life trying to separate soul and body, death is the consummation of philosophy. (This statement produces in me a more total revulsion than any other in Plato.)

The same pessimism appears in the last lines of an earlier poem:

> Whatever flames upon the night
> Man's own resinous heart has fed.

Man's convictions do not represent a supernatural reality. He must convince himself, tell himself stories, invent religions – but the reality mocks his visions, and he only consumes himself.

This is partly an overcompensation for the earlier belief in fairyland; he is throwing out the baby with the dirty water. Many great artists have felt that their best work flows *through* them, using them as an instrument. Yeats is here declaring: 'Not at all. Man consumes himself by his creation.' There was a famous episode in a Marx Brothers film in which the brothers steal a train, the train runs out of coal, and they begin breaking up the carriages and piling them into the fire; finally they break up the engine itself and push it into the furnace, until the train is only a furnace on wheels. This describes Yeats's conception of the working of the creative faculty.

It will be seen that Yeats and Lovecraft have much in common in their way of seeing the world and art. Both see it in terms of a self-destructive pessimism. Yet they both had the good sense to keep their pessimism and their living in separate compartments. Lovecraft may have believed that life is hideous and death is even worse, but he didn't commit suicide at an early age. Although Yeats was regarded, in later life, as the great poet of his time, he cultivated a kind of self-mockery, and deliberately exaggerated some of his crankier notions in order to encourage an attitude of irreverence towards himself. (Even so acute an observer as Mr Robert Graves was taken in, and declared that Yeats was entirely 'phony'.) He often expressed his contempt for his 'sedentary trade' and for thinkers in general, and cast wistful glances at the life of action. He could never escape a feeling that all knowledge is original sin, and that he would be better off as an ignorant urchin in a Dublin slum, or a drunken tramp. So, like Chesterton, he exaggerated the human virtues and vices. 'A proud man's a lovely man,' he writes, and expresses admiration for 'roarers and ranters'. At times, his work expresses a sort of Nietzschean cult of life worship. The young Yeats was simultaneously shocked and fascinated by tales of girls who gave themselves to sailors in a nearby town; the old Yeats writes a series of poems that glory in the physical aspects of sex and in sexual violence.

> Out and impose our leadership
> On country and on town.
> Throw likely couples into bed
> And knock the others down.

From a nihilistic rejection of the world, he now turns to an

15

equally nihilistic acceptance of stupidity and violence as having somehow a meaning in themselves. Yet one always feels that he was not completely taken in by either. Many poets of the late nineteenth century carried their despair to its logical conclusion in death; Yeats was too healthy at bottom to go that far.

OSCAR WILDE

A clearer light is thrown upon his own attitudes and practices by considering the case of his friend and contemporary, Oscar Wilde, for whom Yeats had a qualified but nevertheless deep admiration. Much has been written about Wilde's work and his 'tragic end' but (as far as I know) no one has pointed out the close relation between the two men. Wilde, like Yeats, had in him a great deal of the man of action; this is Yeats's view in his *Autobiographies* and it is confirmed in Hesketh Pearson's book on Wilde. Wilde was a tough and ambitious man who wore a mask of effeminacy and boredom. Yet there remains the mystery of why he went through with the second trial when he might easily have escaped to the Continent. It is true that he seems to have identified himself with Christ, and have believed that he had to live out a tragic destiny. But how did he come to hold this view of himself?

The answer probably lies in a Manichaeism that is similar to that of Yeats. Wilde told Gide: 'My duty to myself is to amuse myself terrifically . . . no happiness, only pleasure. One must always seek what is most tragic.' Wilde's life and work were based on two ideas: pleasure and tragedy. This can be seen clearly in the poem 'The Harlot's House'. The poet stops outside the harlot's house and looks at the party going on inside. While the musicians play the 'True Love' waltz of Strauss, the dancers spin mechanically in a kind of dance of death. The poet's mistress leaves his side and 'Love passed into the house of lust'.

> And suddenly the tune went false,
> The dancers wearied of the waltz,
> The shadows ceased to wheel and whirl,
> And down the long and silent street,
> The dawn, with her silver-sandaled feet,
> Crept like a frightened girl.

After the description of the dance of death, the description of the dawn strikes a curious note, somewhere between irony and tragedy, and shows clearly Wilde's self-division. The 'sin and pleasure' fascinate him (as, of course, they fascinated many writers of the nineties, from Anatole France to Lionel Johnson). But they also seem to give rise to a protestant revulsion and desire for self-punishment. This mood is typical of Wilde. It can be seen again in the sonnet 'Hélas', which begins:

> To drift with every passion till my soul
> Is a stringed lute on which all winds can play . . .

and which contains some obvious sexual symbolism in its last lines:

> . . . Lo! with a little rod
> I did but touch the honey of romance—
> And must I lose a soul's inheritance?

It is also present in *Dorian Gray*, where the pleasures of sin are presented as alluringly as in Swinburne, yet where the corruption that is the result of sin is presented with a George Eliot primness. Edmund Wilson has pointed out that when Wilde feels self-disgust about his orgies of luxury, he turns away to a Christian ideal of humility and abnegation rather than to Yeats's 'sedentary toil of creative art' (so repeating the pattern of Wagner).

When one examines his life closely, it becomes apparent that the basic factor in his conduct was a violent will-to-power about which he felt somehow guilty. Its final motive is contempt for other people, and the refusal ever to be an 'ordinary man'. Wilde conquered London society and became a rich man by jeering at all the standards of Victorian society. When society would have liked to accept him and 'naturalise' him, he made this difficult by an overweening conceit and brutality, again emphasising his separateness. Finally, when everything he touched seemed to turn to gold, when society showed itself willing to idolise him on almost any terms, he again cut himself off by 'seeking out the tragic' and immolating himself. There is here the same insane logic as in *Dorian Gray* and his poems. Only pleasure and superficiality are worthwhile; when they fail, the only alternative is tragedy and death. This perverseness is present in his refusal to try to make himself into a great writer. 'I put my genius into my life, and only my talent into my works.'

Here is an imaginative attitude that takes the world-rejection of Yeats and Lovecraft one stage further. They only declared that they preferred the world of imagination to the real world. Wilde heaped contempt on the real world in every possible way – by denying its basic tenets, preferring pleasure to happiness, superficiality to profundity, talent to genius, by gathering fame carelessly with one hand and throwing it away with the other. Yeats only lived by his imaginative standards in that he pretended to think that fairies really existed; Wilde applied his world-rejection to life in every possible way. It may even be doubted that he was genuinely homosexual. He was certainly heterosexual at Oxford, where he caught syphilis from a prostitute. (It was the mercury treatment for this that discoloured his teeth and gave him such an unpleasant smile.) He was also in love with his wife when he married her. (At this time, he believed – falsely – that his syphilis was cured.) Probably he entered into homosexual relations in the same perverse, self-mortifying spirit that he later went to jail.

Wilde epitomises the imagination as 'escapism'. Yeats and Lovecraft set up the imagination as a faculty for challenging and defying the 'real world'; but Wilde carried the defiance to the point of suicide. For these writers, the imagination was essentially the *alternative* to reality.

AUGUST STRINDBERG

Yeats, Lovecraft and Wilde based their imaginative work on rejection; Strindberg allowed rejection to drive him into insanity. He is probably the only writer who became insane and *wrote* himself back to sanity. From his plays, most readers would recognise the compulsive neurotic bias in his personality. But it can be seen most clearly in the four volumes of his autobiography, the third of which, *Inferno*, has been described as 'one of the most remarkable studies in abnormal psychology in the world's literature'.[7] It is these books that link Strindberg with the 'anti-rational' tradition.

The first part, *The Son of a Servant*, deals with Strindberg's childhood and his life up to his marriage. Strindberg's father was a businessman who became prosperous only after a long struggle; so the writer's early years were spent in conditions of extreme poverty. His mother was a barmaid, whom his father married only after she had borne him two children and was about to produce August. For some reason, Strindberg was ashamed of being 'the son of a servant', and the title of the work reveals that hysterical tendency to public confession that became so apparent later. The first volume of the autobiography is a sensitive but self-pitying book. Certain injustices of his childhood rankled in Strindberg's mind all his life. In his teens, he had a great scare about masturbation which recalls a similar episode in Joyce's *Portrait*. He read books on science and developed the interest in alchemy that appears in *Inferno*.

It is with the second volume that the real interest begins. This is the notorious *Confession of a Fool*, which Strindberg produced in a state of hysteria, and later tried unsuccessfully to suppress. Its first half is a delightful love story. Strindberg was working in the Royal Library when he received a note from the fiancée of a friend, asking for an appointment. The woman was a bluestocking and a coquette; but Strindberg, in his mid-twenties, was susceptible, and he soon thought himself in love with her. She introduced him to her friend Baroness Wrangel, whose unmarried name was Siri von Essen. Siri and the Baron were living in a house that Strindberg's family had once occupied; when he went to visit them there, he had a sense that fate was taking a hand. Soon he was in love with Siri. By this time, his previous siren had admitted her love for him, but his old feeling for her had nothing in common with what he felt for Siri. The new emotion was closer to worship. He had no hope of succeeding; he hardly even thought of succeeding. 'God was deposed, but His place was taken by woman, woman who was both virgin and mother.' (Siri had a little girl.) The Baron treated Strindberg as a special friend; he was a coarse little man who made Strindberg the confidant of his affairs with other women – particularly with Siri's cousin. Strindberg was in a position he enjoyed; Siri also confided in him about her quarrels with her husband. Finally, in the most gentle and gradual way imaginable, Siri discovered she was in love with Strindberg, and the Baron agreed to divorce her. Two years after their first meeting, Strindberg married Siri. Not long afterwards, their first child was born prematurely, and died under the care of a wet nurse. Siri went on the stage and was a success. Strindberg published his first novel, *The Red Room*, a satire on Swedish society and journalism, which achieved an immediate success; it also raised his first storm of moral indignation. His plays were now accepted and presented. It would seem that the couple had good reason to be happy.

But now Strindberg's neurosis began to come to the surface. Like Dostoevsky, he had a compulsion to make himself suffer. He began to suspect Siri of betraying him. His poems came out; they were violent and iconoclastic, and they were violently attacked. This gave Strindberg more reason to believe himself persecuted. A volume of stories, *Married*, was impounded by the authorities and the author and publisher charged with blasphemy. Although he was found Not Guilty, he felt that his enemies were closing in around him. He admits in the *Confession*: 'There were times when I had no doubt that my wife hated me and wanted to get rid of me in order to marry again.' Part of the trouble lay in Siri's desire for a career; Strindberg really wanted a perfectly domesticated wife who would minister to his needs. A strong anti-feminist trend had already appeared in *Married*, and Strindberg was reviled by every bluestocking in Sweden. He felt that women in general, and his wife in particular, wished his destruction. Siri's friends took a hand in breaking up the marriage – including a lesbian. When Strindberg found a love letter from this woman to his wife, he tried to drag Siri to the river to 'drown her like a kitten'. His persecution mania reached a climax. Ten years after they were married, Strindberg wrote his maddest and bitterest play, *The Father*, in which a scheming wife has her husband confined as insane, after torturing him with the suspicion that his child is not his own.

This play, and *A Fool's Confession*, were Strindberg's attempts at revenge on Siri. They were finally divorced in 1892. No one can read *A Fool's Confession* without feeling that the break was entirely Strindberg's fault.

In 1893, Strindberg met Frieda Uhl, a young Austrian writer, who set out to captivate him. He wanted to talk about his loneliness, his unhappiness, his love for his children. She played him carefully, denouncing marriage and praising free love. Finally they married. It was as stormy and uncertain a marriage as his first. One day a German copy of *A Fool's Confession* arrived; Frieda read it, and felt that some day Strindberg would turn on her as he had turned on Siri. The marriage began to fall apart. Strindberg turned to alchemical researches, and soon had samples of gold to show. The authorities agreed that it was gold, but were unwilling to admit that Strindberg had proved the transmutability of metals. They felt, probably correctly, that a man with no scientific training, working in a crude laboratory, had probably deceived himself when he declared that his original copper had been quite pure.

Strindberg and Frieda went to Paris – they now had a child – and finally separated. It is at this point that the *Inferno* begins. He tells how he saw her off at the station, then returned to his room and got out his chemical apparatus. His aim now, he explains, was to prove that sulphur is not an element, but that it contains carbon. Claims such as this need not necessarily be taken as proof of insanity. It must not be forgotten that any schoolboy today knows more about atomic physics than Strindberg learned in his whole lifetime. It is not surprising that Strindberg was not sure about the difference between an element and a compound. What *is* surprising is that Strindberg was soon convinced that he had proved that sulphur contained carbon:

But the skin of my hands, nearly roasted by the strong fire, peels off in scales, and the pain they cause me in undressing shows what a price I have paid for my victory. But as I lie alone in bed, I feel happy, and I am sorry I have no one whom I can thank for my deliverance from the marital fetters which have been broken. For in the course of years, I have become an atheist, since the unknown powers have left the world to itself without a sign of themselves.

'The unknown powers'. The phrase is strongly reminiscent of Yeats – not to mention Lovecraft. But Strindberg is altogether less detached than Yeats. He goes on to tell how he wrote to his wife and told her that he was involved in a new love affair. (This was untrue.) His bleeding hands cause him so much pain that he has a general breakdown, and the Swedish colony in Paris collected enough money to send him to the hospital of St Louis (although *The Father* had recently been a tremendous success in Paris,

21

Strindberg was hopelessly poor.) There his delusions of persecution developed. He believed he was close to death. The sickness around him depressed him. His proof of the carbon in sulphur gained no recognition from the authorities. But he pressed on, and, on leaving the hospital, set out to prove that sulphur is a compound of carbon, hydrogen and oxygen. He declares that he soon established this to his own satisfaction. A minor incident is typical of his state of mind. On the window of a laundry, he discovered a shop-sign consisting of the initials A. S. (his own) on a silver cloud; he read this as a proof that he would succeed in his chemical researches. His fortunes improved slightly; he was allowed to work in the Sorbonne Laboratory. For a time he was happy. He found that his mind was turning against his early Darwinism and atheism; he began to develop a vague religious creed. But his various delusions and manias were catching up with him. He saw signs in everything. Looking through a microscope at a nut kernel one day, he saw two tiny white hands stretched out towards him. Noises disturb him; pianos are played in the next room (three, according to Strindberg) and there are hammering noises. He believes this to be a plot of some Swedish bluestockings, and changes his lodgings. In his new hotel – to which he has been led by 'signs' – strange coincidences worry him and convince him that someone is out to torment him. He makes the acquaintance of an American artist, and becomes convinced that the artist is actually a quack healer called Schlatter who disappeared from America in the previous year; he proves this to his own satisfaction by comparing Schlatter's handwriting with that of his artist friend; but the artist claims he knows nothing about Schlatter. It is possible, of course, that the artist *was* Schlatter – but it seems more likely that Strindberg was becoming insane.

It would be impossible to detail all Strindberg's delusions. He heard a piano playing next door, and was immediately convinced that the pianist was an old friend and disciple, now becoming an implacable enemy since he has married an ex-mistress of Strindberg. Strindberg is convinced that this man intends to murder him, and is relieved when he hears that the man has been arrested in Vienna on a charge of murdering his mistress and two children. But the 'persecutions' continue; Strindberg believes that they are a punishment for the hubris of his youth and for leading the youth of Sweden into atheism. He begins to believe that his 'enemies' are persecuting him with a kind of electric machine which is installed in the next room, and which sends out waves of 'electric fluid' that constrict his chest.

Reading the *Inferno* has the effect of making the reader feel slightly insane. But the strangest part about the book is that its author writes as if he is convinced that his delusions are real. Just as he wrote *A Fool's Confession* to punish Siri, and yet clearly revealed that he was the one who was to blame, so now he explains his delusions to the reader in the absolute certainty that the reader will agree that Strindberg was persecuted by enemies and spirits. His speculations read like Yeats gone mad. Yeats could write about the 'unseen powers': 'They have but one purpose, to bring their chosen man to the greatest obstacle he may confront without despair. They contrived Dante's banishment and snatched away his Beatrice, and thrust Villon into the arms of harlots and sent him to gather cronies at the foot of the gallows . . .' Strindberg declares that the 'powers' turned against him when he began to practise black magic, and the arrest of his 'persecutor' on a charge of murdering his mistress and children leads him to wonder if he is also a wizard who can strike down his enemies by merely willing. He tried committing suicide by leaving an uncorked flask of potassium cyanide on the table, but something interrupted the attempt.

Strindberg now began a 'penitential pilgrimage' that took him first to Sweden, then to Austria, where he stayed with his wife's mother. The 'electric machine' followed him around. An important step towards mental health had been taken when he read Balzac's novel *Seraphita*. *Seraphita* was written when Balzac was under the influence of Swedenborg; it is about an 'angelic spirit' who lives in a Swiss village; to a man who is in love with her she appears as a beautiful girl; to a woman, she appears to be a handsome youth. At the end of the book, she ascends to heaven. Perhaps the most interesting part of the novel is a long account of Swedenborg's life and teachings given in an early chapter. At all events, Strindberg was captivated by it; it made him 'long to be free of the earth'. (It is incredible that Strindberg should also have admired Friedrich

Nietzsche – a man who would have found *Seraphita* wholly poisonous.) In Dornach, Strindberg's mother-in-law lent him volumes of Swedenborg; he now became convinced that he had found the answer to all his sufferings. His torments and delusions were identical with the torments of hell, as described by the Swedish prophet. It was the state that Swedenborg described as 'devastation'. Devastation was the essential prelude to salvation. (William James borrowed from Swedenborg the term 'vastation' to describe an experience of complete horror of his own existence.[8]) From Swedenborg's *Heaven and Hell*, Strindberg discovered that 'devastation' consists in constriction of the chest, the 'electric' sensation, attacks of fear, nightmares and palpitations of the heart. Strindberg wrote in *Legends* (the last volume of the Autobiographies): 'This diagnosis . . . corresponds closely to the sickness that is now so common, so that I do not shrink from drawing the conclusion that we are approaching a new era in which there will be spiritual awakening and it will be a joy to live.' The twentieth century was to be the era of spiritual awakening.

Although Strindberg's period of insanity ended with the discovery of Swedenborg, he was by no means 'a new man'. He continued to be 'persecuted' in various ways, and to see signs and portents in every natural occurrence. Unlike many converts, he does not immediately feel the need to draw others into the fold, and says sensibly: 'Religion is a thing that one must appropriate for oneself; it is no use preaching it.'

After the crisis, Strindberg had an amazing final period. He had seventeen more years to live (until 1912). He had been the founder of a new realism; now he founded a new symbolism. His later plays are deeply subjective, and are less often performed than *The Father* and *Miss Julie*; but there are many who consider the trilogy *To Damascus* – *The Dream Play*, *The Dance of Death* and the *Ghost Sonata* – his finest work.

He married again in 1901 – this time the young actress Harriet Bosse. This marriage was as unsuccessful as the others, and for the same reasons. Strindberg wanted the girl to himself; he resented the theatre. In view of his own clear realisation that he wanted a devoted, domestic woman to make him happy, his three marriages to 'career women' can only be regarded as a kind of masochism. Harriet was flattered to be married to Sweden's greatest literary genius (and a man upon whom his own country was now heaping honours and recognition). Strindberg was still young – he was only fifty. But his manic selfishness and jealousy made him impossible to live with. The birth of a child acted as a brake on the dissolution of the marriage, but by the autumn of 1903 it was over.

Strindberg's sixtieth birthday, in 1909, was widely celebrated. His sixty-third birthday in 1912 was a national event; even in England it was celebrated. But a few months later, on 14 May, he died of a cancer of the stomach.

Strindberg once wrote that he 'began to serve his sentence as a child'. He belongs to the category that William James describes as 'the twice born'. For such men life seems to be a train of sufferings, punctuated by illusory moments of happiness whose purpose is to persuade the sufferer to increase his efforts. And yet, unlike Yeats, Strindberg never created a conscious 'other world' of fairies (although *The Dream Play* comes close to it). His novel *The People of Hemso* is a masterpiece of humorous realism (although the ending is spoiled when he somewhat perfunctorily kills off the hero). And his sickness may be attributed to the stern 'realism' that would have prevented him from permitting himself such a safety valve. Yeats was happy to ease the strain by dividing his personality: half of him believed that reality was a rag-and-bone shop; the other half created visions of the ideal or the heroic. When Strindberg went through his crisis, the whole personality bent and strained, and finally the whole personality accepted the 'supernatural' vision. Yeats managed to simultaneously reject and accept Madame Blavatsky.

In short, it seems that Strindberg clinches the argument for the 'escapist' view of the imagination. If he had been less ashamed of his imagination, he could have lessened the strain that pushed him into insanity (or to the edge of it). As it was, his 'realistic' brain had to manufacture evidence to enable him to finally accept a 'supernatural' view. His illness might be interpreted as his being's revolt against the reality of the 'prison' to which he felt he had been sentenced.

And yet it might be felt that Strindberg's method was more courageous than that of Yeats or Lovecraft. They allowed their dislike of 'reality' and their desire for another world to persuade them of the existence of another order of reality. Strindberg resisted until he was ready to snap, and then gave way unwillingly.

CONCLUSION

Strindberg makes no 'assault on rationality'. He distrusts life and he dislikes society. Yeats wrote of him: 'I have always felt a sympathy for that tortured, self-torturing man who offered himself to his own soul as Buddha offered himself to the famished tiger.' He adds that when he met Strindberg in Paris, Strindberg was looking for the philosopher's stone. This leads one to speculate what outlet Strindberg would have found for his romanticism if he had been born twenty years later, into the age of atomic physics, when such researches would have been demonstrably futile.

The four writers dealt with in this chapter illustrate different attitudes to the 'real world', all based upon rejection. They range from Lovecraft's hysterical assault on 'the real world', through Yeats's guarded respect, to the total acceptance of Strindberg. Strindberg is like a convinced royalist who finds himself forced to condemn the king to death.

In the next chapter, I shall consider the type of imagination that tries a more complicated method of outmanoeuvring 'reality' – that apparently accepts the world as a rag-and-bone shop, and so tries to sidestep the imputation of 'escapism'.

NOTES

1. The following facts are taken from August Derleth's *H. P. L: A Memoir*; I would like also to acknowledge Mr Derleth's help in providing me with additional information about Lovecraft. My other chief source of information has been J. Warren Thomas's unpublished thesis on Lovecraft, which I consulted in the John Hay Library of Brown University, Providence, R. I.

2. See Chapter Four.

3. See the section on M. R. James, Chapter Five, p. 129.

4. It may be mentioned here that in a short book he wrote on the ghost story, Lovecraft makes clear his debt to the English

writer Arthur Machen. Like Lovecraft, Machen is fond of basing his stories on the idea of forgotten people under the earth, ancient legends of evil, etc. He is palpably less obsessed with the horrible and supernatural than Lovecraft; so the extreme clumsiness of his cliché-ridden writing is less forgivable.

5. *A Study of History*, Vol. 10, p. 139.

6. An excellent summary of Yeats's theories can be found in Edmund Wilson's *Axel's Castle*.

7. Eric Bjorkman, Introduction to *The Dream Play*, London; Duckworth, 1924.

8. Quoted in *The Outsider*, p. 111.

Two

The Implications of Realism

EMILE ZOLA

It was Emile Zola who taught the modern novelist the trick of being totally subjective while appearing to be painstakingly, even boringly, objective. Although Zola spent a great deal of time emphasising his 'scientific' technique of gathering information for his novels, he was a frankly ambitious man whose object was to gain money, fame and influence – in that order. He was also the founder of the technique of writing oversexed or sordid books and claiming for them some higher scientific or artistic justification. (One of his novels has a scene in which a son commits incest with his stepmother in a hothouse; to gather information for this scene, Zola went to the Jardin des Plantes and filled a notebook with the names of strange flowers.)

Some modern critics – Mr Angus Wilson among them – have argued that Zola is a very great and underestimated novelist. There can be no doubt at all that he is often a remarkable and powerful writer. He is also a writer who has contributed a great deal of cheapness to the modern novel. When compared with other frankly commercial writers of his century – Dumas and Rider Haggard, for example – there is a nastiness about his work that reveals a more obsessive approach. The reader who makes a study of his books soon discovers that they all have basically the same plan. All move towards climaxes of violence or of sex, all set out to disarm the reader by telling the story in the same precise, objective tone, and all tend to lose their grip towards the end and get swept away into hysteria.

A typical example is *La Bête Humaine*, which cashed in on the Jack The Ripper murders (although the idea of the book came from a French murder case). Its central character, Jacques Lantier, has inherited a sadistic trait from dipsomaniac forebears. Zola's description of the strange compulsion Jacques feels to hurt women, and a scene in which Jacques follows a woman off a train, show a deep

28

insight into abnormal psychology. The beginning of the book demonstrates his ability to create horror and drama without overdoing it. In the first chapter, the stationmaster Roubaud learns that his young wife, Severine, was the mistress of an old man before she married him. He forces her to plot with him to murder the old man. In the second chapter, we are introduced to Lantier and learn about his neurosis; there is a powerful scene in which a girl offers herself to Lantier, and he feels the awful compulsion to kill her, 'to possess her to the point of destroying her'. He rushes away into the darkness, and passes near the railway line. He sees a train flash by, and glimpses in a carriage the stationmaster stabbing an old man while Severine sits on the man's legs. This is the kind of trick only Zola would try. Yet he manages to keep it convincing.

Eventually, Jacques becomes Severine's lover. She is the first woman towards whom he feels no sadistic urge. They plot to murder Roubaud. Now Zola lets the reins slip. There is a gratuitous train wreck, just to stimulate the reader's taste for violence. Then Jacques gives way to his sadistic urge, and murders Severine. Finally, Jacques and the fireman of the train fight on the platform of the engine, and drag one other off while the train hurtles onward. The book ends with the train gathering speed through the night while drunken soldiers sing and shout, unaware that there is now no one on the engine.

One can almost see Zola laying down his pen and taking a deep breath of satisfaction. 'That'll shock 'em.' But it does nothing of the sort. The reader ceased to be shockable several chapters back. (Apparently Zola abandoned the idea of throwing in a pederastic murder as 'too horrific'.)

Angus Wilson has a passage that describes a technique that boxers call 'the old one-two'. He is speaking about *La Terre*:

The atmosphere, the scene, the growing lust of the men, Zola the artist has built these up with complete surety, but two rapes in the afternoon? No; we can't quite take that. All right, says the journalist, what about that cry from the centre of the cornfield – Palmyre, the pathetic cripple girl, the beast of burden, has broken beneath her load, a blood vessel burst in the glare of the sun, and then, in case the reader is still resisting, the tall, gaunt figure of La Grande, the aged peasant woman, advances and prods the body with her stick. 'Dead,' she says. 'Well, that's better than a

29

wretched burden on others.' The episode is complete; the life of the peasantry, one feels sure, is like that – hard, mercenary, brutal.

Mr Wilson implies that the reader is convinced by this piling up of violence; but this is untrue. The whole book is cheapened; it vanishes as a work of art, and can continue only as a piece of sensationalism. And Zola, like a man who realises he has made a complete fool of himself, seems to feel impelled to go on, to plunge deeper into the vulgarity, to shout with defiance to cover his shame. In the final scene, where Françoise is raped by Buteau (and held down by Buteau's wife), Zola tries the preposterous device of making Françoise realise suddenly that she was in love with Buteau all the time. Then he makes the couple murder Françoise with a scythe. This is the book that Mr Wilson describes as the 'culmination of Zola's genius'.

The Zola method, then, is to exaggerate the frightfulness of the world and everyone in it. When his critics accuse him of overdoing the sex and violence, Zola accuses them of squeamishness and hypocrisy. In the same way, Mrs Henry Wood used to defend herself against charges of sentimentality by accusing her critics of being heartless. The truth is that his novels are emotional onslaughts of a kind not unrelated to that of *East Lynne*. But at least Zola was always frank about his purposes and methods. He wrote to his friend Valabrègue: 'If you only knew, my poor friend, how little talent counts in the search for success, you would abandon pen and paper and you would set out to analyse the ways of the literary world, the thousand little tricks that open doors, the art of using other people's credit, the cruelty that is necessary to run over the dear fellow writers.' The novels may reveal this calculating spirit, but the fact that he made no attempt to conceal it is to Zola's credit.

It was because he loved success, and food and wine, and admiration, that Zola was not 'squeamish' about reality. The rag-and-bone shop made the best background for the scenes of violence that would bring him these pleasures. Consequently one need not pay too much attention to his 'realism' as an expression of his imagination. If it had paid him better to write like Mrs Henry Wood or William Morris, he would no doubt have done so. But his realism had a quite definite effect on the imagination of his time, and it is with this effect that I am more concerned in the present chapter.

NATHANAEL WEST

West's work is of interest chiefly because it shows a simultaneous total acceptance and rejection of 'reality'. (I am still using this word to denote the 'world outside' as the writer perceives it.) He finds it as uncongenial as does Yeats, yet he makes no kind of attempt to escape from it.

Nathanael West's real name was Nathan Weinstein. He was killed in a car accident in Hollywood in 1940; he was then thirty-seven. His collected works run to only four novels, two of which are mere *jeux d'esprit*. His two most important works are *Miss Lonelyhearts* and *The Day of the Locust*. The style of both seems heavily influenced by Fitzgerald's *The Great Gatsby*.

An earlier work is worth mentioning. *The Dream Life of Balso Snell* reads like *Alice in Wonderland* written by James Joyce. This is a short, intensely subjective book, that makes no attempt to 'communicate' to its readers; on the contrary, the author seems to enjoy leaving them behind. It is pervaded by a disgust for the body that is reminiscent of Swift, but probably owes more to Aldous Huxley. Alan Ross summarises the quality of the book as 'arrogant obscurantism'.

Miss Lonelyhearts and *The Day of the Locust* are among the most pessimistic and despairing novels written in the twentieth century. The technique is that of *The Great Gatsby* without the glamour, but their content is closer to *The Waste Land* without the underlying religious faith.

'Miss Lonelyhearts' is a young man who runs the Lonely Hearts column for a newspaper during the bootlegging era. He started the job as a lark, but the letters that come in are no joke; they make him aware of the extent of human torment and suffering. Lonelyhearts' attitude is close to that of Ivan Karamazov; but unlike Ivan, Lonelyhearts lacks the metaphysical passion and the love of life. West was obviously aware of the parallel with Dostoevsky, for in an early scene he makes Lonelyhearts read *The Brothers Karamazov*, and decide that he cannot live according to Zossima's injunction to love everything.

The technique of the book shows extreme economy; it

is done in a series of short, tight scenes. There is no plot in the sense of a continuous development; Lonelyhearts' disintegration under a sense of boredom and futility is the only development. His editor Shrike (who is strangely like Joyce's Buck Mulligan) makes jokes about his subordinate's role as the Christ of modern America, the father confessor, scapegoat and remover of sins. But Lonelyhearts is tormented by the image of Christ. Through various episodes he is tortured by the horror of the world. Everybody else in the book is trivial, two-dimensional, shortsighted: West has already answered the question why no one is aware of the suffering and horror of being human. Lonelyhearts has a glimpse of the idea of redemption through love when he meets a cripple, the husband of a nymphomaniac. But it is the cripple who accidentally shoots Lonelyhearts at the end of the book. Lonelyhearts rushes to embrace him in an ecstasy of Christian love; the cripple thinks he is about to be attacked; the gun goes off.

The atmosphere of the novel is stifling; there is not a gleam of hope in it. Probably its nearest literary relative is Huxley's *Antic Hay*. One is reminded particularly of the scene at the midnight coffee stall, where the bored socialites talk about love, and a man with a sick wife talks about his poverty, about how he is forced to overwork an old horse because it is their only means of livelihood. But Huxley's book is gay and hopeful compared to West's.

After *Miss Lonelyhearts*, West went to Hollywood, where he spent the last seven years of his life. *The Day of the Locust* shows no great advance on *Miss Lonelyhearts*. It is the story of a number of people around Hollywood. Two of them are notably sympathetic – a young scenery designer, Tod, and a lonely, middle-aged ex-accountant, Homer. There is only one woman in the book, Faye Greener, an unsuccessful actress, daughter of a down-and-out music-hall comedian. Such plot as the novel possesses is about the way that all the male characters are fascinated by her. There is a dwarf, a Mexican cockfighter and a Hollywood cowboy. As a sex symbol, Faye Greener brings to mind Wedekind's Lulu. She is innocent, good-tempered, and wholly destructive. If *Lonelyhearts* brings to mind *Antic Hay*, this novel brings to mind *Point Counter Point*, except that West knows far more about artistic economy, and lacks Huxley's intellectual exhibitionism. The nastiest scene describes a cockfight with Huxleyan relish. Like *Lonelyhearts*, the book ends catastrophically. The mild-tempered, long-suffering Homer becomes slightly insane when Faye deserts him, and attacks a child who is baiting him. A crowd waiting outside a première thinks he is a sexual pervert and attacks him. Presumably he is killed. Tod, who is also in the crowd, has his leg broken.

It would be easy to interpret these novels as a criticism of capitalist society; West's sympathy seems to be all with the downtrodden masses. He describes the movie extras; 'They loitered on the corners . . . and stared at everyone who passed. When their stare was returned, their eyes filled with hatred . . . they had come to California to die.' Or the people who have come to Hollywood, lured by the glamour and sunshine: 'Their boredom becomes more and more terrible. They realise that they've been tricked, and burn with resentment. Every day of their lives they read the newspapers and went to the movies. Both fed them on lynchings, murder, sex crimes, explosions, wrecks, love nests, fires . . . Nothing can ever be violent enough to make taut their slack bodies and slack minds.'

This is not merely criticism of capitalist society; it is criticism of the human condition.

I have chosen to write about West because his books make no attempt to find a solution. Their despair is static. He seems to have made no advance in the six years between *Lonelyhearts* and *Day of the Locust*. Their atmosphere is agonised need for meaning and purpose. There can be no doubt about the writer's consciousness of sterility and his rejection of it. The only hint of a move towards some kind of religious solution is offered in the title of the second book; presumably this refers to the locusts of the Book of Revelation who appear when the fifth angel blows his trumpet, and who have orders to injure all human beings who do not have the seal of God on their foreheads. 'In those days men will seek death but they will never find it; they will long to die, but death will elude them.' However, the title of a book cannot be taken as evidence; otherwise, Hemingway should have arrived at a religious solution, since he wrote *The Sun Also Rises* in 1923.

WILLIAM FAULKNER

In West, then, the imagination is paralysed. In Faulkner one discovers an imagination that resembles West's in many ways, but that is also closer to Yeats in its romanticism. Faulkner's most violent and 'empty' novel is *Sanctuary*, the story of how a young girl is kidnapped by bootleggers and violated in a way that would have made Magnus Hirschfeld raise his eyebrows. Faulkner admits freely that he wrote it for money; under the circumstances, it is not surprising that it brings Zola to mind. But Faulkner is more of an artist than Zola; even when the horrors fail to convince, the symbolism continues to be effective and to hold the reader's respect. There is the opening description of the gangster Popeye: 'He had that vicious depthless quality of stamped tin.' This also illustrates Faulkner's chief weakness. Stamped tin can hardly be 'vicious'. He is frequently pseudoimpressive, like a gangster talking out of the corner of his mouth. He piles in the adjectives to bludgeon the reader into a state of awe. The style in the later books is incredibly convoluted, and this can also be attributed to the need for impressiveness.

And yet *Sanctuary* is, in some subtle way, a more optimistic novel than *The Day of the Locust*. Perhaps 'optimistic' is the wrong word; it is simply more alive. Like Lovecraft, Faulkner is also out to make your flesh creep. But his horrors are not supernatural; one might borrow Joyce's term and say that he tries for epiphanies of horror – symbolic moments. A typical example occurs in the chapter that has been anthologised as 'Uncle Bud and the Three Madams'. Uncle Bud is a small boy (Faulkner here shows his usual spirit of perversity even in such small details as naming his characters). The three women are three brothel madams, who sit together and discuss the gangster Red, who is about to be buried. (Popeye shot him.) There is a quarrel at the funeral and the coffin gets overturned; the body rolls out and falls on the floor.[1] When they try to pick the corpse up, the wreath comes too, attached to the cheek by a length of wire that has driven into the flesh. The bullet hole in his forehead has been stopped up with pink wax, but this falls out, and they have to pull a peaked cap down over his forehead. Later, as the three madams go on to discuss sentimentally the virtues of the deceased, Uncle

34

Bud gets drunk by taking surreptitious swigs at their beer. Someone catches him at it.

'You boy!' she said, shaking him, 'stan' up!' Limply he dangled, his face rigid in a slobbering grin. Then upon it came an expression of concern, consternation; Minnie swung him sharply away from her as he began to vomit.

The novel ends in an orgy of horrors reminiscent of *La Bête Humaine*; an innocent man is accused of raping the young girl, a mob pours petrol on him and burns him alive. The gangster Popeye escapes, but he is ironically accused of a murder he never committed and electrocuted.

What exactly is Faulkner's purpose in piling up the horror? It is not entirely to make the book a best seller (which it was), for a great deal of his most serious work uses the same devices. To some extent, it is to set the scene for the acceptance of his own romanticism. For Faulkner's mainspring is an exaggerated respect for the past and for the gentry of the Deep South. When Faulkner writes of the past, of the early days of Yoknapatawpha County, of Colonel Sartoris and General Compson, he writes with a nostalgia that occasionally expresses itself in overblown romantic language. The theme of his best novel, *The Sound and the Fury*, is the decay of the Compson family, and when he writes of this decay, his language acquires a crispness that springs from disgust. The family's decadence is symbolised in the 'soiled undergarment of cheap silk a little too pink' that Quentin leaves behind when she elopes with the pitch-man. Popeye had 'eyes like rubber knobs', and his face 'just went awry, like the face of a wax doll set too near a hot fire'. An old man in *Sanctuary* has eyes like 'clots of phlegm'. When he writes about the past, Faulkner talkes about the sound of 'distant bugles on the road to Roncevalles'; when he writes about the present, his symbolism aims at creating revulsion.

Faulkner's County, like Lovecraft's New England, is full of legends of horror; but Faulkner's horror is all physical. He drew a map of Yoknapatawpha County for an anthology of his work; significantly enough most of the places marked on it are connected with violent death. 'Where Lee Goodwin was lynched', 'Where Popeye murdered Tawmmy', etc. One would imagine that Faulkner has a particular score to settle with middle-aged virgins, for at least two of them meet with a horrible fate in his books. In *Light in August*, the frigid Miss Burden becomes the mistress of a Negro and is murdered by him; in the story 'A Rose for Emily', the lady of the title shoots her lover and then sleeps with his body for the rest of her life.

Perhaps Faulkner's most carefully calculated and successful horror story is 'Red Leaves'. This is about the days when Red Indians owned most of Yoknapatawpha County, as well as Negro slaves. The Indians have a curious Egyptian custom of burying a slave with their dead chiefs, to act as a servant in the after-world. Before the burial, they also have a ritual hunting of the slave through the swamps. Faulkner describes this hunting in completely flat language. The Negro is finally recaptured, and given a bowl of water to drink. As he drinks thirstily, the water slops over his chin and cuts paths down through the caked mud on his body. This is the end of the story; the horror – of the Negro being buried alive – is left to the imagination. (There seems to be a chance that the slave will die before he is buried, since he was bitten by a snake in the swamp.)

Faulkner's basic intention is the same as Lovecraft's – to somehow get his own back on 'reality'. He doesn't like the world he lives in. (Hence, perhaps, the tremendous drinking bouts that are so typical a part of the Faulkner legend.) He prefers turning to the past. And, like Lovecraft, he spends much of his creative life making that past more circumstantial and credible. Through a series of books, over thirty years, he has created his own County, a complex myth that he can oppose to 'reality'. Some of his recent books seem to show that the compulsion to live in the past is weakening as he grows older, as it did with Yeats; they deal with the contemporary scene, but without the revulsion shown in *Sanctuary*.

Undeniably, Faulkner's achievement is impressive; yet it is marked, like Lovecraft's, by the underlying feeling of neurotic compulsion amounting sometimes to sadism. His work lacks the Homeric feeling – the feeling that is also present in Scott and Balzac and Dumas – of a man creating because he loves to create, as a bird loves to sing. And some of the stylistic tricks of the later books – the sentences that run on for several pages – reveal a man who is much too aware of the effect he is creating: the prima donna.

For all their diversity of aim, and of literary merit, all the writers I have dealt with so far have one thing in common: they were all born a little too near the 'pain threshold'. There are some men who see the world naturally as an incredibly beautiful place; they carry into adulthood a vision that is the normal mode of perception of some children (if one is to believe Thomas Traherne, Sri Ramakrishna, Wordsworth, for example). If one judges by *A Christmas Carol*, Dickens was one of them; so was G. K. Chesterton; and William James cites Walt Whitman as an example of the 'blue sky philosophy'. These writers need have no *reason* for finding the world an agreeable place; Dickens showed himself to be as aware of evil and malice as any man. They simply *see* it that way. Although Dickens possessed one of the most fertile creative intelligences in literature, he never seems to have felt the need to create his own separate world, as Faulkner did. Characters in one book do not recur in others; each book is a separate unit, like Shakespeare's plays. And this is because Dickens did not feel he was creating a 'Dickensian' world apart from 'reality'. His characters may be like no human beings who ever lived; but, basically, they are people Dickens had known and seen.

Although there may be no reason, apart from temperament, why Dickens and Whitman were able to accept the world they lived in (at least, they had no 'quarrel with God' for creating it), this does not always seem to be true for the 'pessimistic' writers. Childhood injustice or ill-treatment seems to have had a lifelong effect on Strindberg, Dostoevsky, Poe. But this may be an effect not a cause. There is no real evidence that Strindberg's sombre outlook was formed by poverty and injustice, any more than there is evidence that Shaw's optimism was the result of a happy childhood.

At all events, it seems arguable that attempts to create 'systems' and build separate worlds are a romantic phenomenon: that is, they are the result of a tendency to reject 'reality'. This is not to say that the 'born optimists' take the world exactly as it comes. They may, like Tolstoy, be intent on changing it. But Tolstoy's religious system is not an integral part of his creation, as it is with Dostoevsky; it is a later intellectualisation.

If one accepts this proposition – that romantics are system builders – then it would appear that the real division in art is not that which exists between classic and romantic, but the one between the born optimists and the born 'rejecters'. This latter distinction is certainly of more use than the old classic/romantic dichotomy in an analysis of the imagination. One sees, for example, that Shaw and Blake really have less in common than Blake and Zola; for although Shaw and Zola were both social reformers, Shaw was a born optimist, and Blake and Zola were born rejecters and system makers. Blake's vision of the world is Zola-esque:

> I wander through each dirty street
> Near where the dirty Thames does flow,
> And see in every face I meet
> Marks of weakness, marks of woe.[2]

The 'rejecter' may or may not decide to use his observation of the 'real world' in building his system; he may be as faithful to 'reality' as Nathanael West, or as regardless as Blake. He may try to convince on an intellectual level – like Yeats in *A Vision* or Robert Graves in his curious *White Goddess* – or on an emotional level, like Dostoevsky and Faulkner.

EVELYN WAUGH AND GRAHAM GREENE

It is instructive to consider two Catholic writers whose work is an interesting variant on the usual romatic method. Like Zola and Faulkner, they emphasise the sordid aspects of the world to bully the reader's emotions. But unlike Zola and Faulkner, their aim is to create in the reader a sense of total rejection.

Because he is a humorist, Waugh's aims may seem to have little to associate them with the 'rejecters'. But if his world is considered without paying attention to the humour, it is seen that his view of 'reality' is almost as hair-raisingly pessimistic as Lovecraft's. The humour is sometimes like the grin on the face of a skull. His tendency to treat disasters lightly gave him the reputation of a literary *enfant terrible*. In the early books, only injustice and sexual promiscuity are treated as if they were funny. The hero of *Decline and Fall* is kicked out of college for indecency when he is the victim of a debagging incident. The hero of *Vile Bodies* has his novel – his life's work – confiscated by Customs, who say it is pornographic. But it is in *Black Mischief* and *A Handful of Dust* that this type of 'humour' develops into a method. The seduction scene in *Black Mischief* is as deliberately sordid as anything in Joyce. At the end of the book, the hero eats a meal with a tribe of cannibals, and discovers he is eating his girl friend.

The purpose of all this eludes the reader, who assumes it to be simply a peculiar form of humour (the most primitive kind – uncivilised tribes roar with laughter when someone gets hurt). But in *A Handful of Dust*, the purpose is clearer. The book is the story of a woman's adultery, but Waugh shows none of Flaubert's sympathy for the adulteress. Brenda Last decides arbitrarily to have an affair with John Beaver, the son of a female interior decorator who moves in the circles of his mother's wealthy customers. The progress of the affair is described bleakly; John Beaver's complete worthlessness is made so obvious that it hardly makes pleasant reading. Then Brenda's son John is killed in a riding accident. The death has no effect of tragedy or pathos; one even suspects that it is supposed to be somehow funny.[3] Brenda tells her husband Tony that she wants a divorce; he refuses to give her one and goes on a trip to the South American jungle. His canoe overturns, and he struggles to the hut of a half-insane trader who keeps him captive because he wants someone to read Dickens aloud to him. Brenda, abandoned by her lover – who is disgusted that she is not going to get fat alimony – finally marries a friend of Tony's. Tony, of course, is still alive in his captivity, reading Dickens.

Edmund Wilson has called this book Waugh's masterpiece, but that is putting it a little strongly. It is not funny, and it fails to evoke the terror of *The Waste Land*, from which its title is taken. The one thing it does do successfully is to give an overwhelming feeling of the futility of the lives of most of its characters. It does this at the cost of steering very close to the edge of boredom. The great novelist conveys the sensation that he loves his characters; Waugh gives the impression that he is looking down on his characters from a great height, with a sadistic grin on his face. None of Waugh is unreadable (he has too much sense of language for that), but this is the least rereadable of his books; it is hard to imagine anyone who has managed to finish it ever wanting to open it again. If the book is a 'masterpiece', then surely it is the only one in the world's literature with this peculiar distinction.

In his next two novels, *Scoop* and *Put Out More Flags*, Waugh shows his hand more plainly. It now becomes apparent that one of his chief values is the respect he feels for the character of the English aristocracy. *Scoop* is about a naturalist – a country gentleman – who gets sent accidentally on an assignment as a war correspondent, and who keeps demonstrating, in a quiet way, the superiority of the English public-school tradition. *Put Out More Flags* is funnier than *Scoop*, and at first it looks as though Waugh has again decided to treat his aristocrats satirically; but in the end, its ne'er-do-well hero (who also figured in *Black Mischief*) joins the commandos and has a kind of apotheosis. Once again, the aristocratic public-school strain shows it is made of the right stuff.

But it is not until *Brideshead Revisited* that Waugh finally shows his hand. The book is told by Captain Charles Ryder, and it is composed mainly of his reminiscences of an aristocratic Catholic family, whose head is a lapsed Catholic, Lord Marchmain. The first part of the book, which deals with Ryder's acquaintance with the son of the family, Sebastian, at Oxford, succeeds in conveying authentically Waugh's admiration for the eccentricity and glamour of his aristocrats, and his detestation of upstarts, social climbers and vulgarity in general. The snobbery is reminiscent of Wilde. In the second part of the book, Waugh now begins to proselytise for Catholicism, and there is an unconvincing deathbed scene when Lord Marchmain returns to the Catholic fold. Sebastian has gone to live in Fez with a homosexual German, and there is a scene in Waugh's best sordid manner, when Ryder pays them a visit. Sebastian's total humiliation is underscored. Later, Sebastian has a breakdown and enters a monastery as an under-gardener. Ryder is having a love affair with Sebastian's sister Julia, but she finally deserts him at the call of the Church. The second half of the book is the most nauseating mixture of snobbery and sentimentality in Waugh's output.

In a subsequent novel, *The Loved One*, he returns to his earlier manner – satire and black humour. The subject of

his satire is the slickly commercialised Hollywood ceme-
teries. The objection to the book is put pertinently by
Edmund Wilson:

> To the non-religious reader . . . the patrons and proprietors of
> Whispering Glades seem more sensible and less absurd than the
> priest-guided Evelyn Waugh. What the former are trying to do
> is, after all, merely to gloss over physical death with smooth lawns
> and soothing rites; but for the Catholic the fact of death is not to
> be faced at all: he is solaced with the fantasy of another world in
> which everyone who has died in the flesh is somehow supposed
> to be alive, and in which it is supposed to be possible to help souls
> to advance themselves by buying candles to burn in churches.

This remark need not be taken as an attack on Catholicism
so much as on Waugh's sickly brand of Catholic snobbery.
Waugh creates an effect of insincerity that is not the fault
of his beliefs; Eliot managed to embrace Anglicanism without producing an impression of selling out. But one suspects that Waugh's Catholicism has the same roots as his
admiration of the aristocracy – the negative basis of a dislike of vulgarity. His picture of reality is deliberately
depressing; he is telling the reader: 'This is what the world
is like, but I have positive beliefs that save me from despair.'
The 'unregenerate world' is futile and sordid, and destiny
is likely to play sudden horrible jokes. (Auberon Waugh,
the novelist's son, shows the same tendency to black humour
in his first novel *The Foxglove Saga*.) But when the reader
is thoroughly depressed by all this, Waugh offers him his
solution – Catholicism and snobbery. The chief trouble
with Waugh's Catholicism is that Waugh fails to convey
the impression that he is a man with any talent for religious
conviction. He always seizes on the dogmas that seem to
non-Catholics to be least essential to Catholicism – the
doctrine about divorce, for example, which appears in
Brideshead Revisited and later in the 'Guy Crouchback'
series.

The book that is likely to strike non-Catholics as most
interesting is the curious *Ordeal of Gilbert Pinfold*, a
confessional, semi-autobiographical novel that describes
a nervous breakdown; its central character succumbs completely to a persecution mania. For the first time, Waugh
seems to escape from the desire to impress. Readers of his
earlier books may find it hard to avoid a feeling that he is

displaying an ugly form of hubris, which he manages to get away with because he is such an engaging and humorous fellow. In *Pinfold*, this realisation appears to have caught up with Waugh. But the book is curiously unsatisfactory. Having suffered various hallucinations, Pinfold returns home, cured, to write the story of his breakdown. It is as if Waugh started out with a point, and forgot it halfway through. The point, of course, is *why* Pinfold had the breakdown and how he managed to cure himself. But Waugh shrinks from the effort of self-analysis, never having tried to exercise it in his earlier books. One has only to compare it with Tolstoy's *Confession* to realise what is wrong with it. It is a half confession – a quarter confession.

Graham Greene is, in most ways, an altogether more interesting talent than Waugh. But his 'technique of conversation' is identical with Waugh's: his world is meant to depress the reader into feeling the need for religion. Greene brings Zola to mind in more ways than one; all his novels are about sex or violence or both. And there seems to be no doubt that Greene is also deeply interested in success; this makes it difficult to believe in his artistic sincerity.

Greene supplies a great deal more data than Waugh on the development of his personal vision. So far, the two most important sources are the preface to *The Lawless Roads* and several autobiographical essays in *The Lost Childhood*. In an essay in this latter book, 'The Revolver in the Corner Cupboard', Greene tells how he ran away from school, and was psychoanalysed.

I emerged from those delightful months in London spent at my analyst's house – perhaps the happiest months of my life – correctly orientated, able to take a proper extrovert interest in my fellows (the jargon rises to the lips), but wrung dry. For years, it seems to me, I could take no aesthetic interest in any visual thing at all; staring at a sight that others assured me was beautiful, I would feel nothing. I was fixed in my boredom.

Coleridge has described a similar state of mind at the beginning of 'Dejection'.

Greene goes on to tell how he played Russian roulette with his brother's revolver – twirling the chambers, with one bullet in, pointing it at his head, and firing; there was, of course, a six-to-one chance of blowing out his brains. This had the effect of releasing the emotional tension.

In the excellent essay that gives the volume its title, Greene talks about the books that influenced him in childhood. First came *King Solomon's Mines*, which created a romanticism about Africa (of which, curiously enough, *The Heart of the Matter*, that novel of gloomy failure, is the end product). Then came *The Viper of Milan* by Marjorie Bowen. It was not simply the zest and colour of this historical romance that influenced him, Greene writes:

> It was no good in that real world to dream that one would ever be a Sir Henry Curtis [hero of *King Solomon's Mines*], but della Scala who at last turned from an honesty that never paid and betrayed his friends and died dishonoured and a failure even at treachery – it was easier for a child to escape behind his mask. As for Visconti, with his beauty, his patience and his genius for evil, I had watched him pass by many a time in his black Sunday suit smelling of mothballs. His name was Carter . . . Human nature is not black and white, but black and grey. I read all that in *The Viper of Milan* and I looked round and saw that it was so.

He goes on to speak about the sense of doom that becomes most acute when success seems most complete:

> the feeling that the pendulum is about to swing. That too made sense; one looked around and saw the doomed everywhere – the champion runner who would one day sag over the tape; the head of the school who would atone, poor devil, during forty dreary undistinguished years; the scholar . . . and when success began to touch oneself too, however mildly, one could only pray that failure would not be held off for too long.

Failure seems an obsession, and a paragraph later he repeats that perhaps it would have been better if he had gone out to Sierra Leone 'and twelve tours of malarial duty and a finishing dose of blackwater fever when the danger of retirement approached'. This is the expression of a pathologically morbid temperament.

The preface to *The Lawless Roads* explains Greene's sense of evil. He describes his public school (presumably the one from which he ran away) and the

> fear and hate, a kind of lawlessness – appalling cruelties could be practised without a second thought; one met, for the first time characters, adult and adolescent, who bore about them the genu-

43

ine quality of evil. There was Colifax, who practised torments with dividers: Mr Cranden, with three grim chins, a dusty gown, a kind of demoniac sensuality; from these heights, evil declined towards Parlow, whose desk was filled with minute photographs – advertisements of art photos. Hell lay about them in their infancy.

Escaping from the school for a few hours at night, Greene describes how 'one became aware of God with an intensity – time hung suspended . . .'

And so faith came to one, – shapelessly, without dogma. . . . One began to believe in heaven because one believed in hell, but for a long while it was only hell one could picture with a certain intimacy – the pitchpine partitions in dormitories where everybody was never quiet at the same time; lavatories without locks. . . . These were the primary symbols; life later altered them; in a midland city, riding on trams in winter past the Gothic hotel, the super-cinema, the sooty newspaper office where one worked at night, passing the single professional prostitute trying to keep the circulation going under the blue and powdered skin, one began slowly, painfully, reluctantly, to populate heaven. The Mother of God took the place of the brass eagle; one began to have a dim conception of the appalling mysteries of love moving through a ravaged world – the Curé of Ars admitting to his mind all the impurity of a province, Péguy challenging God in the cause of the damned . . .

Greene goes on to give an evocative description of the midland town, too long to quote here, speaking of youths with 'smarmed and scented hair' greeting girls with 'careless roughness . . . sexual experience had come to them too early and too easily'. He speaks of a boy and a girl who committed suicide by lying with their necks on the railway line; she was pregnant for the second time. 'Her first had been born when she was thirteen, and . . . her parents had been unable to fix responsibility . . . among fourteen youths.' He speaks of a woman who murdered her husband by stabbing him with a breadknife. 'The knife went in as if his body was rotten.'

These events are the symbols of Greene's world, just as Yeats's 'storm-beaten old watch tower' and memories of heroism are symbols of his. He goes on to quote the example of Father Miguel Pro, who was executed in Mexico under the regime of President Calles, and was photographed praying for his enemies as he was executed. Here is a symbol of redeeming love and grace in a world that is mostly suffering and boredom.

This is the world that Greene portrays in book after book with dreary consistency, a consistency that is bound to make less pessimistic people suspect an affectation. One is reminded of P. G. Wodehouse's remark about a Russian novelist in *The Clicking of Cuthbert*: 'Vladimir specialised in grey studies of hopeless misery, where nothing happened till page three hundred and eighty, when the moujik decided to commit suicide.' With unfailing accuracy, Greene seizes on the most depressing details to characterise a scene. But his stylistic effects sometimes come dangerously close to bathos. This, from the opening of *The Power and the Glory*: 'A few vultures looked down from the roof with shabby indifference: he wasn't carrion yet. A faint feeling of rebellion stirred in Mr Tench's heart, and he wrenched up a piece of the road with splintering fingernails and tossed it feebly towards them.' The 'splintering fingernails' are intended to make the reader wince; the adjective 'feebly' produces a sense of futility. But 'he wasn't carrion yet' is a cheap dramatic trick, a gratuitous comment by the omniscient novelist offered as if it were one of Mr Tench's thoughts. The opening of *The Confidential Agent* uses the device even more flagrantly: 'The gulls swept over Dover. They sailed out like flakes of the fog and tacked back towards the hidden town, while the siren mourned with them; other ships replied, a whole wake lifted up their voices – for whose death?' At the beginning of *The Ministry of Fear*, a man entering a fairground is walking 'towards his doom'. In the first sentence of *Orient Express*, the passengers 'cross the grey wet quay, over a wilderness of rails and points, round the corners of abandoned trucks . . .' (One feels like asking: 'Who abandoned them?') In the second sentence of *Brighton Rock*, the journalist Hale is described: 'With his inky fingers and his bitten nails, his manner cynical and nervous, anybody could tell he didn't belong.' Somehow, the world that is described so effectively and movingly in the preface to *The Lawless Roads* fails to come across. All these dramatic devices make it look like stage scenery. A road in *Brighton Rock* looks like 'a razor scar slashed in the chalk'. This is in fact, a slightly different use of the Lovecraft technique. Greene also wants to make our flesh creep, so he constantly uses

45

overcoloured words and images to do it. But as with Love-craft's constant use of 'eldritch', 'horrible', 'miasmic', etc., the final effect is one of self-parody. Edmund Wilson commented on the enormous relief of turning from Lovecraft's overcoloured prose to Mérimée's cold and detached horror story 'The Venus of Ille'. The same is true of Greene; one finally feels irritated by the 'pathetic fallacy' that is always lurking behind the most innocently objective description. It is a relief to turn to the novels of Robbe-Grillet, for he at least tries to keep himself out of his descriptions.

Some of Greene's short stories are less overloaded with the pathetic fallacy, and his description of childhood torments and miseries produce an effect of sincerity that is absent from most of his novels. But the obsession with failure is still there, pervading everything. In *Mr Polly*, Wells described provincial-town seediness and boredom with the same realism as Greene; but one feels that he is waiting impatiently for the point in the book where Mr Polly achieves his freedom and realises that 'if you don't like your life you can change it'. Greene's equivalent of Mr Polly, the butler Baines in 'The Basement Room', is accidentally betrayed by the child who adores him. (Baines has killed his wife by pushing her over the banisters.) The story is told from the point of view of the child, suggesting that it is the author who is trying to exorcise a painful memory. Yeats has a poem in which he refers to memory that makes him writhe with embarrassment, 'my conscience or my vanity appalled'. But Greene positively dwells on these moments of retrospective agony, finding in them a justification for his refusal to enjoy being alive.[4] (His one portrait of a healthy-minded, cheerful woman – Ida Arnold in *Brighton Rock* – bristles with a Jansenist hatred.)

A story called 'The End of the Party' can be considered as a brief epitome of Greene's method. It deals with a pair of male twins, Peter and Francis, about eight years old. One is self-confident, the other timid. They have a kind of telepathic contact. They go together to a New Year party, where there will be games in the dark. Francis is terrified of the dark and tries hard to get out of going, but the grown-ups cannot comprehend that any child should want to avoid a party, and the twins are packed off. A great deal of emphasis is laid on Francis's sensitivity and his terror. Finally, the moment arrives; games in the dark are announced. Francis tries to excuse himself, but the other children call him a coward, and he agrees to play. As he and his brother crouch in the dark, Peter can feel the vibrations of fear coming from him. Finally the lights go on; Francis has died of terror. But Peter wonders 'why it was that the pulse of his brother's fear went on and on, when Francis was now where he had always been told there was no more terror and no more darkness'. Francis is a frightened ghost, perpetually doomed to terror now he is outside the body's protection.

A whole attitude to existence emerged in the story. The incomprehension of adults, the agonised sensitivity of children, and finally the horrible unknown behind life that justifies every terror. A 'healthy-minded' reader who finds the story hysterical and unconvincing would argue that there *are* sensitive adults who remember their childhood; that although the agonies of childhood are real, we outgrow them and are better for outgrowing them; and that, finally, Greene knows no more about 'the other side' than any 'once born' optimist. No doubt the self-induced agonies of the hypochondriac are also 'real'.

But from the viewpoint of the unconvinced reader, the most irritating thing about the story is a kind of emotional double-shuffle. Greene appears to be condemning the incomprehension of adults and, by implication, asking for more understanding. But, as we know from Greene's other work, his pessimism is not of the sort that will be modified by a little comprehension. The universe is a black and a horrible place, and it would still be black and horrible even if children and adults were in constant telepathic contact. The story asks for the reader's sympathy under false pretences; while appearing to plead for children, Greene is actually preaching his Jansenist doctrine that life is pretty awful anyway.

This is the final objection to Greene. His fundamental position, as explained in the autobiographical work, is valid enough. Like all writers born a little too close to the 'pain threshold', he needs to compensate for the futility and meanness he sees around him. His 'world view' is not unlike that of Nathanael West. 'Birth, copulation and death', failure, seediness, suffering. You feel that even if he had to describe an oak tree in early spring, he would take care to explain that the leaves have a coating of coal dust from the nearby foundry and that the tree is dying anyway from the polluted river that flows past its roots. But unlike West, he failed to take Scott Fitzgerald for a master. So instead of the tight, classical control, the delicate irony and self-mockery, there are tremendous melodramatic gestures. One can imagine Henry Irving hamming the opening of *The Confidential Agent*, and sinking his voice to a hoarse whisper on the words 'For whose death?'.

Greene's admirers will object that I have quoted his serious novels and his 'entertainments' as if there is no distinction. But can any author divide his work into two categories and declare that one half of it is 'unrepresentative'? The case of Faulkner's *Sanctuary* argues against it. At the most, it means that the author throws off certain restraints in writing a potboiler. Greene admits that *Brighton Rock* was conceived as an entertainment, and turned into a 'serious novel'. This is precisely what is wrong with it. Pinkie, the teenage killer who is also a Catholic, is a character out of a B film, frankly incredible in his evil. And this is not because such youths *could not* exist; most probation officers have a Pinkie among their charges. It is because Greene takes no trouble to take the reader inside the character; instead, he relies on overcoloured adjectives, in the Lovecraft manner, to frighten the reader into accepting the boy as wholly wicked, 'tight-lipped', 'rigid', 'brutal', with 'anger grinding at his guts' and 'hideous and unnatural pride'. Every other sentence contains an attempt on the part of the author to bludgeon the reader into the right state of mind; the sea is 'poison-bottle green' (what is the difference between that and ordinary bottle green?), Pinkie's eyes have 'an effect of heartlessness like those of an old man in whom human feeling has died', and his hatred is like 'handcuffs to be fastened around [someone's] wrists'. But Pinkie is also a Catholic, so in spite of his evil, he is closer to God than the good-natured Ida Arnold, who tries to bring about his downfall.

Pinkie marries a young girl (also, of course, a Catholic) to prevent her from 'talking'. On a fairground, he makes a record for her and confesses that he hates her. She does not play it immediately. After Pinkie's death, the girl visits a priest, who speaks to her of 'the appalling strangeness of the mercy of God', and says that if Pinkie loved her, it shows he was not beyond redemption. She goes home to play the gramophone record. The book ends, 'She walked rapidly in the thin June sunlight towards the worst horror of all'. The ending is reminiscent of Zola's *Bête Humaine*; the final assault on the reader. But, as with Zola, Greene has lost the reader's credence two hundred pages back; he has cried wolf too often.

But there is one effective scene in the book – the final scene with the priest. For a moment, the reader becomes aware of what Greene is trying to say. He mentions Peguy: 'There was a Frenchman . . . who had the same idea as you. He was a good man, a holy man, and he lived in sin through all his life because he couldn't bear the idea that any soul should suffer damnation . . . He never took the sacraments, he never married his wife in church. I don't know, my child, but some people think he was . . . well, a saint.'[5]

Greene, like Peguy, is objecting to the usual idea of damnation. He is trying to say, in effect: 'The world seems foredoomed to damnation, and if the mercy of God is rational, there is no hope for us. But one can never tell.' If *Brighton Rock* had said this successfully, it would be an important book, perhaps even a great book. But it fails every possible test; its religious theme is cheapened by its melodrama, its pseudo-impressive writing, its hysteria.

In some of his more recent books, there are signs that Greene is becoming conscious of these shortcomings. *The Quiet American* is told in the first person, and so lacks those annoying interpolations from the author, those similes that are all cut to the same pattern of disgust. The narrator is a non-believer, and there is no sign that Greene disapproves of his cynical agnosticism. The only sign of Greene's usual bias is his attitude towards Pyle, the 'quiet American', who represents innocent and meddlesome humanitarianism; he is a kind of transformation of Ida Arnold. An entertainment, *Our Man in Havana* (1958), reveals a sense of humour that has apparently been in abeyance for the past thirty years. His most recent book at the time of writing, *A Burnt Out Case*, is set in a leper colony in Africa, and is overweighted with the usual sense of failure and futility, but seems to have an element of 'confession' in it (like Waugh's *Gilbert Pinfold*), since the main character, a successful architect, confesses that his enormous success is just a bore, and has left him spiritually empty; it is hard not to identify this viewpoint with Greene's. The conse-

49

quent feeling of sincerity makes the book more convincing than his last African novel, *The Heart of the Matter*, another protracted study in bad conscience, agony and humiliation that ends, after two hundred and fifty pages, 'when the moujik commits suicide'.

In certain matters of technique and outlook, Greene's nearest literary relative is Aldous Huxley. Huxley's world is also a gloomy place, divided between weaklings and fools. And both Greene and Huxley place great emphasis on humiliation. It is significant that when Greene speaks of his 'symbols of evil' – the thin partitions in the dormitories, lavatory doors without locks – they are actually symbols of embarrassment. (One is reminded of a scene in *Eyeless in Gaza* where the schoolboys peer over a dormitory partition to spy on a boy masturbating in a rupture truss.) Shaw could accept the necessity for humiliation and embarrassment with the cheerful comment, 'You cannot learn to skate without making a fool of yourself'. One suspects that Greene and Huxley have allowed early humiliations to colour their whole lives.

But when he is compared with Huxley, it is immediately obvious that Greene is the lesser writer. To begin with, he is no thinker; he lacks the analytical faculty. A writer who professes to speak about the condition of man is gravely handicapped if he refuses to try to define his position in intellectual terms. It is even difficult to treat such a writer as serious. It is not that Greene has an *a priori* objection to using a novel to express ideas, as Joyce had. It is significant that the most effective pages of *Brighton Rock* are the ones in which he comes clean and allows the priest to express the idea of the book. It would appear that he simply objects to the exercise of thinking, and indulges in it as little as possible.

JEAN-PAUL SARTRE

The work of Sartre is as uncompromisingly 'realistic' – that is to say, as sordid – as that of any of the writers dealt with in this chapter. But he differs from West, Faulkner, Greene, in being an 'intellectual' whose interest in depicting human lives and their environment is largely analytical. Like them he wants to pass judgment on human life; unlike them, he does not decide in advance on the answer.

In an essay on Mauriac, Sartre makes clear his notion of the novelist's responsibility. His objection to Mauriac is that he takes 'God's standpoint on his characters. God sees the inside and outside . . . In a like manner, M. Mauriac is omniscient about everything relating to his little world. What he says about his characters is Gospel.' He finished with the famous comment: 'God is not an artist. Neither is M. Mauriac.' These objections, of course, might also be applied to Graham Greene; in essence, they are an objection to the 'pathetic fallacy', to the novelist interposing himself between his creation and the reader and 'explaining' it. (There is an example in a Trollope novel – I forget which – where Trollope writes: 'Well, reader, what shall we make Miss X do? Shall we make her marry the squire?' This is an extreme example of what Sartre is objecting to.)

The technique of allowing reality to speak for itself can be extended in many directions. The novelist might, for example, behave as if he were simply a camera and a recording machine. Joyce tried this in the newspaper-office scene of *Ulysses*, where the cries of newsboys, the noise of machinery, the ringing of telephones and the snatches of overheard conversation are all recorded impartially. The result is a tremendous confusion. The camera-technique may be effective when the action is simple, as in the early chapters of *Ulysses*, but it has its limitations. Another alternative is Robbe-Grillet's technique of allowing a whole novel to be observed through the eyes of a single character, and providing long and careful descriptions of everything he sees – the size, shape and measurements of every table and chair. This may appeal to purists, but it makes for incredibly tedious reading.

But in his first novel *Nausea (La Nausée)*, Sartre has taken the idea of objectivity to a curious extreme. The novel is the diary of a man whose feelings keep drying up completely and leaving him confronted with objects that seem to crush him. The human mind selects and interprets what it sees as a matter of course; it rations out its attention, deciding what is important and what can be ignored. Sartre is saying: 'How can we judge what deserves attention?' We are, of necessity, egotists who allow our feelings to dominate our lives. But if a man went to an extreme of Christian humility and sat waiting for the meaning to emerge from the objects that surround him, the result might be that sudden collapse of individuality in the face of the world.

A simile might make this clearer. When I pick up a book, I know that the author had an overall impression that he wanted to make, and I try to read it with an open mind, to grasp what he wants to say. If I have just been reading Thomas Hardy, and I turn to Tolstoy assuming that Tolstoy sees the world in the same way as Hardy, I shall be mis-interpreting Tolstoy's intention until it dawns on me that he is saying something totally different. Yet no matter how much I try to keep an open mind as I read some new author, I find it impossible not to impose my own ego on the book in certain ways. I remember certain things with clarity and forget others; I pay more attention to some things than to others. If it is a difficult book – let us say, an experimental novel by a new author – I try hard to interpret his intention, and keep trying out different patterns of my own on the book, to see if they fit. And I may feel aware that I am distorting the book in reading it, and try hard to keep my own ideas and personality in complete abeyance until I have grasped what the writer wants to say.

In the same way, we hold a dual attitude towards our experience. To some extent, we are willing to learn from it, so we try to preserve an open mind; but we are also critical and selective; there are some things we try to avoid, and if they are unavoidable, we try to pay them as little attention as possible.

If a man should try to suppress completely his critical and selective faculty – perhaps because he has a low opin-ion of himself – he would find himself in the position of being bullied by the physical world, crushed by it. For even if you are reading a book with a completely open mind, you still need to keep enough of your critical faculty to be able to distinguish the words and the meaning of the par-agraphs; a book read with a *completely* open mind would be only a series of black characters on paper.

Unfortunately, the world is not written by an author, so there is no point in gazing passively at one's experiences and waiting for the author's meaning to become apparent. This has the effect of causing the world to dissolve into black squiggles.

That is the theme of *Nausea*. Antoine Roquentin becomes periodically aware that he imposes order on his experience. But he has an extremely low opinion of himself; he feels himself to be completely ignorant of the purpose of his life and of life in general. Like many heroes of modern novels, he comes to feel that life is a meaningless ritual. When he occasionally becomes aware that he is imposing his judgments on his experience, he immediately suspends his judgment-making faculty, and is suddenly confronted with the crushingly 'real' reality that he happens to be looking at: so he is suddenly frightened and disgusted by a stone in his hand, by an ink bottle on the table. While he is writing the life of a historical character he realises that he is also imposing his meanings and judgments on it, just as the character himself did in the act of living it. So he stops writing it. He feels that people who impose meaning on their lives by a smug self-conceit are 'swine'; this feeling becomes very strong when he walks round a portrait gallery, with its pictures of eminent local citizens. He feels, as it were, that no one has a right to begin living until he knows why he is alive. He then goes on to recognise that no one has ever had any idea of why he is alive; so all men would experience this total moral collapse, the 'nausea', if they saw as clearly as he sees. This is the nineteenth-century nihilism, the H. P. Lovecraft pessimism: we can choose truth or life, but life depends on self-delusion. Sartre is one of the first novelists to express this nihilism in basic, non-emotional terms.

There is, of course, no answer when the problem is expressed in this way. At the end of the book, Roquentin decides that one *must* choose, that since we shall never know why we are alive, he must select an arbitrary purpose and commit himself to it.

This may seem a stoical and uncomforting philosophy, but Sartre has continued to expound it for the past twenty years. In one of his later plays, *The Hermits of Altona* (1959), he still makes one of his characters talk about 'the basic horror of existence'. Most of his works are dramas of choice. The novels (influenced by Faulkner) are as gloomy and full of disgust as Greene's. An early volume of stories, *The Wall*, is typical. Its opening story, 'Intimacy', deals with a frigid woman of lesbian tendencies who has married an impotent man because he makes no physical demands; she leaves him temporarily for a lover, but goes back to him. Sartre goes to a great deal of trouble to focus all kinds of distasteful detail of physical intimacy, trying to defeat the mind's tendency to impose a sexual meaning on them. The story is, in that sense, anti-pornographic; it uses the technique of *Nausea*, making physical details so oppressive that they eventually become meaningless. (An English paperback edition of the book has a blurb that declares it 'leaves Lady Chatterley standing at the post'; nothing could be more misleading.) Another story deals with a woman who chooses to live in the insane world of her husband's paranoid delusions. All are concerned in some way with the act of choice. His major novel *The Roads to Freedom* (in four volumes) is also a gallery of different kinds of characters confronting different choices. It is also a 'historical' novel about the second world war, and the experimental techniques of the latter two volumes, together with the atmosphere of unfailing gloom and physical oppression, make reading it a feat of endurance.

The play *The Hermits of Altona* reveals Sartre's strength and his weakness very clearly. His vision of the world continues to be as gloomy as Greene's, but the dramatic sharpness of the play gives it a sense of heroism. It deals with the son of a wealthy shipbuilder of Hamburg, who tortured Russian prisoners during the war. After the war, tormented by conscience, he locks himself in an upper room of the house and clings to the delusion that Germany has collapsed. All but a few close relatives believe him dead. His ill-treatment of the Russian prisoners had been a reaction against his horror of the Nazi regime. Early in the war, he had tried to shelter a Jewish rabbi; his father, realising that his son was endangering his own life, betrays him to Goebbels. His father's position saved him, but the rabbi was shot before his eyes. He feels Ivan Karamazov's obsession with suffering; the fact that he is not allowed to suffer torments him, so that he goes to the other extreme and tortures Russian prisoners. At the end of the play, he and his father, both having faced their own immorality, commit suicide together.

The play is convincing provided one accepts Sartre's premise of 'the basic horror of existence'. If not, all its dramatic conviction becomes confidence trickery, and the final suicide a contrivance, as unnecessary as that of Scobie in *The Heart of the Matter*. But although Sartre has argued convincingly that all human beings live upon a delusion of their 'necessity', he has never tried to argue logically that human life is basically horrible. His feeling about this is simply the viewpoint of a man close to the 'pain threshold', and therefore no more necessarily valid than the pessimism of West or Greene.

Sartre's one certain contribution is the concept of 'nausea', the breakdown of man's form-imposing faculty under self-contempt. He has thus emphasised the form-imposing faculty, which had so far been recognised only in psychology. (Brentano called it 'intentionality'; this intentionality became the basis of Gestalt psychology, as well as of Husserl's phenomenology.) But 'form-imposing faculty' is obviously related to the imagination. What Sartre has done is to write a kind of psychological commentary and interpretation on Yeats's lines about the Shakespearean fish. When Roquentin feels he has no right to imagination, he becomes the most breathless of the fish that lie 'gasping on the strand'.

Even so, Sartre had touched upon a valid answer in *Nausea*. Roquentin has certain moments of absurd affirmation listening to a Negro woman singing 'Some of these days', watching the sunset over the sea. These seem to be moments when a super-rational, non-imposed meaning *emerges* from the real world. But perhaps this was too close to mysticism. The war came, and Sartre never again wrote about the moments of 'absurd affirmation'.

Nevertheless, in the final analysis one has to admire Sartre. Temperamentally he is close to West; and like West he does not try to find the easy way out. But while applauding his honesty, one cannot help protesting about his lack of vision. The objection to Sartre – as to the other writers in this chapter – is that no one can 'sum up' life as being 'finally horrible'. We possess a tiny beam of consciousness that is capable of lighting up a small space around us and a certain period of time behind us. It also has a power of abstract 'identification' with other consciousnesses and other periods in history, but this identification is a very thin carbon copy of actual experience. Our consciousness is selective. There are millions of things in the world around us; only a few of them get into our perceptions at any particular moment, or into our memories. Therefore, our state of mind, our attitude to existence at any given moment, is based upon very few 'facts' indeed. If *all* the facts in the universe could be simultaneously present to one consciousness, we might admit that any comments it chose to make would be valid for our universe. But no man's remarks on 'life' can be taken as any more than one possible view out of millions. Sartre is ignoring the strange, dual nature of all experience. He might have given closer attention to the Negro woman singing 'Some of these days', and to the nature of the blues in general. The *ideas* expressed in Negro blues are pessimistic and defeatist; and yet, as Bessie Smith remarked, 'singin' about them makes you feel good'. When the defeat is sung, it is reconnected to the basic, dionysiac energy of existence, and is somehow overcome. For this reason, the 'defeated' world-view can never be an absolute. Great art may speak of defeat, but it also speaks of the apparently absurd reasons why defeat is not absolute. When this absurdity is rationalised into the 'supernatural', or simply into the force of heroism and endurance, it becomes a dangerous nuisance, an obstacle to an effective grapple with the defeat.

Consideration of Sartre's basic preoccupations leads one to recognise that all his work is *an act of protest at the limitation of human consciousness.* In asking: 'Why am I here?' Roquentin is also asking why his consciousness is so limited that he doesn't know the answer. But as soon as this generalisation is accepted, it immediately becomes plain that all art is such a protest. In some cases, it takes the form of an attempt to remedy this limitation – as, say, in *War and Peace* or *The Old Wives' Tale*, which aim at breaking the time and space barriers. But, more frequently, it is an attempt to create an alternative 'reality', or simply to ask why we are so limited. The protest may be overt, as in *Faust*, or implied, as in *Madame Bovary* or *Bouvard et Pécuchet*.

Edward Upward has a story called 'Sunday' in which the archetypal situation occurs. A bored young clerk reflects on the dullness of Sunday (very much as John Osborne's characters would be doing in another twenty years):

'I am going back to my lodgings for lunch. Who will be there? Only the table, the flower with protruding stamens . . . the glass of custard, pleated apple green satin . . . The whole afternoon and evening will be free. Realise that, realise what I could do. All the possibilities of thinking and feeling, exploration and explanation and vision, walking in history as among iron and alabaster and domes, focussing the unity of the superseded with the superseding, recognising the future, vindicating the poets . . . foreseeing the greatest of all eras. But unless I am very careful, I shall sit on the sofa trying to decide not to go on reading the paper. I shall look out of the window. People will pass carrying neatly rolled umbrellas . . .'

In *Crome Yellow*, Huxley's hero has a similar reflection:

'Oh this journey! It was two hours cut clean out of his life; two hours in which he might have done so much, so much – written the perfect poem, for example, or read the one illuminating book. Instead of which . . .'

This kind of consciousness came into literature with Tchekhov, who documents it exhaustively; to a lesser extent, it had existed in Pisemsky and Goncharov. The twentieth-century novel became the novel of protest at limitation, the novel of dissatisfaction. It is the subject of Barbusse's *L'Enfer*, in which a man spends his days looking through a hole in his hotel wall. It is present in *Ulysses*, until the last chapter brings a kind of reconciliation in the affirmation of Mrs Bloom. It is the underlying feeling of Saki's *Unbearable Bassington*, and it is the subject of Hesse's *Steppenwolf*. It is also the subject of Camus's *L'Etranger*.

All this is only to say that much of the most serious literature of the twentieth century is a complaint addressed to human destiny. Its essential feeling resembles that of a stanza of Omar:

Ah, love! could thou and I with fate conspire
To grasp this sorry scheme of things entire,
Would not we shatter it to bits – and then
Remold it nearer to the heart's desire!

It is worth noting that the protest of earlier poets was often directed against the violence and unpredictability of human affairs. Macbeth complains that life is a tale told by an idiot because he feels the meaninglessness that underlies his own destiny. If this was also Shakespeare's feeling, then it would seem that Shakespeare was the first writer since Ecclesiastes to attempt to convince his readers of the 'vanity of human wishes' by *illustrating* them in a work of art. Even as late as the 1890's, poets were unwilling to confess that it was boredom and dullness that worried them. Dowson could reconcile himself to human life by writing:

> They are not long, the weeping and the laughter,
>> Love and desire and hate . . .

It took the frankness of the twentieth century to make poets drop complaints of boredom into the universal Suggestions Box. The romantics of the nineteenth century, when they admitted boredom, took care to suggest that it was the result of a satiety of experience. Barbusse's voyeur expresses a new feeling of underprivilege; not merely social underprivilege, but the feeling that destiny has given man a poor deal. Thomas Wolfe was later to express this feeling of underprivilege as a violent hunger for every kind of experience, a tragic because finally insatiable hunger.

THE ANTI-NOVEL

It might seem that it would be impossible to take the novel further in the direction of the static and the subjective than Sartre has ventured. But a group of writers in postwar France has attempted to do so. They are grouped together as 'anti-novelists' for obvious reasons, and the best-known names among them are Alain Robbe-Grillet, Nathalie Sarraute, Michel Butor and Marguerite Duras. In the remainder of this chapter, I propose to examine briefly the work of the first two of these writers.

ALAIN ROBBE-GRILLET

Two of Alain Robbe-Grillet's novels which have been published in England are *The Voyeur* and *Jealousy*. Both show this theory of 'total detachment' in action. Neither can be regarded as a successful novel.

Robbe-Grillet's true precursor is Ernest Hemingway. Robbe-Grillet is an anti-romantic, who objects to the way that most novels are overloaded with 'human' overtones, saturated with the human viewpoint. He seems to feel that a novel should be like a block of factory-made ice cream, 'untouched by hand'. He objects particularly to the 'pathetic fallacy' in novels, the habit of speaking of a 'brooding sky' or a 'threatening landscape'. But his objection is not simply to the Lovecraft–Poe–Mary Webb type of fiction. Even the most detached novelist, in describing some dramatic scene, allows the lifeless objects to reflect the emotions of the participants. A novelist describing a suicide may comment on a fly buzzing on the windowpane, or children's voices outside, using a device of dramatic contrast. For Robbe-Grillet, objects are objects – rather as in *Nausea*; human beings should have no excuse for imagining that their emotions are somehow noticed by Nature.

Hemingway had already utilised a similar technique. In *The Sun Also Rises*, the hero's emotional agonies are left unstated; the external world is described in photographic detail. Hemingway tried to make this a consistent attitude. A situation involving pain is described clinically; only 'the facts' are presented. So in 'Today Is Friday' two Roman soldiers talk casually about the Crucifixion, and then return to discussing their own affairs. In 'A Canary for One', a train journey is described minutely. During the journey, an American woman mentions that her daughter fell in love with a Swiss, but that they couldn't allow her to marry a foreigner, so they took her away. The girl stopped sleeping, and refused to eat; her mother is taking her a canary to try to console her. This part of the story is 'thrown away' in a few sentences. In the final sentence, the author mentions that he and his wife were returning to Paris to set up separate residences. He seems to imply: 'The world is full of incredible misery and heartache, people fall in love and think their emotions are everything, then they fall out of love and live separately, and the world goes on, indifferently.' Only the title indicates that the heartbreak of the girl separated from her lover is the real centre of the story. In 'A Sea Change', a girl is about to leave the man who loves her and to go off on a sea voyage with a lesbian. But most of the story is devoted to describing the bar where their last meeting is taking place, the tourists who wander in and out, the casual chitchat that forms a background to his misery.

Hemingway, then, is also concerned with breaking away from the romantic way of telling a story. Auden makes the same point in his poem 'Musée de Beaux Arts':

> About suffering they were never wrong.
> The Old Masters: how well they understood
> Its human position; how it takes place

> While someone is eating or opening a window
> or just walking dully along. . . .

But it should be noted that Hemingway pushed the method to its limits, and still refused to drop it. The technique of hints and understatements can be applied only to a narrow variety of situations. There has to be some powerful emotion with which the reader can sympathise. The technique is at its most moving in *A Farewell to Arms* where the hero, instead of describing his agony after the death of Catherine, merely mentions that he walked back to the hotel in the rain. But in *Across the River and into the Trees* the love affair of the dying Colonel with a teenage girl succeeds only in being mawkish and embarrassing, and the continual attempt at understatement strikes the reader as a confidence trick. He is reminded of Roy Campbell's epigram:

> You praise the firm restraint with which they write—
> I'm with you there, of course:
> They use the snaffle and the curb all right,
> But where's the bloody horse?

This is the chief criticism to be levelled at Robbe-Grillet. Hemingway is overwhelmingly successful in at least two of his novels and half a dozen short stories, where the studied detachment of tone is more poignantly effective than any amount of emotional rhetoric. So far, Robbe-Grillet cannot boast of any comparable artistic success. The subject of *The Voyeur* seems to promise that the detached technique will yield rich results. A travelling salesman returns to the island of his birth, where he talks to old friends and sells watches. A young girl is found raped and murdered on the rocks. Did the salesman commit the murder? All is ambiguous. The salesman recapitulates his movements on the day of the murder; the reader suspects that he himself is not sure whether he is the killer. A magnificent subject, that compares with Dürrenmatt's *Pledge*. Unfortunately, Robbe-Grillet seems to have no talent whatsoever for building up tension. Page after page of flat, undistinguished prose meanders past, with lengthy descriptions of anything that can be measured. This, for example, is a description of a buoy on the last page: 'It was a heavy iron buoy, the portion above water constituting a cone surmounted by a complex appendage of metal stems and plates.

The structure extended three or four yards into the air. The conical support itself represented nearly half this height.' And so on for another dozen lines. There is no particular significance in this buoy, except that the hero happens to be looking at it at that moment. In a short novel, this kind of thing occupies about ninety per cent of the space.

Jealousy is told through the eyes of a jealous husband who lives with his wife on a tropical banana plantation. Nothing much happens, except that the husband observes minutely every act of his wife and her every gesture. An act like the killing of a centipede by the 'other man' is described microscopically. The book begins and ends with precise physical descriptions. As in Hemingway the reader's mind is supposed to be full of the agony of the jealous husband, which is made more intense by its isolation from the surrounding objects and emotional overtones. There is supposed to be an effect like that of those 'three dimensional' photographs one can buy, that one looks at through a pair of red and green glasses. The emotion stands out in the foreground, naked and clear, and the background is separated from the foreground by a clear gap. Objects are indifferent, cold; man's agony is therefore all the more tragic because it is a self-enclosed circuit, burning itself out. The effect is not new. Joyce uses it in the opening scene of *Ulysses*, where Stephen's agony of conscience about his dying mother is contrasted with the sunlight on the sea and Buck Mulligan's cheerful obscenity. Granville-Barker uses it in the opening scene of *The Secret Life*, where the music of Wagner's *Tristan* is contrasted with the cynical or practical attitudes of the 'men of the world' who have just taken part in an amateur performance. But Hemingway, Joyce and Granville-Barker communicate with the reader; their detachment covers an emotion that needs no rhetoric for its communication. It would seem that, so far, Robbe-Grillet has not yet found himself a subject that, told with scientific precision, will make its own impact of pity or horror on the reader. But even supposing that Robbe-Grillet finds this ideal subject, it still remains a matter for conjecture how long it will be before, like Hemingway and Joyce, he finds himself at the end of his artistic tether, pushed to an absurd extreme by his adherence to a technique. Economy and precision are undoubtedly of immense importance to the artist. But it is significant that the greatest achievements in the field of the novel have been created by writers who were not afraid to produce 'fluid puddings' (Henry James's contemptuous epithet for the *War and Peace* type of novel). Dickens, Balzac, Dostoevsky, Tolstoy, Mann, Kazantzakis, J. C. Powys, are all highly unsatisfying as craftsmen; one never ceases to wish that they possessed Joyce's fierce preoccupation with technique, James's scientific intellect, Hemingway's detachment. But their slapdash technique always expressed what they meant, even if it often expressed more than they meant. Where novelists are concerned, it would seem that we have to choose between diarrhoea and constipation, except in the very greatest works. But one thing is certain: no amount of technique can ever form a substitute for having something to say.

NATHALIE SARRAUTE

The first impression gained on reading Nathalie Sarraute's two novels *Tropismes* and *Portrait of a Man Unknown* is of a conglomeration of influences – Henry James, Proust, Sartre, even, at times, the early T. S. Eliot. But to say this is to be unfair to Mlle Sarraute, who is a sensitive and original writer. The chief complaint one can make against her – and her fellow anti-novelists – is that it is a pity she was never influenced by Eliot's essay on Marie Lloyd, in which Eliot emphasises the importance of the artists keeping in touch with the 'general public'. It is true that she never writes for effect, or to impress her highbrow readers; there is never obscurity for its own sake. But the involuted complexities of her novels make the later Henry James seem straightforward.

Sartre has written of her:

If we take a look, as the author invites us to do, at what goes on inside people, we glimpse a moiling of flabby, many-tentacled evasions; evasion through objects which peacefully reflect the universal and the permanent; evasion through daily occupations; evasion through pettiness. I know of few more impressive passages than the one which shows us 'the old man' winning a narrow victory over the spectre of death by hurrying, bare-footed and in his nightshirt, to the kitchen in order to make sure whether or not his daughter has stolen some soap.

Her work, Sartre suggests, is deliberately about the 'inauthentic', a picture of human beings as trivial, frightened ghosts: in short, *salauds*. But this fails to give an impression of the pathological nature of her writing. *Portrait of a Man Unknown* reads like extracts from a psychiatrist's casebook dealing with an oversensitive neurotic who is about to develop delusions and persecution mania. The sensitivity to fine shades of emotion in the late James has here become an agonised awareness of every single strand of feeling in each human relation. It is as if an adolescent boy wrote with complete honesty about his miseries and embarrassments in all his everyday dealings, and assumed that everybody in the world was as concentrated on their own feelings as he is. One is reminded continually of cases that William James cites in that chapter of *The Varieties of Religious Experience* called 'The Sick Soul'. The basis of this psychological state is the self-unsureness of *Nausea*; but the narrator of *Portrait of a Man Unknown* is overaware of people, not of things. Its near-paranoiac character can be seen in a typical passage like the following:

Now the conversation had a different sound for me; it had lost its apparently banal, harmless aspect, and I sensed that certain words that were being spoken gave on to vast craters, immense precipices, visible only to initiates, who were leaning, restraining themselves . . . I was leaning with them, restraining myself, trembling and attracted as they were – over the abyss.

This is part of a description of an ordinary conversation over a meal. It is interesting to note its affinity – in mood – with Lovecraft: the concealed horror of existence. And it is characteristic of her method: to look at every grain of a human relationship under a microscope, until the most harmless fragment is seen, like a piece of cheese, to be swarming with wormlike grubs. This frequently has the same effect as the microscope of Proust or James; to quicken the reader's insight and deepen his sense of the implications of a situation. But it also goes over continually into the abnormal, and one becomes aware that, in magnifying her awareness, she has forfeited the ordinary, vital response to existence that is the basis of good writing. She seems to know this. After describing a public square with 'wan little gravel plots' (Robbe-Grillet would hardly approve of the adjective) and a hedge 'like the fringe of beard that . . . grows so thickly on corpses', she admits that this is not far from a case in a psychiatric handbook where the patient believes everything to be dead. She goes on to invent a passage that might be a parody of Graham Greene:

Everywhere you go, you feel dead childhoods. No childhood memories here. Nobody has any. They fade and die as soon as they form. They never seem to succeed in getting a grip on these pavements, or on these lifeless housefronts. And the people, the women and the old men, sitting motionless on the benches, in the little plots, look as if they were in a state of decomposition.

Elsewhere in the book, she seems to be describing herself:

I know that she needs so little, the merest nothing makes her tremble, this Hypersensitive, lined with quivering little silken tentacles that sway at the slightest breath . . . Like dogs sniffing along a wall at suspicious odors they alone recognise, with her nose to the ground, she picks up the scent of the things people are ashamed of; she sniffs at implied meanings, follows through the traces of hidden humiliations, unable to break away from them.

In Mlle Sarraute can be seen most clearly the objection to the increasing preoccupation with technique; her fish are not merely gasping on the strand; they are dangerously close to disintegrating altogether. Mlle Sarraute has this in common with Robbe-Grillet: she is the latest development of the school that believes that the purpose of literature is to represent reality more minutely than ever before (in Robbe-Grillet, objective reality; in Mlle Sarraute, psychological reality). But this is to forget that literature must also have a component of movement, of gusto.

In Mlle Sarraute's case, there is the possibility of development in another direction. Her *Portrait of a Man Unknown* has close affinities with Eliot's *Prufrock* and 'Portrait of a Lady'. The young man in the latter poem has just this kind of overawareness of every shade in a relationship, and the same ear for banal conversation. After some clanging piece of sententiousness, his 'smile falls heavily among the bric-a-brac', or:

I feel like one who smiles, and turning shall remark
Suddenly, his expression in a glass.
My self-possession gutters; we are really in the dark.

But it is not a long step from satirising 'inauthenticity' to denouncing it, as in *The Waste Land*, and then to searching for authenticity, as in *Ash-Wednesday* and the *Four Quartets*. Mlle Sarraute's way is less of an obvious dead end than that of most of the writers dealt with in this chapter. At least the static quality of her writing does not spring from a sense of futility, or a misguided attempt at total objectivity.

NOTES

1. Faulkner may here be indebted to *Ulysses*, where the same thing happens – in Bloom's imagination – to Paddy Dignan's coffin.

2. NB. This is an earlier version of 'I wander through each chartered street'; it can be found on page 170 of the Nonesuch Complete Blake, 1957. Blake later changed 'see' to 'mark'.

3. Though a point emerges when Brenda receives a phone call about the accident: she assumes that it is John Beaver who has been killed, and is relieved to hear that it is only her son.

4. There is a curious and significant remark in the travel book *Journey Without Maps*, where Greene admits that the danger of the African journey revealed in him something he had never been aware he possessed – a love of life. It seems a pity that Greene forgot this piece of self-discovery so promptly.

5. Greene is here not quite accurate; Péguy took the sacrament twenty days before he was killed in the war.

Three

The Implications of Total Pessimism

Even for a reader who knows his modern literature, it is difficult to explain how the novel came to a halt in the present cul-de-sac. 'The evolution of realism' is not a convincing explanation. Are Tolstoy and Balzac so much less 'advanced' in realism than Joyce and Robbe-Grillet? Does the evolution of technique really demand a complete suspension of plot? The idea is absurd. The novels of C. P. Snow are as 'true to life' as Mlle Sarraute's and as full of psychological delicacy, and yet they have a great deal of 'plot'.

Plainly, the avant-garde writers have somehow performed a neat conjuring trick. They profess to be completely uninterested in ideas, and yet their whole technique is dictated by a pessimistic Weltanschauung.

This proposition is easier to follow if one considers the work of Greene, Waugh, Sartre and Faulkner. These writers have one feature in common: all represent the world as an appalling place, and all succeed in ending on a note of uplift by declaring their faith in some abstract idea (catholicism, 'engagement', romantic stoicism). For readers who may be neither Catholics, Communists nor Southerners, these solutions will appear to be either limitedly true, or downright nonsense, and the authors convicted of a greater or lesser degree of self-deception.

It is interesting to compare the writers in the previous chapter with two writers who have had the courage to declare for a total and unrelieved pessimism, with no claim to 'artistic detachment' or even to an uplifting stoicism.

The first of these, Leonid Andreyev, was never popular in England, and is today almost totally forgotten.

LEONID ANDREYEV

The best book on Andreyev is Gorki's short study. From this and the few biographical facts that are available in English (particularly in A. Kaun's thesis on Andreyev), his life and personality can be pieced together. Born in Orel in 1871, of middle-class parents, he suffered from the youthful romanticism that was so common in the nineteenth century. He studied law at St Petersburg and Moscow and wrote short stories. The rejection of his first story made him attempt suicide, in a way that had something in common with Russian roulette. Certain trains had low furnaces that almost touched the tracks; Andreyev lay down between the rails, willing to accept an unpleasant death if this type of train was the first to pass. It was not; a train with a high furnace passed over him, leaving him untouched. However, he later shot himself near the heart with a revolver; the bullet missed his heart, but caused the permanent heart complaint from which he died at the age of forty-eight. His third suicide attempt occurred at a gay student party, when Andreyev suddenly stabbed himself with a knife; again, the wound was not serious. He also shot himself through the hand on another occasion, and Gorki records that the hand was twisted permanently.

Gorki, who was already a well-known young writer in 1898 when he read Andreyev's first story in a Moscow newspaper, wrote to the author, and later arranged to meet him at a railway station. The meeting was brief but warm; Gorki records the friendliness of Andreyev's personality, and his impulsive words: 'Let us be close friends.' One of their earliest conversations was about suicide and lying under trains. (Gorki had often played this game for a dare as a child.)

Within a few years, Andreyev had become the most famous and popular writer in Russia, surpassing even Gorki. Now they were on more equal terms, their friendship could develop with less restraint on Andreyev's side. To the English ear, some of Gorki's descriptions make it sound as if a homosexual relationship existed between them, Andreyev often kissing Gorki passionately, or even embracing his knees and wetting them with tears. (This is most unlikely.) Their characters were completely opposed. Gorki was the son of poor parents who had educated himself late in life, who had tramped from end to end of Russia and seen all kinds of miseries, which he described in his early short stories. Tolstoy once told Gorki that he liked him because he was so good-natured, although he had every right to be vindictive. Gorki was easygoing, good-tempered, totally honest, an avid reader, and a romantic who took no deep interest in the physical side of sex. Andreyev, although he had often starved as a student, was 'middle class'. He loathed culture and never read more than he had to. He was a heavy and gloomy drinker, who easily became drunk. (He attributed this to the fact that his father was a dipsomaniac.) 'The flesh' fascinated him in the same morbid way it had fascinated Baudelaire and Wilde, and he took perverse pleasure in sexual orgies with unclean prostitutes. Physically they were also opposites, Gorki being strongly built, with his heavy, almost comic face, with its large nose and drooping moustache, while Andreyev was physically delicate, with a neat, pointed black beard and small, handsome features.

In spite of Andreyev's alcoholism and morbidity, Gorki emphasises that he was a delightful companion, continuously witty, as enthusiastic and affectionate as a child, delighted with his own ability to express ideas concisely and imaginatively. On one occasion, when Gorki was pleased with his friend's neat summarising of a certain type of woman, Andreyev beamed like a schoolboy, and began to boast naïvely about his power over words.

These two extremes of Andreyev's character should be understood in order to gain a fair picture of his achievement. He was in no way a fully integrated personality. His harshest critics have always failed to realise this. Tolstoy said contemptuously; 'Andreyev says Boo, but I am not frightened.' When his stories 'Abyss' and 'In the Fog' caused such a storm of hysteria, and all kinds of libels appeared on him in the Russian press (usually asserting that he was a sexual degenerate) he went frantic with worry, and had to be dissuaded from courting further misunderstandings by writing letters of protest to all the newspapers. His enemies regarded him as a mature and malignant Satan when he was actually a kind of brilliant, bewildered schoolboy, craving affection. His success erected further barriers of envy. A stronger personality might have gone its own way, developing as an artist and thinker. But the inherited morbidity of Andreyev's constitution could not bear the strain; there was no basic resilience, no fundamental hunger for life that would always triumph over the doubts. The more one studies Andreyev, the more inescapable becomes the conclusion that he would have been a great writer if his constitution had not betrayed him.

As it is, Andreyev is always the brilliant schoolboy. Gorki's accounts of his conversation show his ability to throw off ideas at considerable speed, and to quickly dramatise them into stories or plays. These ideas are never really profound, but they are always connected with religious and philosophical issues. For example, Andreyev threw off a suggestion for a story about a man who wants to test the stupidity of believers; he practises asceticism and becomes a saint with thousands of disciples, to whom he preaches his own doctrines; then one day he announces to his disciples that it is all nonsense. Unable to live without their belief, they kill him and go on believing.[1] Moreover, Andreyev was quite capable of writing such a story overnight, and showing it to Gorki the next morning.

But even more typical of Andreyev's imagination is the following anecdote. Gorki told Andreyev of how a revolutionary comrade had taken refuge in a brothel, hunted by the police. A prostitute realised this, and sympathised with him. The revolutionary, being something of a puritan, rejected her advances, whereupon, losing her temper, she slapped his face. The revolutionary had the good sense to recognise his own priggishness, and apologised to her, whereupon they became friends. Andreyev wrote this idea into the story 'Darkness' in which a puritanical revolutionary flees into a brothel. But the key line of the story occurs when the prostitute screams at him, 'What right have you to be good when I'm bad?' This, for Andreyev, was the whole point of another of his ironic stories about the futility of human life and the impossibility of communication. Gorki recounts this anecdote with disapproval, adding that he thinks the original story more moving than Andreyev's distortion of it.

It is difficult to say whether Andreyev should be regarded as a revolutionary or as anti-revolutionary. Like so many Russian intellectuals at the time of the abortive revolution, he served some time in prison for lending his flat to revolutionaries as a meeting place. He later wrote the most moving testimony of all to the bravery of revolutionary comrades in 'The Seven Who Were Hanged'. And yet the pessimism of his work is the opposite of the revolutionary spirit.

From the biographical point of view, Gorki's most interesting chapter describes how Andreyev spoke one day at length on the futility of thought. Their opposed views are an interesting epitome of one of the theses of this book – the two views of imagination. Gorki took the Shavian view that thought is all human power, the imagination a searchlight on the future, that even in its failure to solve ultimate questions, thought is noble. Andreyev held that all thought is anti-life, all imagination a consolation against the horror of life. 'True wisdom is calm, but all great men suffer torments,' Andreyev declared, stating the Dostoevskian position. After a quarrel, during which Andreyev admitted that there were times when he hated Gorki, they went out into the yellow fog of St Petersburg, drank in a café, and went home with some prostitutes. Gorki then describes a scene that might have come out of Andreyev, or Kuprin's 'Yama, the Pit', when one of the women stripped and danced drunkenly on the table, while Andreyev talked about the hopelessness of life. Finally, Andreyev went into the bedroom with one of the women. Gorki seems to have abstained. Andreyev ended by plucking all the feathers of the prostitute's hat (for which she promptly made him pay) and insisting that one of the women accompany him on a drive around St Petersburg. Gorki finally got rid of the woman while Andreyev slipped into a drunken sleep, and took his friend back home. But as soon as Gorki had gone, Andreyev went out again, and went on drinking for three days, after which he left for Moscow. The picture of Andreyev's joyless debauchery is of exceptional power.

The chief events of Andreyev's life can be summarised briefly. He became famous at the turn of the century, at the age of thirty. He married his first wife in 1902, a meek, attractive girl named Alexandra, on whom he became completely dependent, clinging to her like a child, demanding that her life should be completely pivoted on his own, objecting if she even wanted to leave him to go into St Petersburg. When she died in 1906, he was completely shattered, and confirmed in his pessimism. He married again in 1907, this time a girl named Anna Denisevitch, and clung to her with the same childlike tenacity. Friends who saw her some time after their marriage could hardly recognise her because the former beauty had become so haggard and worn. Nevertheless, she managed to outlive her husband. Andreyev moved to a house of fantastic architecture at Kuokkala in Finland, where he spent the rest of his life. He continued to drink heavily, to travel, and to waste time on such fads as painting. Because of the heart ailment, his health was never strong, and the impact of a bomb near his home brought on the final heart disease. He hated the Russian revolution of 1917, and edited a reactionary newspaper from 1914 onward. He died an enemy of the Soviets, and his work is very much out of favour in contemporary Russia, although occasional stories are printed.

Andreyev's literary quality is very uneven indeed. His early stories are gently gloomy, in the Tchekhovian manner. They might all be said to derive from Tchekhov's story 'Heartache' in which an old cabman tries to tell his passengers about the recent death of his son; but no one is interested, and he is at last forced to talk to his horse. One of Andreyev's least unpleasant stories, 'Vania', tells of a small boy who has been brought up by an aunt and uncle. His mother, who had been deserted by her husband, decides that she wants custody of the child and, after a legal battle, finally succeeds. The aunt and uncle are shattered, and Vania is unsatisfied. He loved his aunt, and his mother seems false and hysterical. At the end of the story, he is taken to the small, untidy room where he will now live with his mother, and she shows him some toys. Vania is indifferent to toys – he prefers reading – and shows it. His mother flings herself on the bed and bursts into tears. Vania strokes her hair, tells her that he will love her, and offers to read her a story about a water nymph.

This story is the exception. Far more typical is 'The Little Angel', the story of a thirteen-year-old juvenile delinquent named Sashka, whose father, a pathetic and drunken clerk, is the only person he cares for. Sashka shows every sign of growing up to be a criminal. One day, much against his will, he is sent to a children's party, where he sees a wax angel on top of the Christmas tree. This fascinates him; he begs for it until he gets it. Possession of the angel exalts him. Back in his dingy home, where his mother is drunk, he falls asleep. 'Sashka's dreams were formless and vague, but they stirred his agitated soul profoundly. All the good that radiated over the world, all the anguish of a soul that longed for joy, rest and peace, that longed for God, this little angel united in herself . . .' But Sashka hangs the angel up over the stove, and it melts completely in the night. The complete pointlessness of this tragedy – for nothing is less likely than that a child would hang a wax angel over a hot stove – reveals an element of cruelty in Andreyev that recalls Maupassant. All the same, the psychology of the story is penetrating; it was not generally felt in 1900 that juvenile delinquency was the result of lack of affection.

Andreyev shows the same interest in morbid psychology in 'The Thief'. His thief, a young man named Yurasov, is the son of peasants who wants to be taken for a middle-class youth. He dresses in what he imagines to be the style of a German clerk and sometimes calls himself Heinrich Walter. The story tells how he steals a wallet at the beginning of a train journey, and how an accumulation of upsets and humiliations makes him hysterical, so that he becomes convinced that men have boarded the train to arrest him. He finally jumps off the train in a panic and is killed by an oncoming locomotive. Typical of the Andreyev cruelty is a final touch in the story – as Yurasov falls on the tracks, his teeth are smashed in, and he lies dazed, his toothless mouth upturned, as the lights of the oncoming train hang over him. Andreyev is determined that the reader should shudder. But the chief interest of the story lies in its Sartrean psychology. Yurasov wants to escape the feeling that he is a thief with three convictions behind him, and he keeps escaping into his dream personality of Heinrich the clerk, whom everyone will accept as a solid, honest, pedantic member of the middle classes. But he cannot understand why he is snubbed when he tries to show off his knowledge of the stock market or open a conversation about the weather. He does not realise that his own unsureness of his identity makes him too pressing; he feels that people can see that he is a fake, and that no amount of disguise will alter this. At one point, the stillness of the countryside when the train stops makes him understand what is wrong with him – that he is too much concerned with other people and his relation to them. ('Hell is other people.') Later still, when he recalls a song that evokes memories of humiliation, the language becomes even more reminiscent of Sartre: 'Something monstrous and formless, turbid and clinging, attached itself to Yurasov with a thousand thick lips and kissed him with impure wet kisses.' And later, when the sound of dance music suddenly appeals to him – he is an excellent dancer: '. . . when he danced he was good and gentle; he was no longer either the German Heinrich Walter or Yurasov the thief, but a person of whom he knew nothing'. It becomes obvious that Andreyev knows far more about criminal psychology than Dostoevsky. Yurasov has the basic psychology of any number of master criminals – Lacenaire, Deeming, Holmes, Chesney; Stavrogin is like no man who ever existed.

One of the best-known stories of Andreyev's 'ironic' period is 'The Grand Slam', about four aging people who always play cards together. One of them dreams about getting a grand slam. One day, his luck is amazing; as he declares a grand slam and reaches out to take the next card, he dies of heart failure. When they look at the next card, they discover that he would, in fact, have had a grand slam. One of the characters suddenly realises the meaning of death – that the dead man will never know that he had a grand slam, for which he had been longing for so many years. This is perhaps the nearest Andreyev ever approached to a religious insight: these people who have no idea of what life means, and who waste the capacity for hope on a card game, who are hopelessly out of touch with the reality of both life and death.

All these early stories are told in simple, human terms. Andreyev had not yet allowed his preoccupation with symbolism to interfere with his artistry. Even so, as Gorki points out, these stories are completely devoid of humour, as if Andreyev was afraid to express his natural personality in his work. This is undoubtedly his chief weakness. But even more fatal to his power as an artist is his tendency to twist everything to fit a preconceived scheme of nihilism. His insights are never allowed to express themselves simply as observation of life; all have to be dragooned into proving his basic idea, the futility of life. Perhaps the most famous example is the story 'Abyss'. Two young and idealistic students are taking a country walk. They are in love, but shy of one another; they talk about love in a manner that recalls Shelley. They pass three tramps, who follow them and finally attack them, knocking the youth unconscious and raping the girl. When the student wakes up, he finds the girl unconscious and naked. At first he is horrified and tries to cover her up; then the contact with her excites him, and he takes her himself. Andreyev's last sentences are typically melodramatic: 'For a single instant, flaming horror lighted up his mind, opening before him a black abyss. And the black abyss swallowed him.' But Andreyev's point is well made, and relates him to Wedekind and Maupassant: man is unconscious of the power of the sexual instinct, which is more dangerous than a bomb.

As a famous writer, Andreyev felt the need to play the prophet of nihilism. He was also jealous of the success of Artzybasheff. His stories became steadily more symbolic. The impossibility of human communication dominates them. In 'The Life', a man suspects that his mistress is deceiving him, and kills her with a knife; having killed her, he realises that he will now never know the truth, that he has immortalised the lie. (Andreyev may have been influenced here by the death scene of Mélisande in Maeterlinck's play.) In 'Silence', the neurotic daughter of a priest commits suicide after refusing to explain what is tormenting her, then the priest's wife becomes paralysed, and cannot reply when he begs her to forgive him. In 'Laughter', a young man who is unhappily in love puts on a fancy dress costume of a Chinese noble, together with a mask whose complete wooden immobility makes everyone laugh. When the young man pours out his misery to a girl at the party, she listens seriously while her eyes are turned away from him, but bursts into helpless laughter when she looks at him.

There is something faked about these stories; Andreyev is loading the dice. Admittedly, his mask is only a symbol of the immobility of human flesh, with its inability to express the suffering of the mind; but the story still rings hollow. Tolstoy is right; Andreyev is now shouting Boo, not writing out of some inner need.

In his biblical trilogy, 'Judas Iscariot', 'Lazarus' and 'Ben-Tobith', the interest in religion is only superficial. 'Judas' is another of Andreyev's intellectual handstands, like the story of a man who becomes a saint to test the stupidity of believers. He is interested only in asking whether it is not possible that Judas wanted to help Christ

74

to live out his destiny as the crucified man-god, and did so in spite of the label of traitor that his act would bring. Judas, in short, might have displayed an altogether unusual degree of self-sacrifice, and might be the greatest of the apostles. Again, Andreyev seems to be out to dazzle his admirers and confound his enemies by turning all 'values' upside down. But over fifty years after its publication, all its shock value has disappeared, and it seems merely a period piece.

'Ben-Tobith' is briefer and more straightforward; it tells how a man called Ben-Tobith had an appalling toothache on the day of the crucifixion, and the story is told from the viewpoint of Ben-Tobith's toothache; the execution of a cranky Jewish prophet is just another unimportant event that forms a background to Ben-Tobith's pain. Andreyev's theme is here more universal than in 'Judas', and B. G. Guerney is right to compare the story with Anatole France's 'Procurator of Judea'. But the comparison brings out Andreyev's ignorance of the period. An enemy of culture, he is not at his best in historical fiction.

'Lazarus' is probably the most pessimistic story Andreyev ever wrote, the essence of his nihilism. It tells how, when Lazarus came back from the dead, he had seen some vision that made him aware of the total futility of human life. Anyone who looked into his eyes was seized by the same conviction. A famous Roman sculptor comes to see him, and goes away and carves a monstrous black shape, under which rests a beautifully chiselled butterfly. One of his friends smashes the black shape, leaving only the butterfly. But when his friends talk at length about beauty, he retorts: 'All that is a lie.' Finally, the emperor Augustus summons Lazarus because he wishes to accept the challenge of looking into his eyes. He also comes to feel that life is futile, but decides he must overcome his distaste for the sake of his people. He has Lazarus blinded, and Lazarus ends his life sitting on a rock, staring sightlessly in front of him.

The biblical trilogy brings to mind Oscar Wilde. There is the same fake biblical language as in Wilde's prose poems ('And it came to pass . . .' etc.). Moreover, one has only to consider the anecdotes that Andreyev produced in such abundance in conversation with Gorki to realise that, like Wilde, he tended to ruin his original inspiration by overelaboration. There is the same romantic pessimism as in Wilde, expressed in Wilde's anecdote about Christ. Christ walks though a city, and reproves a drunk, who replies: 'I was a leper once; you healed me. What else should I do?' He then reproves a man who follows a prostitute, and the man replies that he was blind once and that Christ had healed him; finally, he sees an old man weeping, and when he asks why he weeps, the old man replies: 'I was dead, you brought me back to life. What should I do but weep?' Like Wilde, Andreyev is fond of talking in hushed whispers about the sins of the flesh. 'Let there be a feast of the flesh,' he exclaimed to Gorki. He romanticises prostitutes, and would no doubt have admired Wilde's poem about the harlot's house. Moreover, as Gorki points out, Andreyev's nihilism did not extend to his own affairs; he was hungry for fame and praise. The need to make an impression is more important to him than the honest expression of his feelings.

Andreyev's writing life was barely twenty years long, and the last ten were a continual decline. His work became more 'symbolic' and in every way poorer. A story called 'The Wall' reveals all the worst and most theatrical elements in Andreyev taking charge. It is wholly symbolic, told by a leper who stands at the foot of an immense wall that extends as far as the horizon. For several pages Andreyev describes the misery and apathy of the other people who are with him; some of them play pointless games, and ignore a man who is starving to death a few feet away. There are legends of an old hermit who managed to burrow a hole in the wall (symbolising the saints or mystics) and some of them spend their lives looking for this mythical hole. They try various devices to get over the wall, but without success. Finally, urged on by the narrator, waves of people rush at the wall to try to break it down, but many are crushed to death. The narrator tries to persuade them to keep charging the wall, because every additional body is a steppingstone towards the top of the wall, but they ignore him and fall into apathy again.

The story recalls James Thompson's 'City of Dreadful Night', and it is ultimately just as unconvincing. It makes no attempt to argue a case that life is futile – as Schopenhauer does; it simply states it. No doubt the 'waste land' vision is deeper than the ordinary acceptance of life that

76

Andreyev attacked in his earlier stories. But it is still a halfway house. A man who genuinely possesses it is tormented by it; it drives him to keep looking for the 'hole in the wall'. The solutions are not always the same; they may differ as widely as Nietzsche's pessimistic vitalism and Eliot's acceptance of Anglo-Catholic Christianity. But there is no sign in Andreyev that he made any effort to get beyond the 'waste land' stage. His later works might be described as complacently nihilistic.

There are two exceptions that should be mentioned, and they are arguably among Andreyev's finest works. These are the story 'The Seven Who Were Hanged' and the play *Anathema*, written respectively in 1908 and 1909. The story deals with the last days of five young revolutionaries and two murderers. It is, for the most part, a careful study of the seven condemned, showing their different attitudes to death. As usual, Andreyev reveals himself to be a psychologist of considerable depth. All the revolutionaries go to their deaths cheerfully, and the two women are the bravest among them. The two murderers are cowards in the face of death. The final scene, when the bodies are cut down in the snow and sent back to the prison, is strangely moving. As a work of art, it is perhaps Andreyev's most undeniable *tour de force*. Its content is a different matter. Although all seven refuse the consolations of a priest at the end, Andreyev implies that their souls are now in heaven. Moreover, it is impossible to believe that Andreyev was really convinced that his revolutionaries were somehow worthwhile; his outlook in his other work argues against it. It seems more probable that he wrote the story as a bid for popularity with the revolutionary movement, which had begun to condemn him as a pessimistic reactionary. His extreme sensitivity to criticism and to fluctuations in his own fame adds credibility to this view.

Anathema is Andreyev's version of the Book of Job. Anathema is the devil, who asks the Guardian of the Gates of Eternity to show him the answer to the problem of existence, so that he can help mankind. When he is refused, the devil goes down to earth and proceeds to tempt an old Jew, David Leiter, who is dying of starvation in a Russian town. The Jew cannot be tempted. The devil urges a mob to stone him to death. Later, the devil asks the Guardian of the Gates whether David's death does not demonstrate the futility of life and the failure of love and virtue. The Guardian answers that the devil will never succeed in understanding the purpose of goodness and life. The devil replies with defiance and curses.

It would seem as though Andreyev has here changed his whole viewpoint, if he is on the side of David Leiter and the Guardian. The old Jew is certainly one of Andreyev's most memorable figures. But if Andreyev was inclining to an irrational vitalism in *Anathema*, the tendency was left undeveloped. Other plays, like *The Black Maskers*, *The Life of Man* and *He Who Gets Slapped*, are heavily symbolic and, on the whole, very bad. *Savva* has some touches of the old Andreyev, in its story of the revolutionary who wants to blow up a miracle-working image with dynamite to show the mob that dynamite is stronger than religion; he is finally torn to pieces by the mob. One of the late plays, *Professor Storitsyn*, is a touching portrait of the personal failure of an idealistic intellectual – a familiar theme in Russian literature since Turgeniev's *Rudin* – but it failed to redeem Andreyev's tottering reputation. His long novel, *Sasha Zegulev*, of 1912 was received with indifference. His last piece of writing was a plea to the Allies to save Russia from the Bolsheviks.

Andreyev is a curious example of artistic dishonesty. His success began with a novel called *The Red Laugh*, a story about the sufferings of war which began with the words: 'Madness and horror.' Eighteen years later, his last novel (unfinished), *Satan's Diary*, still takes the same nihilistic view of the world. In the course of his career, Andreyev came under many influences. *The Red Laugh* derives from Garshin's anti-war stories; 'In the Fog' from Tolstoy. At some point, Poe became an influence – the Poe of 'The Masque of the Red Death' – and the 'symbolic' period began. Andreyev had no real development, only a progression from influence to influence. The same old defeatism was dressed up in different clothes.

However, it would be a mistake to dismiss Andreyev as an insincere pessimist. Gorki's memoir alone refutes this. The early works are the outcome of a genuine moral ferment; they bubble with life. The tragedy of Andreyev the artist was that he ceased to pay attention to life; his later works are all mathematical propositions, devoted to asserting his nonsensical theme, that life was not worth living. I use the word nonsensical because the demonstrations were all faked; if life is not worth living, then stories are certainly not worth writing. A large part of Andreyev remained undeveloped: an affectionate, oversensitive adolescent with a longing for fame and public approval, and a tendency to be deeply hurt by misunderstanding. He made no attempt to 'live with' his pessimism; like Schopenhauer, he enjoyed the good things of life. In *The Day of Wrath*, he could even write an overblown dithyramb on freedom. Andreyev is almost a Dostoevsky character, and he demonstrates the truth of Aldous Huxley's remark that Dostoevsky's characters are fundamentally unreal. They may seem to be working models for real people, but if they were ever translated into reality, it would soon become apparent that there is something wrong with their clockwork. The inventor has done a little faking somewhere, and disguised some human weakness as metaphysical agony. This is not difficult to do. Andreyev advertised himself as the genuine Dostoevskian article, the metaphysical man, Stavrogin made flesh, intent only on his vision of the pointlessness of life. When we examine him, we discover that the metaphysical angst is partly hurt vanity and partly toothache. And yet he is by no means wholly a fake. Given a stronger constitution, a more searching temper, he could easily have been greater than Dostoevsky. The temperament was there but not the strength, the perception but not the will. He remains perhaps the most interesting artistic failure of our century.

SAMUEL BECKETT

I can think of only one other writer who has accepted the implications of pessimism as stoically and logically as Andreyev: Samuel Beckett. A comparison of the two provides some interesting observations, for Andreyev thought of himself as post-Dostoevsky, while Beckett obviously thinks of himself as post-Joyce and Kafka. Considering the similarity of their Weltanschauung, the difference in their method is astonishing. A knowledge of the relation of Andreyev's pessimism to his literary creation also provides some fascinating insights into Beckett.

Beckett's work has gone farther than that of any other

contemporary in the direction of 'static' experimentalism. He has taken the protest about human boredom and misery to a point where it defeats its object – to communicate the protest to other people.

Beckett's work has often been compared to Joyce's – the connection may have been suggested by a myth that Beckett was once Joyce's secretary. Such a comparison is nonsensical. The only similarity is that both are Dubliners. Joyce was preoccupied with language; Beckett's sense of language is about as lively as Hansard. *Ulysses* has been compared to a city, open it at almost any place and the reader will find unfamiliar alleyways, vistas he never noticed before. Any page of Beckett reads pretty much like any other page of Beckett. Nor does there seem to have been any development in his view of life. If all his works except one were destroyed in a holocaust, it would make no difference; any one is completely representative.

What exactly has Beckett to say? In *Endgame*, one of the characters tells a story that seems typical. A man goes to a tailor for a pair of trousers, but the tailor keeps delaying, saying first that he has spoiled the seat, then that the crotch is giving trouble. Finally, in a fury, the man shouts: 'In six days God made the world. And you're not capable of making me a pair of trousers in three months.' The tailor replies: 'But my dear sir, look at the world, and then look at my trousers.' It is the old Omar Khayyám complaint.

Beckett's work has its precedents – notably certain stories of Tchekhov's, such as 'Goussiey', which might have served as a model for all Beckett's novels and plays. It begins: 'It was already dark, and would soon be light. Goussiev, a private . . . raised himself a little in his hammock and said in a whisper: "Do you hear, Pavel Ivanitch? A soldier at Soushan told me that their boat ran into an enormous fish and knocked a hole in her bottom." The man on the bunk . . . was silent, as though he had not heard.' This is the atmosphere of *Waiting for Godot*. Goussiev lies in his bunk and makes pointless conversation; he also has long spells of remembering his home. Finally, he dies; his body is thrown into the sea, and sinks slowly through the green water; a shark swims up and eats it. The reader is reminded of Eliot's lines about 'Phlebas the Phoenician, a fortnight dead'.

Beckett utilises this method, but employs the technique of Kafka. All is vague and uncertain. In his first novel, *Murphy*, a young man sits naked in a rocking chair and reflects on the meaningless of existence, which is mainly putting his clothes on and taking them off. It is as if he sits there waiting for a sign from God: 'Tell me what life is all about and I'll do something. But why *should* I go out and live?' It begins: 'The sun shone, having no alternative, on the nothing new.' But Beckett is somehow ashamed to embark on questions or statements about life. The nearest he comes is when Murphy remarks to a friend that life is 'a wandering to find a home'. There is a kind of febrile, erudite brilliance about this, Beckett's first novel, that immediately calls to mind West's *Dream Life of Balso Snell*. The elaborate and ironical style is more reminiscent of George Meredith than of Joyce. And Murphy's accidental death at the end seems as pointless as that of Goussiev or Miss Lonelyhearts.

The Beckett trilogy (*Molloy, Malone Dies, The Unnamable*) is very nearly unreadable. It is a kind of Mrs Bloom monologue that goes on for four-hundred-odd pages. It opens with Molloy sitting in his room; the book is his 'stream of consciousness'. Eight pages are devoted to describing how he collected sixteen pebbles, distributed them between four pockets, and worked out how to suck each of them in turn without sucking any twice. This kind of lame comedy seems to owe something to similar passages in Gertrude Stein's *Making of Americans*. After ninety pages of this kind of thing, the book switches to a narrative by another character who has been told to 'see about' Molloy. This narrative seems more purposeful than the first part, with a touch of the detective novel. It begins: 'It is midnight. The rain is beating on the windows.' This soon turns into a Kafka-esque dream (all Beckett springs from Kafka's 'Country Doctor'). The reader who flicks over the pages quickly might think he is reading a novel by John Buchan. One is not sure what is supposed to be happening; the new character seems to be looking for Molloy, and is told to write a report. At the end, he says; 'Then I went back into the house and wrote, It is midnight. The rain is beating on the windows. It was not midnight. It was not raining.' The reader who has ploughed through this with increasing bewilderment feels a certain lack of sympathetic interest at the opening words of the second novel, *Malone Dies*: 'I shall soon be quite dead at last in spite of it all.' Malone takes about a hundred pages to die. There is the usual Beckett ambiguity: 'This room seems to be mine. I can find no other explanation to my being left in it.' The last words of *The Unnamable* are '. . . you must go on, I can't go on, I'll go on.' Upon which the only possible comment is 'God forbid'. The whole trilogy seems to be a very long elaboration of Eliot's 'Gerontion', the old man sitting in his room 'waiting for rain', with the same fragmentary or cryptic references to characters and events from the old man's past life.

There is good reason for feeling that Beckett is only a long-winded elaboration of the early-Eliot mood. The epigraph for his collected works could be Eliot's lines:

> I have heard the key
> Turn in the door once and turn once only
> We think of the key, each in his prison
> Thinking of the key, each confirms a prison . . .

How, in that case, has Beckett achieved his rather dubious celebrity – that of an author who is quoted by 'cultured' people but never read? The answer is quite certainly on the strength of the success of *Waiting for Godot*. *Godot* is about two tramps standing under a tree; they exist in a nightmare world. One of them has been beaten, but it is not certain by whom. They are waiting for Godot, but they are not sure who he is or what he looks like. It is, in fact, the straightforward Kafka atmosphere. What makes the play a success is that the tramps have the quality of knockabout comedians. Just as the fun is beginning to flag, Pozzo, a huge piglike man (a symbol of capitalism?) comes on leading his servant on a length of rope. There are flashes of a Rabelaisian wit that Beckett can show occasionally:

POZZO: Which of you smells so bad?
ESTRAGON: He has stinking breath and I have stinking feet.

When the curtain finally falls on the first act, Beckett has made his point and written an entertaining and weird play, sustaining his pessimistic undertones with humour and invention. Incapable of guessing when his audience has had enough, he goes on for another hour, repeating the same situation, the same jokes, and bringing on Pozzo and his servant again to break the monotony.

Apparently Beckett was not entirely pleased with the success of *Godot*, particularly with the London performance, which treated it as a hilarious metaphysical comedy. He felt that his pessimism had been overlooked. So he produced another play, *Fin de Partie (Endgame)* to try to drive home his point. The play takes place in a tower with very high windows. There are four characters: a man in a wheelchair, his servant, and his parents, who are legless and live in two dustbins. One of the high points of the play occurs when the father begins to say the Lord's Prayer, and the man in the wheelchair interrupts with a scream: 'The bastard! He doesn't exist!' Finally, one or both of the characters in dustbins die. The servant (Clov) makes a final speech that seems to summarise Beckett's nihilism: '. . . I don't understand, it dies, or it's me, I don't understand that either . . . I open the door of the cell and go. I am so bowed I only see my feet . . . I say to myself that the earth is extinguished, though I never saw it lit.' This is true of Beckett: he also never saw the earth 'lit'.

The play, naturally, had not the success of *Godot*. Encouraged, Beckett went on writing more plays, as though he had a mission to convince the world that life is not worth living. *Krapp's Last Tape* is a monologue in which a tired old man talks into a tape recorder and reminisces about his past. A radio play, *All that Fall*, has several tired, broken characters who wonder painfully why life is so meaningless and so full of suffering. Another radio play is virtually a long monologue of another dying old man on the sea-shore.

There is, it would seem, a fundamental fallacy in Beckett's work. It is possible to create good literature with a defeatist theme – as Andreyev sometimes did; it is even possible to advocate suicide – as Artzybasheff did in *The Breaking Point*. It is possible to write at considerable length about someone dying – as Tolstoy did in *Ivan Ilyich*. But to write about dreariness demands that one should offer a counter-attraction – as Zola well realised when he spiced his work so heavily with sex. Beckett accidentally brought off the right combination in *Godot*. But apparently he decided he was betraying his own pessimism by sugaring the pill. His later works make one think of a man trying to write a symphony using only one note.

The main objection to his work is its unoriginality. It might have been concocted from a mixture of Eliot and Kafka, with a dash of Joyce. Suffering and bewilderment must be expressed dynamically – as by Wilfred Owen in such war poems as 'Futility' and 'Exposure'. In its context, Owen's agonised cry 'What are we doing here?' expresses volumes of Beckett.

CONCLUSION

The fallacy that has reached a kind of limit in Beckett is also the fallacy underlying our notion of science and philosophy; it is the idea that man's only task is to survey the universe, to look outward. Certain modern philosophers (Russell, for example) give the impression that they believe that all they have to do is to sit in an armchair and consider the 'facts'; that the perceiving mind and the logical faculty can be relied on completely to deal with those facts and come up with an answer. There is, of course, an opposite fallacy: Nietzsche's cry of 'Ignore the philosophy and look at the philosopher'. Neither is true. The mind and perceptions are partly reliable; but no philosopher has a right to think of himself as a pure reasoning force (unless his field is mathematics). The right state of mind for a philosopher is an active looking-both-ways, outward and inward simultaneously. It is not enough to be a Pascal, preoccupied only with his own shortcomings, or a Russell whose good sense is often marred by a smirk of self-congratulation.

In literature, the trouble is less easy to define. The 'Shakespearean fish' tried to portray the world objectively, to represent it as it might seem to any man. The romantics became more personal and spoke boldly of the world as it seemed to *them*. This has led eventually to a kind of self-conceit; the artist sits in his armchair and writes about his vision of the world as if he is delivering the gospel. He also takes himself for granted, like the philosopher. He is inclined to offer his *temperamental reactions* to life as if they were the result of a most careful weighing up of the whole universe. In the Edward Upward story 'Sunday', the central character finally has a kind of vision of the purpose of history that leads him to decide to engage in left-wing political action. In this way, the intuitions that were bewildered by the boredom of a Sunday afternoon reach out beyond the boredom, out into a world in which they *can* discover meanings. Hesse's Steppenwolf has a similar vision of the purpose of his own life after a boring day: 'A refreshing laughter rose in me . . . The golden trail was blazed, and I was reminded of the eternal, and of Mozart and the stars.'

What appeared to be a blank wall of meaninglessness proves to be not really a wall. But it does so only because the artist's intuitions and emotions keep thrusting out and trying to grasp something, trying to break through the incomprehension. The artist has to recognise himself not merely as being able to see the world, but as also being able to *alter his perception* of it. Both Beckett and Russell are fixed in the static fallacy, accepting the original form of the perceptions. In closely related ways, they fail to grasp that man has a *will to perceive* as well as perceptions, and that the perceptions can be adjusted like the range on a telescope.

It is the static fallacy that has led to the 'fish gasping on the strand'. The realist vision began with Balzac and Zola, and was an attempt to give 'reality' its due, instead of using it merely as a backcloth against which stories took place. After the coming of Joyce, 'reality' began to demand more and more of the stage, although – as can be seen in Joyce – it cramped the 'story'. The realist vision becomes more and more microscopic, more concerned with techniques and 'ways of seeing'. Because it wanted to render 'reality' with more delicacy of detail than ever before, it tended to dispense with story. This can be traced in the writing of the last half century, from Joyce and the later Henry James (who, as much as Joyce, wanted to render minutely the reality of a situation), through Proust, Dorothy Richardson and Virginia Woolf, to Sartre and the young French school of novelists.

The general reader may well feel that the essential quality of literature is being lost in all this refined experimentalism, just as the music lover may find it hard to go beyond the music of Schönberg and Webern to the 'far out' experiments of Boulez, Stockhausen and the rest. In fact, both modern literature and modern music have split into two streams, one 'esoteric', one of immediate appeal. In music, if you find Schoenberg and Dallapiccola incomprehensible, you can turn to Sibelius, Poulenc, Carl Orff. In literature, the free imagination has sought expression again in various types of fantasy: in ghost stories, detective stories and science fiction.

To summarise on 'realism' and 'pessimism': the study of the 'nausea' school of modern literature leads to some important conclusions about the imagination. As Sartre points out: man lives from moment to moment. He uses very little will power. Like a drifting log, he lets events carry him along. Hence the importance of that sentence in *La Nausée* about the café proprietor: 'When his café empties, his head empties too.' This being so, man is enormously susceptible to the feelings of boredom and of meaninglessness. (A certain penetrating modern critic has used the illuminating phrase 'the great mystery of human boredom', a lightning flash of insight.) Beckett tends to blame 'life' for the boredom. He complains that all his characters feel like people who have been abandoned in a dentist's waiting room. It never seems to strike him that perhaps he himself – or his characters – are to blame for the meaninglessness. Perhaps this is because he can see no example in history of men who have behaved otherwise, and he believes in the unchangeableness of human beings. But an existentialist critic might interpret the agony and boredom of his characters – like the 'ordeal by pettiness' in Sartre's *Huis-Clos* – as a frenzied demand for a 'new deal' for human beings – in fact, as a demand for a new type of human being, capable of will and the act of choice.

This, then, is the basis of any theory of the imagination: the picture of men jammed miserably in the present, will-less and futile. The realisation of lack of will is 'nausea'. This feeling permeates twentieth-century culture; it is expressed by thinkers as distant as Sartre and Gurdjieff. (The latter wanted to do something about it.) Man as the slave of the present; man in the Time-trap; man as the creature of circumstance, the sport of destiny. When 'destiny' feels inclined, it fills him with enthusiasm and well-being and illusions; when it ceases to require his service, it leaves him high and dry and bored.[2]. The agony of modern literature is the agony of this realisation. The 'fish gasping on the strand' are gasping because they have

86

relied on 'reality' and 'truth' to free man, to exalt him, and they are faced with the reality of man's lack of will, his helplessness in the face of boredom. Sartre's café proprietor is also left gasping on the strand when his café empties.

How shall man gain detachment from this 'present' against which his nose is jammed so tightly? How will he escape the enormous hand that holds him by the scruff of the neck? In asking this question, we have started to define the prime function of imagination.

NOTES

1. It will be noticed that this story anticipates Sartre's play *Le Diable et le Bon Dieu*. I shall later point out that Andreyev frequently anticipates Sartre.
2. In 'The Beast in the Jungle', Henry James has a study of a man 'whose destiny is that nothing shall ever happen to him'. It makes an interesting counterweight to the novels of Thomas Hardy, in which people are always being raped by destiny.

Four

The Vision of Science

Whitehead once wrote: 'The notion of life implies a certain absoluteness of self-enjoyment.' This goes to the heart of the problem of imagination. Steppenwolf's moment when he becomes aware of 'Mozart and the stars' is a moment of absolute self-enjoyment.

In a sense, one might say that nature has always aimed at producing a being capable of absolute self-enjoyment. The early animals were too concerned with keeping themselves alive and finding food. 'Self-enjoyment' was the indulgence of the stupidest and least active creatures; they fell prey to the more violent mammals. Survival meant directing the attention away from inner satisfaction, towards the dangers of the outside world. Man, we assume, was the first creature to think of uniting with others of his own kind to divide the labour of self-protection. Once he had learned the secret of building a house in a tree or on a lake, he might have found leisure for the relaxation that had killed off the diplodocus and the vegetarian dinosaurs. Instead, he preferred to increase his labour, spurred forward, admittedly, by natural catastrophes. Today one of the chief problems of Western man is the problem of too much leisure. The rise in juvenile delinquency and petty crime, the increase in neurosis, are its direct outcome. Yet in spite of his leisure, man seems as far as ever from this 'absoluteness of self-enjoyment'. It is true that there is still plenty to be done on the social and scientific level. This does not alter the fact that the trend of civilisation is towards increased control of the outside world, and that when (and if) this control is achieved, man will still know nothing about the art of 'self-enjoyment' as distinguished from the pleasure of material achievement.

The purpose of the artist and philosopher has always been to re-emphasise the need for the subjective. Their task is difficult; since all life has been involved in a fight for survival for millions of years, there is an automatic brake on inward-looking self-enjoyment in human beings.

H. G. WELLS

This is worth analysing at some length; its connection with the problems of imagination is immediate. H. G. Wells has certain passages in his *Experiment in Autobiography* that are worth quoting in this context. Wells begins the book by complaining that he is not getting the freedom of mind he needs for work. He goes on:

Entanglement is our common lot. I believe this craving for a release from bothers, from daily demands and urgencies, from responsibilities and tempting distractions, is shared by an increasing number of people who, with specialised and distinctive work to do, find themselves eaten up by first hand affairs... Most individual creatures since life began, have been 'up against it' all the time, have been driven continually by fear and cravings... and they have found a sufficient and sustaining interest in the drama of immediate events... But with the dawn of human foresight and with the appearance of a great surplus of energy in life such as the last century or so has revealed, there has been a progressive emancipation of the attention from everyday urgencies. People can ask now what would have been an extraordinary question five hundred years ago. They can say: 'Yes, you earn a living, you support a family, you love and hate, but – *what do you do?*'

Conceptions of living, divorced more and more from immediacy, distinguish the modern civilised man from all former life... We originative intellectual workers are reconditioning human life...

We are like early amphibians, so to speak, struggling out of the waters that have hitherto covered our kind, into the air, seeking to breathe in a new fashion...

I do not now in the least desire to live longer unless I can go on with what I consider to be my proper business... I want the whole stream of this daily life to flow on for me... if what I call my work can still be, can be more than ever the emergent meaning of the stream. But only on that condition.

This is the 'artist' pleading quite clearly for more 'self-enjoyment' and less commitment to the outside world.

And yet it would be a mistake to suppose that the artist's only problem is the distraction of events. The inner brake is just as real. It is worth trying to define the nature of the inner brake.

For any civilised human creature, then, the conflict is between the demands of environment and the desire to sit back and enjoy life for 'what it is'. This phrase 'what it is' deserves analysis. Supposing a businessman has had a long and hard career, and has at last provided undoubted security for himself and his family, and has met all other obligations that he feels to be pressing – to a political party, for example. He now has the right to relax in his country house, turn his mind away from the practical worries of business, and at last contemplate life and the world. If he has hobbies, he will presumably now indulge unlimitedly in these. If he has a taste for less innocent pleasures – Parisian cocottes, for example, or blue films – no doubt he will also indulge these. His 'duty' is now done. Duty may be conceived as a religious imperative or simply as a responsibility to civilised society. In either case, it is a meaning imposed from outside. He can now, as it were, impose his own meanings on life. It is at this point that his conduct answers the tacit question: What is life really worth? What can be got out of life by a man with no material worries and no obligations to fulfil?

One type of answer to the question is given by Charles Lamb in his essay about the superannuated man. His old clerk, who is finally retired on a pension and exults in his freedom, declares: 'Man, I verily believe, is out of his element as long as he is operative. I am altogether for the life contemplative.' Freedom, for him, means pottering around the bookshops, walking around public gardens, watching the 'poor drudges' on their way to work. But here the old clerk's notion of freedom halts. There is no mention of strange intuitions of 'other modes of being', of mystical ecstasies as he stares at an ear of corn, nothing that Wordsworth or Traherne or Blake would consider the essence of freedom.

Unless a man is a poet or a mystic, his notion of the 'value of life' is bound to be defined in terms of certain material symbols. Hence we have people committing suicide when they read in the newspapers about a new hydrogen bomb test, threatened inflation, a rise in the rate of sex crime. Their lives are like a grocer's scales; on one side is a certain number of weights, on the other a bag of sugar; if another spoonful of sugar is added, the weights rise. Life has ceased to be worth living; there is more pain than pleasure.

In a sense, this is inevitable. Each human consciousness is limited; it cannot contain everything in the universe and weigh up every single factor before it decides about the value of life. But here lies the value of the artist. He protests, in effect, that the value of life always exceeds any possible misery or discomfort. He attempts to keep open the door to the irrational, to the powers of affirmation. In order to live and act, human beings *must* make certain makeshift judgments on life. A youth who has just left school and is thinking about a career may want an answer to the question: 'What are my fullest potentialities?' But he does not postpone finding a job until he has answered the question. He has to make the best choice between available alternatives. And his choice constitutes a kind of judgment on the value of life; he will continue to act in a way that implies such judgments all his life. The poet is attempting to remind us all the time that such judgments *are* makeshift, that they leave out of account most of the universe.

When Wells declares that he wishes to go on living *only* if 'life' means pure mental activity, he is declaring, in effect, that from now on he will no longer regard makeshift judgments on life as having any meaning or validity. Self-enjoyment is synonymous with purposeful evolutionary activity of the intellect and the senses; and the notion of a living creature, capable of absolute self-enjoyment, is the notion of a man-god, no longer plagued by tiresome necessities over which he has no control. When a man commits himself to this definition of meaning, the 'value of life' ceases to be a matter of material symbols, comparable to a bag of sugar on the grocer's scales, and therefore limited by the consciousness and the physical aims of the individual; it becomes instead a function of the limitless realm of the intellect and imagination, of the creative will.

One could make a convenient, if oversimplified statement of this part of the argument by saying: The great artist would be incapable both of suicide and of murder, for his awareness of a wider scale of values would make either act absurd. In a practical sense, it may be true that we 'each think of the key, each in his prison', and the

91

criminal may attempt to force the door. The artist recognises that there is only one valid way out of the prison (and therefore only one valid meaning of the word freedom): to demand a way of life that is immediately connected with the values of evolution.[1]

THE DEVELOPMENT OF SCIENCE

Although I have spoken of the 'artist' as the champion of the 'anti-necessity' values, the word is used only as a convenience to cover every type of creative mental worker. In fact, science has probably done more for the emergence of new values in four centuries than art and religion have managed in two thousand years. It is unfortunate that intellectual fashions in the past century have obscured the nature of science by opposing it to religion (so that when the 'conflict' is spoken of today, many people immediately think of T. H. Huxley versus T. E. Hulme, or Bertrand Russell versus T. S. Eliot, and thus confuse the issues completely). But 'science' is one of the basic human intellectual activities, and consists of a certain faith in the concept of order.

The primary attitude of the living organism towards its environment is acceptance, and instinctive adjustment to changes. The first man who noticed that the seasons rotate at yearly intervals, and used this knowledge to become a successful farmer, was the first scientist. Instead of merely adjusting himself to the pressure of events, he attempted to anticipate events. In the same way, the first men to regard the thunder and lightning as gods were also scientists; they attempted to base a theory upon their observation, even if the theory was inaccurate.

But this is by no means a definition of the scientific spirit. Man's natural attitude in the face of confusion is defeat; if the confusion threatens him personally (as, say, in an earthquake), it is fear, and his response is retreat.

But even where there is no fear, man's attitude to basic problems need not be an attempt to solve them. There are tribes known to anthropology today who cannot count above five. This is understandable enough. The world is 'given' to our senses; there is no good reason why our response to it should be other than immediate and sensory. Besides, as all children know, attempts to apply reason to our problems are likely to be a waste of time. A child who gets lost may sit down and try to reason out his position by remembering what turnings he has taken. If he is in New York, or some other city with a simple geometrical street system, he may succeed. But he is more likely to find his way home by wandering around until he finds a street he recognises, or by asking directions from an adult. *Reliance on powers of reason does not come easily; it is opposed to our basic animal instinct.*

The spirit of science is not merely faith in the powers of reason; it is also a belief that our problems may be simpler than they appear to be; the true scientist is a gambler with a faith in long shots. Faced with utter confusion and a minimum of knowledge with which to solve it, he proceeds upon the assumption that it is worth making the attempt. Archaeology affords abundant examples. The decipherment of Egyptian hieroglyphics is a relatively simple one. Guessing the meaning of hieroglyphics from their shapes was unreliable. The solution depended upon finding a fairly lengthy inscription in both hieroglyphics and a known language. As everyone knows, the Rosetta stone, written in Egyptian and Greek, furnished the basis for a solution. Even so, it was only Champollion's inspired guess that the 'cartouches' (hieroglyphic words with a circle round them) represented the names of kings that provided the final key.

A more striking example of the scientific spirit is provided by Rawlinson's decipherment of the 'wedge-shaped' cuneiform script of the Behistun inscription. The inscription was in three languages, Old Persian, Elamite and Babylonian. The difficulties of the wedge-shaped ideograms were enormous; Rawlinson soon discovered that a certain sign might stand for a syllable or a word, or even several syllables or words; on the other hand, several signs could stand for the same word. Everything was changeable; there was apparently no possible basis for interpretation. Even to attempt such a task would seem absurd. Rawlinson's success is an amazing example of a man's faith in the powers of deduction and logic.

It has been objected by many writers of the past century that science is *not* a religion, and ought not to be treated as one. It is merely a method, a plodding, two-dimensional method, with no relation to the higher realms of poetry and religion. But examples like that of Rawlinson demonstrate why, for certain men, science could become a religion. Reason also has its miracles. This was seen again in 1917, when Einstein's prediction about light rays and gravity was verified by the eclipse. This 'miracle' made Einstein the most famous scientist since Newton, and became a symbol of the triumph of science in the twentieth century.

These examples bring us closer to the truth about the 'scientific spirit'. It represents a new, aggressive policy towards nature on the part of human beings, a policy completely opposed to the animal acceptance of defeat in the face of confusion.

All this makes it possible to understand the impact of science on the human imagination. The primitive imagination is stimulated mainly by violence and fear. Early epics and sagas deal either with battles or with plots and counterplots. Such works of imagination, from *Gilgamesh* to *The Thousand and One Nights*, represent the world as an alien and dangerous place in which only heroes can hope to find happiness. The supernatural – ghosts or jinns or magicians – is very seldom on man's side; usually it is a symbol of alien menace. With the development of science and humanism, all that changed. In Plato there is a new kind of imagination, based on his faith in truth and knowledge. Socrates' attitude to the universe is wholly positive – although not materialistic. He expresses the feeling that there is a fundamental rightness about nature, that the main evil of the world is human stupidity, which will be slowly dissipated by philosophy. This spirit is present in Campanella's *City of the Sun* and More's *Utopia*; it is even present, in a negative way, in *Gulliver's Travels*.

Since the time of William Law, scientific humanism has been under attack in England. Newman satirised it and Hulme and Eliot dismissed it irritably. But a distinction should be made here. The shallowness and blindness of certain types of humanism (the kind that Eliot attacked in his essay on Irving Babbitt) is not a final argument against humanism as such. Even Blake, who detested Newton for 'closing up his senses' and reducing the universe to lines and angles, could write at the end of *The Four Zoas*:

94

The dark Religions are departed, and sweet Science reigns.

Blake is not denying the human capacity to grasp 'truth', but he insists that a man must be wide awake in every particular in order not to falsify it. Man must possess 'fourfold vision'; he must allow that the physical senses or the emotions are as likely to reveal 'truth' as the intellect. Blake is not attacking science, he is widening its definition.

Still, it must be allowed that Newtonian science made no impact on Blake's imagination. This would hardly have been necessary; in spite of his pessimism about the dirty streets and degraded human beings of the industrial revolution, he needed no stimulus to imagine a new race of supermen, men who would live in total harmony with God and the universe, perpetually renewed by 'the divine vision'. And his use of the word 'imagination' is here revealing and valuable. For Blake, the basic trouble with human beings is the narrowness of their vision. His 'Immortal', Los, has senses that stretch throughout the universe. After his 'fall' (which Blake explains by various symbolic legends, all amounting to the same thing: the domination of intellect), Los's senses 'close up' and enclose him in 'a narrow circle'. He becomes like the rest of us, tied to the present, identifying truth with 'fact' (i.e., with what is at the end of our noses). In all his legends in the prophetic books, Los begins the long struggle to recover his vision by building 'the city of art'. The exercise of the imagination is the first step towards liberating men from the tight prison of the present. If Blake mistrusts Newton and the new chemistry of Priestley, it is because he believes that mere scientific ratiocination, exercised in the narrow prison, is likely to produce a totally distorted picture of reality. It is interesting to speculate what Blake would have thought of modern science fiction.

UTOPIAS AND ANTI-UTOPIAS

Any examination of the scientific imagination should begin with a brief survey of Utopias. More's *Utopia* is the earliest of these, and gave its name to the ideal state. More used the form of fiction, and took care to preserve an attitude of self-mockery. Utopia means 'the good place' in Greek, and it is described to the narrator by a man called

Hythloday – meaning 'a talker of nonsense'. The chief points to note about More's Utopia are its democratic ideals – the 'prince' is elected by the majority – its communistic features – meals are communal, family welfare is a matter for the State, 'culture' is encouraged by the State – and its religious basis – all religions are tolerated, but atheism is not permitted.

Tommaso Campanella's *Sun City* is more authoritarian than Utopia. Although he advocates communism of goods – and of women (unlike the puritanical More) – his city is ruled by philosopher-priests, and the duties of its citizens include military service. Campanella was an advocate of experimentalism in science, but he accepted 'revealed theology'.

Francis Bacon's *New Atlantis* is again written in the form of a novel. Bacon's Utopia is closer to the scientific spirit than More's or Campanella's, although its citizens are Christians (having been mystically converted by Christ after his death). But all the emphasis is on the increase of knowledge, and Bacon is one of the first to voice the humanist daydream, the day which human beings know so much that they will be able to perform 'all things possible'. In this respect, Bacon differs not only from More and Campanella, but from most later creators of Utopias. His vision is of 'men like gods', not simply of a Welfare State. He is, in a sense, interested in ultimates, and his exalted idea of scientific knowledge, expounded in his *Novum Organum*, has earned him the title of 'the high priest of modern science'.

Until H. G. Wells's *Men Like Gods*, later Utopias tended to be Welfare States. The most famous is *Looking Backward* by Edward Bellamy, published in 1888. In Bellamy's novel, a man falls asleep, like Rip Van Winkle, and awakes in AD 2000. The Boston of the future is part of a socialist Utopia. Money has been abolished, and all crime is treated as a mental disease. (This is not a satirical suggestion, as in Butler's *Erewhon*.) There is a universally high level of culture, and women have achieved an unusual degree of self-expression.

All this, like More's Utopia, may be regarded as strictly practical from the social viewpoint. Much of it has already been implemented in the Scandinavian countries. Bellamy could hardly have known about the steep rise in sex crime and suicide that has been one of the results of the welfare state. (Nor do I mean to imply that these disadvantages are necessarily permanent objections to a welfare state.)

William Morris's Utopia, in *News From Nowhere*, is not unlike Bellamy's. The most interesting thing to note about Morris is that although his aspirations may have been in a socialist future, his heart was in the medieval past. Like Bacon, he also had an ultimate in mind, but it was a strangely dreamy ultimate. The keynotes of the future socialist state would be simplicity, dignity and beauty. He might have lost faith in socialism if he had been told that modern Stockholm and Leningrad are not at all unlike New York, with a perpetual rush of traffic and people. Neither socialist nor capitalist countries have much use for hand-made furniture and hand-printed books. The fourteenth century of *A Dream of John Ball* is more reminiscent of Jeffrey Farnol's fictionalised rural England than Cobbett's. Everything is cleanliness and light. The truth of fourteenth-century England was probably closer to Zola's *Earth*. Morris's ideal is a poet's dream of *'luxe, calme et volupté'*.

WELLS AGAIN

This, in many respects, is also true of H. G. Wells's many Utopias. (His first, *A Modern Utopia*, is actually the least important of these.) Wells's chief hope for the future is of a highly educated and reasonable humanity. This, for example, is typical:

> And yet ... in little more than a century, this antiquated obdurate [Jewish] culture disappeared. It and its Zionist state, its kosher food, the Law and all the rest of its paraphernalia, were completely merged in the human community. The Jews were not suppressed; there was no extermination ... yet they were educated out of their oddity and racial egotism in little more than three generations. [*The Shape of Things to Come.*]

In most of his books about the future, Wells reveals himself very much the blue-eyed optimist. And yet he can also be astoundingly accurate. The book quoted above was published in 1933; yet a chapter of it deals with the World War 1940–50.

In the Days of the Comet is typical of Wells at his most

optimistic. He imagines that a comet made of gas strikes the earth, and the gas has the effect of completely reforming human nature. The hero of the book is in love with a girl who is in love with a rich young man, and he is on his way to shoot them both when the comet strikes. After being changed by the gas, the three of them live together happily, without jealousy. More than one critic has jeered at this idea, yet there is a certain nobility in it, as in all Wells's visions of the future.

The weaknesses of his scientific optimism become apparent in *Men Like Gods*. This is partly because the book is very badly written. Wells had almost no artistic conscience about the novel: he realised that a novel will attract a wider public than a volume of non-fiction, so he frequently set his ideas in the feeblest of stories rather than write another social treatise. The consequence is that the modern reader finds it very hard to accept *All Aboard for Ararat* and *The World of William Clissold* (although the latter is well worth reading). At the start of *Men Like Gods* two motorcars which are driving along a country road suddenly find themselves on a completely different road in another world – a Utopia, everyone is beautiful, free and happy; men and woman go naked; they communicate by telepathy. The party of 'earth-people' include a Roman Catholic priest, a famous politician, an English lady. Wells gets some conventional fun out of satirising them. But it is all so poorly conceived and badly written that it creates in the reader a very determined Utopia-resistance. There is a stifling feeling about his happy and healthy Utopia. This can be traced to a kind of authoritarian trend in Wells's mind. It is all rather like the picture of the Good Child painted by a Sunday school teacher to persuade his pupils to become little angels; any healthy child promptly does the opposite. The trouble with Wells's men-like-gods is that they are nothing like gods. The godlike contains elements of power and mystery; it may be symbolised by lightning in darkness or by a mountain half hidden in clouds; but it is not likely to be evoked by a Garden of Eden picture of innocence and happiness. Moreover, although Wells pokes fun at the politician with his lifeless parliamentary language, his evasions and clichés, his own faults are not unrelated to these. There is a mechanicalness about the whole book, a superficial way of dealing with the world and human psychology. Wells's virtues are immense – especially in the books he wrote between 1896 and 1910 – and there can be no doubt, in the final analysis, that he is a great writer. But a point arrived in his development when he might profitably have studied Dostoevsky. As it was, the great crisis came only shortly before the end, producing the extraordinary *Mind at the End of Its Tether*. Unlike Strindberg, Wells was not able to benefit from it by 'curing' himself and at the same time deepening and broadening himself. At his best, Wells is as stimulating as pure air and sunlight; his incredible mental energy carries the reader along. At his worst, he has all the faults that anti-Shavians attributed (falsely) to Shaw: head-without-heart, superficiality, and lack of insight into human psychology.

Men Like Gods makes anti-Utopia books comprehensible. The ancestor of these is Dostoevsky's *Notes from Underground* in which his beetle-man rejects mathematics and logic, and declares that freedom is synonymous with the irrational. Valéry Briussov's story 'The Republic of the Southern Cross' owes something to the beetle-man's reasoning. It tells of an ideal welfare state at the South Pole, where the workers are kept as happy as well-fed pigs. A strange insanity called 'contradiction-mania' breaks out and ends by wrecking the city; it is man's subconscious need for freedom rather than mere happiness.

ZAMIATIN

The only anti-Utopia novel that has pretensions to greatness also owed something to Dostoevsky: Eugene Zamiatin's *We*, from which both Aldous Huxley and George Orwell would appear to have borrowed liberally. It is, however, a finer novel than either *Brave New World* or *Nineteen Eighty-Four*. Orwell's novel is ultimately a failure because it has no artistic detachment; it is hysterical, rhetorical, exaggerated. Like Greene's *Brighton Rock*, its black is too black, and its implied white is too white. Huxley's novel also fails because its antinomies are oversimplified: on the one hand, overmechanised civilisation; on the other, Shakespeare and 'culture'. If Huxley had been a Catholic, he might have simplified his task by taking up some of the attitudes of the priest in *Men Like Gods* who is horrified with the birth control in Wells's Utopia ('refusing to create souls', etc.). This would not have been a great deal more naïve than the attitude he actually takes up.

Zamiatin's book, on the other hand, projects itself very thoroughly into the mind of an enthusiastic inhabitant of the 'brave new world'. The book is told in the form of a diary kept by D-503 (all inhabitants of the city have numbers instead of names). He is the engineer of a new rocket. The city is enclosed in a wall made of greenish glass; outside is the old wild-life of the earth: inside there are only huge glass buildings. All inhabitants of the city live in full view of everyone else. The city is ruled by The Benefactor, a Stalinist dictator who is re-elected periodically on 'democratic' principles. (He is never opposed, of course.) Sex life is run on a basis of free love, and any inhabitant of the city can sleep with any other inhabitant merely by handing over a pink ticket to the person he or she desires. Zamiatin is a poet, and his pages have none of the atmosphere of neurotic disgust that hangs over Orwell:

Spring. From beyond the Green Wall from the wild plains that lie out of sight, the wind brings the honeyed yellow pollen of certain flowers. The lips become dry from this pollen; you run your tongue over them every minute or so and, in all probability, all the women you come across have sweet lips now . . . This interferes with logical thinking to some extent. But then, what a sky! Blue, cloudless . . . [B. G. Guerney's translation.]

Zamiatin has no need to resort to an atmosphere of claustrophobia to suffocate the reader into the right frame of mind. And the engineer's lyrical outbursts about mathematics and order are entirely convincing. They actually have the reader convinced that such a perfectly ordered city is thoroughly desirable. The engineer goes to a concert where he hears a piece of Sciabin's music; he is repelled and yet strangely, almost masochistically, attracted by the emotional disorder. Then a piece of modern 'mathematical music' is played, and he is soothed. (Music is written by machines, presumably the originals of Orwell's novel-writing machines.) Finally, as in Orwell, the hero is attracted by a woman who whispers revolt to him. She steals his affections from a pretty, innocent, round-faced girl with whom he has been having an affair for years. She

100

persuades him to fake illness so that he can visit the House of Antiquity with her – a house in which relics of the 'old world' are preserved. The day arrives when the Benefactor is to be voted to power again; but this time he is not unopposed. The engineer is horrified by this revolt against the perfect city, and yet he feels himself irrationally drawn into it. A revolution follows. The engineer goes beyond the glass walls for the first time, and discovers a race of people who live in freedom. They want him to help them steal the rocket. But the plot fails, the rebellion is crushed, and the Benefactor discovers a new way for combatting the anarchy of the human soul. Someone has discovered a simple brain operation that destroys the imagination. Everyone in the city is ordered to submit to the operation. The engineer does so, and at the end of the story he is again as 'sane' and balanced as at the beginning.

It is interesting to note that this book was written in Soviet Russia in the early 1920's, and that Zamiatin was allowed to leave Russia and end his days in Paris (where he died in 1937 of heart disease).

The book's central thesis is that of Dostoevsky's Grand Inquisitor: that most people cannot bear freedom, so it is better to take away the freedom and give them happiness and bread. (The Grand Inquisitor fascinated Russian intellectuals of the pre-revolutionary decades; Rozanov wrote a commentary on it that is among his best books.) Zamiatin often brings Dostoevsky to mind: as, for example, when his engineer writes: 'Liberation? It's amazing how very tenacious of life criminal instincts are in human kind . . . Liberty and crime are just as indissolubly bound together as – well, as the motion of an aero and its speed.' In other places, he anticipates the tone of *La Nausée*: 'The number seated on my left looked at me out of the corner of his eye – and sniggered. One detail has, for some reason, remained with especial distinctness in my memory: I saw a microscopic bubble of saliva pop up on his lips – and burst. That bubble sobered me. I was I once more.' One suspects that the seminal influence of *We* may have been very wide indeed. (It was translated into both French and English in the 1920's.)

SCIENCE FICTION AND SPACE OPERA

Science fiction sprang from the progressive beliefs that are the essence of science. The spirit of science is a spirit of enterprise; it follows naturally that writers should ask themselves how far the human race can advance through enterprise. It is natural that the first type of science fiction should be portraits of Utopia. It is also natural that space travel should be the next possibility to engage its attention. Cyrano de Bergerac's two novels about a voyage to the moon and a voyage to the sun were published about 1660. One of Poe's best stories tells how one Hans Pfaal travelled to the moon in a balloon. Jules Verne was one of the first seriously to apply his imagination to the problem of space travel; his moon voyagers are shot out of an enormous cannon! Shortly after this came Wells and his first novel, dealing with time travel.

LOVECRAFT AGAIN

But it would be a misrepresentation of science fiction to suppose that it is entirely devoted to portraying the scientific conquests of the human race. H. P. Lovecraft had occasional recourse to the medium; and his purpose, as usual, was to undermine man's conceit in his scientific knowledge. 'The Whisperer in Darkness' is an uneasy combination of horror story and science fiction. 'The Colour out of Space' is frequently anthologised as science fiction; its 'hideous thing' is a kind of cloud that sucks the life out of living things, and finally returns to space. But Lovecraft's best work of science fiction – and perhaps the most satisfying work in his whole output – is a novel called *The Shadow out of Time*. In it he loses the tug of war to keep it within the bounds of the horrible, and becomes a good writer of imaginative science fiction.

The Shadow out of Time utilises an idea that had already appeared in 'The Thing on the Doorstep': that minds can be pushed out of their bodies by alien intelligences, and the body 'used' by the alien. It begins: 'After twenty-two years of nightmare and terror . . . I am unwilling to vouch for the truth of that which I think I found in Western Australia on the night of July 17–18, 1935.' The professor who tells the story lost his memory abruptly, and did not recover it for several years. While his memory was lost, he appeared to continue to live and work as usual, travelling and studying. But his family felt that he had become 'alien'. What happened, one learns, is that the professor's body was borrowed by a member of a civilisation from the distant past. While this alien was carrying out research in twentieth-century America, the professor's psyche was banished back to the past, and occupied the body of the alien. When his memory eventually comes back (i.e., when he finds himself back in his own body), he can no longer remember anything about the past few years; the strange beings have imposed a memory block. But the block is not strong enough to stop him from having dreams about the city to which he was banished.

The 'aliens' are iridescent cones, ten feet high, that move around on a contractible base like the suckers that hold shellfish to rocks; they have three tentacles and a kind of head on the end of another tentacle. They belong to a civilisation that predates humanity by a hundred and fifty million years. (According to Lovecraft's myth, men replaced a civilisation of winged beetles.) The conelike beings came from another planet, and wrested the earth from 'a horrible elder race of half-polypus'; the semi-material polypuses were driven underground, and the entrances were covered with great trapdoors, secured with iron bands. The cone creatures then built an impressive civilisation of huge stone blocks. They had no stairs – only inclined planes. Eventually, the polypus creatures staged a comeback, and the cones all migrated forward in time into the bodies of winged insects. Lovecraft makes no attempt to explain the absurdities occasioned by this postulated ability to shuttle back and forth in time: that, for example, if the creatures could anticipate the re-emergence of the polypuses, they could also take measures to prevent it, or simply go back in time to a period before the polypuses got loose.

While the psyche of Lovecraft's professor is confined in the body of the conelike creature of a hundred and fifty million years ago, he is allowed to study in the huge libraries of the city, and to make notes (on the understanding, of course, that all this will vanish from his memory when he returns to his own age).

The point of the story occurs when the professor goes

on an archaeological dig to Western Australia in 1935. He discovers signs of the vanished civilisation of the cones. (He has been hoping that his dreams about the past were all delusions.) One night he wanders out of camp, and comes upon an entrance to an underground palace. He goes down, and finds himself back in the city of his dreams – now in ruins. Finally, he makes his way to the library where he studied, gets down a notebook off the shelves, and finds notes written in English in his own handwriting. (Lovecraft does not bother to explain how a ten-foot cone with tentacles could come to have the same handwriting as a human being with hands.). He hurries out of the city, pursued by the semi-material polypus creatures (who have broken out from under their trapdoors).

The Shadow out of Time would suffice to make Lovecraft a minor classic, if it were not so overwritten and full of unnecessary adjectives and occasional tautologies (such as a reference to dreams as 'the unchecked caprices of sleep'). But its chief fault is bound up with Lovecraft's intention. He tries hard, by the liberal use of his usual adjectives, to give the story an atmosphere of terror. ('The incalculable age and brooding horror of this monstrous waste began to oppress me as never before, and I could not keep from thinking about my maddening dreams of the frightful legends . . . And yet I plodded on, as if to some eldritch rendezvous.' Here, in a passage of less than fifty words, there are six unnecessary adjectives.) But most readers will find his conelike beings interesting rather than horrible; in fact, why should they be horrible? The final effect of the story (if you are not irritated by the overloaded language) is to produce an authentic impression of awe and mystery, resting on the evocation of vistas of time and space.

Edmund Wilson has jeered at this example of Lovecraft's invention as being wholly preposterous. But Lovecraft's strange city and its inhabitants are not intended in themselves to create a sense of horror. The horror lies in the concept that they can move about in time and take over human bodies. For this reason. *The Shadow out of Time* is an unusually good example of the difference between the authentic and the inauthentic use of imagination. The 'sick' aspect of Lovecraft that produced absurdities like 'The Lurking Fear' and 'Pickman's Model' is intent on maintaining his usual spooky atmosphere, and for this reason he sets the story in 'Arkham' where most of his horror stories take place, and throws in the usual references to the *Necronomicon* of 'the mad Arab Abdul Alhazred', the Comte D'Erlette's *Culte des Goules*, etc., but it would seem that, whether he likes it or not, Lovecraft is growing out of these childish fantasies (the novel was written towards the end of his life), and his imagination is becoming more at home in the mysteries of the common daylight. If all Lovecraft's adjectives were removed, the reader would suppose that the story had been created in the spirit of *The Time Machine*. Its impact is not the impact Lovecraft intended to make, but that of good science fiction. And science fiction aims at 'daylight' effects. Aristotle stated that tragedy purges through pity and terror. Science fiction is not an attempt to 'purge', but to liberate the human imagination; it achieves this liberation, not by pity and terror, but by attempting to evoke wonder and amazement. (At its best, it may also evoke awe, but this is rare. Wells achieves it at the end of *The Time Machine*, but I can think of few other examples.) By this definition, *The Shadow out of Time* is good science fiction. But it is not, by any stretch of language, a good horror story.

It is obvious that the above attempt at a definition of science fiction covers every type of fantasy, from the *Odyssey* to Baron Munchausen's Travels. All that science has done is to provide fantasy with a kind of classical framework, in the same way that Aquinas provided Dante with a theological framework. Munchausen, like Lucian of Samosata in the *True History*, produces humorous absurdity after absurdity, but the effect is like eating too much ice cream at a party: the extravagances sicken. There is no inner coherence, to draw the reader from page to page. In fact, the reader could almost lay the book down and continue to write it himself. Compare this with the careful scientific explanation that makes Poe's account of Hans Pfaal's journey to the moon so absorbing, or the details given by Jules Verne in his four space novels. In these the reader's credulity is captured; the story appears to unfold according to a logical process. Combined with the spirit of science, the imaginings have a certain authority – the kind that Dante must have possessed for his contemporaries.

(This can be seen also in Poe's detective stories, as well as in the Sherlock Holmes stories which are so closely related to them.)

BELL'S *Before the Dawn*

A typical example of this scientific framework is provided in E. T. Bell's novel *Before the Dawn*. Bell, who published his novels under the pseudonym of John Taine, is best known as a mathematician, and author of the classic *Men of Mathematics*. The novel appeared in 1934, and the publishers called it 'a work of fantascience', evidently feeling that 'science fiction' is not an accurate description. Like Wells's *Time Machine* and Lovecraft's *Shadow out of Time*, it is an attempt at the imaginative evocation of another epoch. But Bell is logical enough to realise that time travel is an impossibility. Wells had explained that time is merely the fourth dimension, and that men will one day travel in time as they now walk along Oxford Street. Like Lovecraft, he did not bother to face all the obvious paradoxes that would arise: for example, that a 'time traveller' could travel back to yesterday and pick up his 'self' of the day before, then travel back another day and pick up his 'self' of two days ago, and accumulate an army consisting of an infinite number of 'himselves'. In short, it would involve an infinite number of parallel worlds, each one a fraction of a second behind its neighbour, so that time travel would be a 'sideways' progress from one world to another. As a mathematician, Bell is aware of all this. So he makes an alternative suggestion. Sound can be recorded on wax discs; why should the rocks of the distant past also not contain records of everything they have '*seen*'? The Russian science-fiction writer Yefremov makes a similar suggestion in a story called 'Shadow of the Past', in which an enormous crystal cliff has 'photographed' a prehistoric monster.[2] But Yefremov's 'photo' is static; Bell suggests that if we could find the means to 'play them back', crystals might reveal moving pictures of the past.

In his novel, a group of technicians who are investigating electronic techniques for assessing the age of archaeological objects stumble on a method of playing back the record of the rocks. A tiny needle of light travels over the surface of the object, searching out the changes due to the impact of light. The book is written as if it is an actual scientific record; each chapter tells of some small advance in knowledge. The result is a moving and vivid picture of past geological ages that has an effect similar to that of Wells's *Outline of History*. Bell describes great lakes, carboniferous forests, the emergence of the amphibians, and finally the passing of the dinosaurs. He is particularly effective in creating a picture of the meaningless brutality of nature, Tennyson's 'nature red in tooth and claw'.

Bell's novel is a classic of the purest type of science fiction – that is to say, fiction that depends for its effect solely on the vision of science. Pure science fiction attempts to evoke the same type of wonder that watching a chemical experiment produces in an eleven-year-old. It attempts to be realistic. It might be judged by the following hypothetical test. Suppose the existence of an alien being from another planet, similar to our own. Suppose that this being is offered such scientific works as Darwin's *Voyage of the Beagle*, a life of Madame Curie, Schliemann's account of his discovery of Troy, and a popular history of the development of science since Newton. Suppose also that the alien can read and understand these books, but is unable to judge whether they are fact or fiction. If someone tried to slip in Wells's *First Men in the Moon* and an issue of *Astounding Science Fiction*, the alien would certainly be able to spot the works of imagination. But if he were offered Bell's *Before the Dawn*, Olaf Stapledon's *Last and First Man*, Wells's *Shape of Things to Come* (with its title suppressed), and certain novels of Robert Heinlein, he might find himself hard pressed to distinguish fact from fiction. (Such an observer would also have difficulty in deciding whether *Kon-Tiki* is a boy's adventure story.)

'Pure science fiction' could pass this test. It is an attempt to communicate the authentic vision of science through fiction, but it forms a very small proportion of the science fiction that has been published since 1925.

POPULAR SCIENCE FICTION

The American science-fiction magazine *Amazing Stories* came into existence in the mid-1920's and was the first of its kind. (Lovecraft published some of his stories in it.) In the 1930's the form became suddenly popular; there was a new and slicker *Amazing Stories*, a *Thrilling Wonder Stories, Astounding Stories, Fantasy Magazine*, etc. Most of these were by no means as bad as their titles suggest; in fact, they fostered some excellent writers. The late Stanley G. Weinbaum (who died young) occupies a comparable position as a writer of science fiction to Lovecraft's as a writer of weird tales. The writing of science fiction was, and still is, a fairly disinterested occupation; its rewards are small compared to those of 'straight fiction' or detective novels. It has its hacks, but a large percentage of the writers for *Amazing Stories* were men whose imaginations were genuinely possessed by the 'vision of science' and who wrote in almost a proselytising spirit. If the imagination was sometimes feeble, the intentions were often idealistic.

As a typical example of the best type of popular science fiction, consider A. E. van Vogt's volume of stories *Destination Universe!* Its opening story, 'Far Centaurus', deals with the problem of reaching the stars. A scientist discovers a drug capable of keeping men in a state of suspended animation. This partly answers the problem of how men could keep alive through the enormous periods of time that it would take to reach the nearest stars – even for a space ship that could travel at the speed of light. Several drugged men are shot towards Alpha Centauri. They wake up after fifty years or so, take more of the drug, and sleep on for another fifty years. In this way they are still young men when they reach the star. But when they arrive, a surprise awaits them. Since their space ship set out, human science has made immense advances, and has constructed space ships that can cover the journey in a fraction of the time. When they arrive, the star is already colonised by men from earth. Unfortunately, the author has no idea of how to finish his story, but the first part is impressive because it makes the reader aware of the immensity of space. The men who leave earth on a two-hundred-year voyage are severing themselves from all their human connections, and from the human race. By the time they arrive on the star, all their relatives on earth will be dead. The story jars the reader's imagination to a new viewpoint. Our imaginations are anthropocentric, earthbound; they prefer to deal with the emotions with

108

which they are familiar – human love and hate. In this sense, a story like van Vogt's can be considered as a new departure for the human imagination, which since Homer has dealt with warmer and more familiar emotions. Van Vogt brings this home at the beginning of the story, where the narrator mentions a pretty girl who kissed him as he climbed into the space ship and then reflects that she is now either a grandmother or dead, although it seems only a few hours since she kissed him. But towards the end, the space travellers decide that they are uncomfortable in the world of the future; van Vogt does a little juggling with scientific terminology, 'time vortices', etc., and his space travellers go plunging back in time, so that the narrator can rejoin the pretty girl who has kissed him. The 'strangeness' created by the story is broken in favour of the emotions we are familiar with. The author looks into the abyss and then turns tail.

Still, it is something to have looked into the abyss. And for its first half, the story is an excellent example of the almost theological note sounded by the best science fiction. It recalls Pascal's phrase about the 'eternal silences of these infinite spaces', but it also has the merit of bringing it home to the imagination more forcibly than Pascal does.

At its best, science fiction has this effect of jerking the imagination out of its anthropocentric prison yard and stirring it into a new kind of perception.

As Edmund Crispin points out in his introduction to the first volume of *Best Science Fiction*, many science-fiction stories take an extremely pessimistic outlook on contemporary history. Some end with the destruction of the human race in atomic warfare. Others take a gloomy pleasure in emphasising that the human race is a mere passing episode in the history of the earth: this type of story is not particularly profound or original – its great-grandfather is Gulliver's visit to the land of the Houyhnhnms – and we need not take seriously Mr Crispin's assertion that its pessimism constitutes a genuine 'moral content'. Others again take the opposite attitude – that humanity may only be another of nature's experiments, but that it is a highly successful one, and we all ought to be rather proud to be human.

But there are also many stories that achieve an exciting

pressure of ideas, on the same level as van Vogt's 'Far Centaurus'. *A Case of Conscience* by James Blish deals with a distant planet inhabited by semi-reptilian creatures of extraordinary gentleness and intelligence. A group of earth-men have to decide whether the planet is suitable for colonisation by the earth. A Catholic priest advances the argument that the planet is a snare of the devil. Its inhabitants seem to be an example of perfect goodness who are thus without the need for redemption by Christ; it is therefore a trap set by the 'Ultimate Enemy' to convince men that Christianity is unnecessary, and its colonisation would lead to the spiritual ruin of the whole human race. Strangely enough, all the members of the expedition agree with this, and the planet is put on the 'Index'. The discussion is on a level that compares with the Russian novel of the nineteenth century; it is astonishing to realise that this story was printed in a pulp magazine for sale on newsstands.

A favourite science-fiction theme is the problem of identity. Brian Aldiss has an excellent story called 'Outside' that achieves an intensity that is reminiscent of Kafka. It uses the Kafka technique – a favourite with science-fiction authors – of writing about a situation from 'inside', making no effort to relate it to the ordinary world of the reader; it is up to the reader to keep his wits about him and to grasp the situation from odd hints and clues dropped by the author. In Aldiss's story six people are living in a windowless house – four men and two women. Every day food appears; no one asks where it comes from. They play cards to pass the time. No one seems to wonder what there is outside the house. The situation is not unlike Beckett's – or human life on earth. But one man, Harley, is troubled and begins to investigate. He discovers that creatures of an alien race, known as Nititians, have been infiltrating among human beings, and constitute a great threat. Nititians can 'kill a man, dispose of him, and turn into exact replicas of him'. A space ship with a load of these fake human beings has been intercepted; the Nititians have been subjected to artificial amnesia, and placed in the sealed house, with one real human being among them as an observer. They all continue to maintain their human form by a kind of self-hypnosis; only great stress can cause a breakdown. At this point, Harley points out that he is a human being; as he speaks, he feels himself dissolving and turning into a Nititian. He is told: 'Like earth insects that imitate vegetables, your cleverness cripples you. You can only be carbon copies. Because Jagger did nothing in the house, all the rest of you instinctively followed suit. You didn't get bored – you didn't even try to make passes at Dapple . . .'

In a story of less than five thousand words, Mr Aldiss has succeeded in creating an effective symbol of the human condition and posing the problem 'Who am I?' in a new and startling way. His treatment of the problem of identity is certainly more economical and artistically successful than, say, that of Max Frisch in his highly praised novel *Stiller* (which has been compared to Kafka and Mann). All the same, it should be noted that some of Aldiss's themes appear elsewhere. Van Vogt has a story called 'The Sound' about 'aliens' who can impersonate human beings; Philip K. Dick's *Imposter* uses the idea of a fake human being who does not know that he is an alien. Stock themes appear in science fiction as much as in folklore and fairy tales.

A story called 'Hobson's Choice' by Alfred Bester treats the theme of time travel with unusual thoughtfulness. It sets out to explode 'escapist' ideas about the past; its moral is that a man is most comfortable in the age he has been born into, even if he casts wistful glances back to the Ancient Greeks or the Elizabethans. It sounds a note of breezy 'realism that recalls Shaw and Wells; but it is interesting that Bester should have needed to choose the medium of science fiction to express his ideas on escapism. Again one becomes aware that science fiction seems to have escaped the general sense of defeat, the cult of 'the little man', that pervades so much modern writing.

The writings of Robert A. Heinlein deserve special mention in this context. Like Lovecraft, Heinlein has tried to build up a kind of mythology – only in this case, it is a mythology of the future. Most of his volumes have an appended chart of 'Future History, 1951–2600'. Heinlein's work varies in quality; at its worst it can be sentimental, whimsical or melodramatic; but at its best it combines imagination with a careful realism; he might almost be described as a Zola of the future. Among living writers of science fiction, he has the most consistently high quality

111

and, together with Weinbaum, is the writer whose work most deserves to be considered simply as literature.

Another writer of curiously inconsistent quality is Ray Bradbury. As a writer of pure fantasy, he sometimes compares with Wells. Indeed, a short novel called *Lorelei of the Red Mist* (written in collaboration with Leigh Brackett) is an exercise in the heroic that, although it is set on Venus, recalls the Norse sagas and the *Odyssey*. (The resemblance may be intentional.) But Bradbury also has a curious obsession about children, and this makes some of his stories seem near-pathological. In one of them children act as spies for aliens from another planet, and when the aliens invade earth, join enthusiastically in hunting down the adults. In another story in *The Illustrated Man*, children plot to get their parents devoured by wild beasts. This unhealthy side of Bradbury can be seen at its worst in a story called 'The October Game' (which is not science fiction). In this tale, a husband plots how to get revenge on his wife, who is frigid and hates her husband for giving her a daughter. He throws a children's party at which they all play a rather gruesome game in the dark; the game consists in dismembering a dummy, and passing around its head, arms, etc., with an incantation about witches. The husband actually dismembers his daughter and passes around fragments of her body. The last sentence of the story reads: 'Then . . . some idiot turned on the lights.' (The dots are Bradbury's, intended to increase the tension.) The most charitable description for this kind of thing is puerile. It is unpleasantly reminiscent of Graham Greene's obsessions. Fortunately, not all Bradbury's work is on this level. A story called 'The Fire Balloons' (anthologised by Edmund Crispin) shows a preoccupation with the nature of goodness. A group of priests go to Mars to try to Christianise the planet; one of them hears about strange beings in the form of balloons of blue light, who live in the hills; he takes several colleagues with him to try to 'save' the balloons, but ends by having to acknowledge that these alien beings have already achieved a level of disinterested benevolence that goes far beyond human beings. It is a pity that Bradbury touches this level of perceptiveness very occasionally indeed; too many of his stories combine a magazine-ish slickness with facile pessimism.

But this is not a fault confined to Bradbury; it would seem that one of the great temptations of science-fiction writers is to make the story end with a big bang to startle everybody. There is also the Lovecraft tendency to try to make the reader's flesh creep; but this is often simply a reflection of the feeling that the universe is a cold and hostile place, and that the reader ought to be shaken out of his parochialism.

One of the worst and most irritating tendencies of science fiction is its fondness for scientific jargon and 'alien-ness' for its own sake. Some writers seem to feel that science fiction ought to read like an obscure textbook on wave mechanics. They clothe their stories in an armour of technical terms that makes them as impenetrable as the later Henry James, and that frequently conceals a mushiness of stereotyped emotion and attitudes that would do credit to Amanda McKittrick Ros.

Nevertheless, at its best there is a great deal to be said for science fiction. It often shows a vitality and inventiveness that have been absent from literature since the nineteenth-century romantics. Its writers have, it might seem, become slightly delirious at being told that they needn't worry any more about *Ulysses* and the end of the modern novel, and have plunged into a debauch of pure fantasy. Bradbury exemplifies this in its best and worst aspects; when he is being subjective and 'individual', the result is often morbid rubbish; when he decides to write a straight adventure story, he reveals himself as a powerful creative talent. As a 'Shakespearean fish' he is completely successful; when he tries to be 'modern', he goes to pieces. This makes one wonder how many other authors are doomed to mediocrity in a straitjacket of 'honesty' and realism.

CONCLUSION

Sartre's *La Nausée* stands at the end of a cul-de-sac of the imagination, a symbol of 'mind at the end of its tether', honesty that has fumbled its way to a standstill. Self-analysis has ended in total enfeeblement.

I have tried to show that this complete blankness in the face of 'reality' is also the basic animal response to nature – ignorance and acceptance; and, when catastrophe

113

strikes, defeatism. In contrast to this, the spirit of science stands for action and progress. Before the rise of science, men looked to religion and the day of judgment to achieve the final liberation of the spirit from its bonds. Francis Bacon was among the first to transfer this role to science – i.e., to human knowledge. But the kind of liberation forecast by Bacon and the Italian humanists was purely intellectual. It must have seemed to them that the human spirit had entered a new domain, achieved a new power of conquest. In religion, all was 'revealed' and the theologian was the slave of the scripture. In science, a man was his own master; he could construct a system of the world with no reference to the Old Testament; its only necessity was internal consistency.

This is the spirit of science fiction, from More's *Utopia* onward. It is a spirit that often betrays its enthusiasts into naïvety, the kind of oversimplification of human nature revealed in *Men Like Gods*. It applies to the imagination the stimulus of intellect, but shows no psychological grasp of human nature. (Psychological insight, while it mixes well enough with religion, seems to find no special interest in science. Writers like Blake, Dostoevsky, Joyce, D. H. Lawrence seem to be actively anti-scientific. In Pascal, psychological insight was pressed into the service of religion, but science remained in a watertight compartment.)

And yet there can be no doubt that the stimulus applied to the imagination by science is somehow more 'authentic' than the kind of stimuli Lovecraft and Yeats applied. Wells's novels may be criticised for oversimplifying the reality of human nature, but their distortion is innocent compared to Lovecraft's.

But the problem of imagination is the problem of its relation to 'reality'. The answer to be gathered from Joyce, Beckett, Sartre and Yeats (in 'The Circus Animals' Desertion') is that imagination cannot live with reality; it must be annihilated by it. Imagination is lies. (What theme had Homer but original sin?) In *Crime and Punishment*, Svidrigailov admits that he sometimes imagines that eternity is the corner of a stuffy room, covered with spiderwebs. This, Beckett and Sartre imply, is the truth of it. When you consider it honestly, reality is that coat hanging on the door, that fly perched in the corner of the ceiling. Reality

114

is defeat, old age and death. Man is chock full of illusions and vitality, thoughtfully provided by life to stop him from facing the awful reality. But the day has to come; one day man has to lie down in the rag-and-bone shop of the heart.

The answer of science is more optimistic. Imagination is the herald of change. This is the view that Yeats took in his more optimistic moods, and in 'Under Ben Bulben' he declares that Michelangelo's figures on the Sistine chapel roof are there to inspire men to strive for greatness, the final aim being 'profane perfection of mankind'. So although he is 'anti-rational', Yeats ended his life holding the same views on imagination as Wells and Shaw. His 'profane perfection' is another way of saying 'men like gods'.

For Wells, the imagination inspired by science can look to the very near future for the fulfilment of its dreams. The world state is around the corner; men grow wiser every year, learning by their mistakes. Shaw takes a slightly more metaphysical view of the imagination. Michelangelo is also one of Shaw's favourite examples, although he preferred the sibyls and prophets to the muscular young men and cherubs. Shaw has a great passage in *Back to Methuselah* that summarises his vision of the purpose of imagination. Eve has just finished a tirade about the stupidity of digging and fighting; she goes on to talk about her children who have become artists:

Some of them will neither dig nor fight . . . but one gives them what they want because they tell beautiful lies in beautiful words. They can remember their dreams. They can dream without sleeping. They have not will enough to create instead of dreaming; *but the serpent said that every dream could be willed into creation by those strong enough to believe in it.*[3] There are others who cut reeds of different lengths and blow through them, making lovely patterns of sound in the air; and some of them can weave the patterns together sounding three reeds at the same time, and raising my soul to things for which I have no words. And others make little mammoths out of clay, or make faces appear on flat stones, and ask me to create women for them with such faces. I have watched those faces and willed; and then I have made a woman-child that has grown up quite like them. And others think of numbers without having to count on their fingers, and watch the sky at night, and give names to the stars, and can foretell when the sun will be covered with a black saucepan lid. And there is Tubal, who made this wheel for me, which has saved me so much labour. And there is Enoch, who walks on the hills, and hears the Voice continually, and has given up his will to do the will of the Voice, and has some of the Voice's greatness. When they come, there is always some new wonder, or some new hope; something to live for. They never want to die because they are always learning and always creating.

This passage says fundamentally the same thing as the extract from Wells quoted at the beginning of this chapter, but it says it more forcefully and with more awareness of its implications. The artist, the scientist, the mathematician, the religious man, are all seen as embodiments of the imagination, all striving for the same 'profane perfection of mankind'. The view is diametrically opposed to that of Beckett with his 'nothing to be done'. According to Shaw, there is always something to be done, if it is only sitting still and willing something to happen. 'Every dream can be willed into creation by those strong enough to believe in it.' But the Beckett school has lost not merely the strength to will; it has lost even the strength to dream.

NOTES

1. My book *The Outsider* dealt with the attempts of various men to disown the 'limited' scale of values and live according to the 'unlimited'. This way of defining the problem provides the only satisfactory answer to the question: What is the Outsider outside? He is not finally 'outside' society or religion or humanity; only outside the 'necessity' scale of values. Hence Nietzsche's declared aim: the transvaluation of values.

2. Yefremov is surprisingly unknown in England and America (some of his works are issued by the Russia Today Book Club, printed in Moscow). He is one of the few science-fiction authors who can be seriously compared to Wells.

3. My italics.

Five

The Power of Darkness

I have borrowed the title of a play by Tolstoy for this chapter, because the play symbolises a certain practical attitude to the problem of evil. Tolstoy's peasants commit murder, adultery, theft and finally infanticide in the mean and narrow spirit of Zola's peasants in *Earth*. The scene of the murder of the baby must be one of the most harrowing in dramatic literature. But plainly, Tolstoy's feeling is that evil is basically stupidity. It is insensitivity to the suffering of others. Finally, and most important, it is a *miscalculation of the value of life.* If a millionaire died of chagrin when he lost half-a-crown down a drain, it would prove a breakdown in his sense of values, a failure to assess the extent of his possessions. The study of, for example, the Burke and Hare murders produces the impression that they had miscalculated the value of their own lives (not to mention those of their victims). It is obvious that the miscalculation was caused by the appalling social conditions of Edinburgh in 1810; that in a sense Burke and Hare had very little 'to live for'. No doubt Traherne and Nietzsche are right: no human being has ever yet had the smallest glimpse of the value of life. A man about to be executed may have more idea of it than most of us; but even he can form no real estimate. And yet Shaw is also right: a sense of the value of life can only be cultivated by people who have the money and leisure to study beautiful things. The 'miscalculation' of Burke and Hare was a social rather than a moral matter.

There is hardly need to comment that Lovecraft would have found this view completely repellent. So, no doubt, would Graham Greene. There is a certain type of writer for whom it is necessary to believe in the positive existence of evil, evil as a batlike monster, as the Eternal Adversary, waiting to drag human beings to perdition. With most of them – as with Lovecraft and Greene – the view does not make for serious literature. It has the same effect as the scientific optimism of Wells – a certain oversimplification.

117

But it has another quality in common with scientific optimism: it acts as a powerful stimulus on the imagination.

The present chapter is concerned with the preoccupation with evil, and its effect on the imagination.

I have already commented that science provides the imagination with a framework, analogous to the theology of Dante. The 'power of darkness' school of writing has no such framework, and is always striving to provide itself with one. This is the reason that so much of the literature of evil seems so curiously lacking in backbone. This seems to be true on all levels of merit, from Dostoevsky to Lovecraft. Dostoevsky was temperamentally opposed to Tolstoy's pragmatic, unmystical view of the nature of evil, and yet his own honesty led him continually to endorse it. When the devil appears to Ivan Karamazov, he admits he is a figment of Ivan's imagination; instead of being a figure of terror and evil, he is a seedy and brash individual. Stavrogin in *The Devils* tries hard to be sinful, and ends by having to admit that he is not stupid enough to be evil. What is more, there is something unconvincing about Dostoevsky's attempts to write about evil; for all its power, there is an adolescent quality about *The Devils*. Aldous Huxley's remarks on Dostoevsky are pertinent and valid: 'All Dostoevsky's characters . . . are . . . emotional onanists, wildly indulging themselves in the void of imagination . . . But however agonising they may be . . . these tragedies . . . are fundamentally ludicrous and idiotic. They are the absurdly unnecessary tragedies of self-made madmen.'

The sheer length of *The Devils* and its accumulation of detail make it difficult to judge as a whole; but anyone who has read Camus's potted stage version of it cannot fail to agree with Huxley. 'If Stavrogin could have gone to bed with women he liked, instead of sleeping, on satanically ascetic principles, with women he detested; if Kirilov had had a wife and a job of decent work; if Pyotr Stepanovitch had ever looked with pleasure at a landscape or played with a kitten – none of these tragedies, these fundamentally ludicrous and idiotic tragedies, would have taken place.'

If this is true of a writer of Dostoevsy's stature, what

can be said for Lovecraft and other writers of subjective fantasy?

Nevertheless, if taken on its own level, the literature of evil and the supernatural provides some interesting glimpses into the working of imagination. To begin with, its lack of a framework or a background of belief, throws into relief the peculiarities and obsessions of individual writers. Dostoevsky, for example, twice associated the rape of a ten-year-old girl with his vision of evil; yet it would seem, to judge by his work and his life story, that he was, if anything, under-sexed. Is it possible to find a connection between lack of sexual development and preoccupation with supernatural evil?[1] A respected English critic has suggested that the stories of M. R. James are full of symbols of repressed homosexuality. Poe's views on sex were certainly affected by his unhappy love life. The Reverend Montague Summers, who was a believer in witches and a connoisseur of supernatural lore, seems to belong to the type of the repressed homosexual. E. T. A. Hoffmann was sexually inadequate. And Edmund Wilson has some interesting speculations on James's 'Turn of the Screw' and its author's curious fear of sex. (On the strength of this novelette, Franz Höllering declared that James was a *Kinderschänder* – a child violator.)

This question is not important, it is only an interesting example of the questions that arise out of the study of the tale of supernatural evil.

E. T. A. HOFFMANN

Consider, for example, the relation of Hoffmann's personality to his fantastic tales. Hoffmann's work is, for some reason, almost unknown in England, although it maintains a high level of invention more consistently than Poe. The author died at the age of forty-six, after six months of agony; yet his life cannot be described as tragic; there is only a sort of muffled unsatisfactoriness about it. It seems to have been forty-six years of prolonged boredom and unfulfilment. Born in 1776 in Königsberg, Hoffman was a stunted, ugly child. He became a musician, fell unhappily in love several times, had an affair with a married woman that was finally broken off because of Hoffmann's indiscretion, sank into poverty and became a drunkard, and

119

finally – in the last ten years – became famous. Unrequited love was a recurrent theme in his life. When his poverty finally lifted, he was attacked by arthritis and partial paralysis. (Offenbach's *The Tales of Hoffmann* is a remarkably accurate portait in many ways; it reveals his fatalistic belief in his bad luck, his drunkenness and his sexual failure. Hoffmann, himself a talented composer of operas, would have been delighted by it.)

Certain parallels with Poe are obvious. And yet Hoffmann's stories are totally unlike Poe's. Poe's tales all exist in a ghostly half-light; Hoffmann's take place in a brighter-than-day daylight. They are full of colour and movement; they remind the reader of the opening of such operas as *Carmen* and *Faust*, with their gaily dressed crowds and sparkling music. Everything is solid and circumstantial. This would seem to be the revolt of Hoffmann's imagination against the dreariness of his life. The moment you begin to read a story by Hoffmann, you are in a highly eventful world; you have only to read the first few sentences of the story to feel that it might lead to a thousand different developments. This is simply the incredible strength of Hoffmann's imagination, that seems to exude power and vitality. He launches his stories with the first sentence. 'Huddled into a wretched post-chaise, which the moths had left from instinct – as rats desert a sinking ship – I stopped at last at the inn in the Glogau market place, feeling as if half my bones had been dislocated.' Or: 'Councillor Krespel was one of the strangest, most fantastic men I ever came across in my entire life . . .' Immediately, the story is underway and travelling fast. Hoffmann's tales reveal the storyteller's art in its purest form, like a man turning somersaults for the fun of it. He brings to mind Pushkin rather than Poe.

And yet, as might be expected, the stories are full of sexual failure and of tragic fatality. The three stories that Offenbach used are typical. The first, 'The Sandman', tells how a young student falls in love with a mechanical doll created by the cranky Professor Spalanzini, with the help of the evil magician Coppelius. The figure of Coppelius has obsessed the student's mind since childhood (when he associated him with the sandman who comes to see that naughty children are in bed), and after the love affair with the doll has ended in tragic farce, Coppelius somehow induces the student to throw himself from a high building. The second describes how a young German falls in love with the courtesan Giulietta, and gives her his reflection as a token of his love. Giulietta and her sinister associate Doctor Dappertutto now try to force the young man to murder his wife and child. He finally succeeds in banishing them; but he never regains his reflection. Here, Hoffmann seems to be expressing a feeling that freely offered love must be a trap. In 'Councillor Krespel', a beautiful young girl is not allowed to sing because she is consumptive; but she finally prefers to sing herself to death rather than live without self-expression. (Thomas Mann seems to have borrowed this plot for *Tristan*.) In these three stories, Hoffmann's fatalism is apparent. In the first two, the hero is already attached to a solid, decent, unimaginative woman before he falls tragically in love. The implication is that man must choose between the pleasant, dull life of the earth or the high fevers of the imagination. Story after story deals with the man of genius pursued by tragic fatality, and usually there is the solid, decent girl in the background, who cannot save her lover from his destiny. This is also the theme of 'The Jesuit Church in Glogau' and 'The Mines of Falun'.

In all Hoffmann's work, vitality and humour fight with morbid fatalism. When Hoffmann decides to be funny, he is very funny indeed. 'Salvator Rosa' was the basis of Donizetti's comic masterpiece *Don Pasquale*. 'The Fermata' deserves a high place among the world's best humorous stories; it is also one of the few moving and convincing accounts in fiction of the development of musical talent. Hoffmann could also write a straightforward tale of intrigue and mystery like no other writer of his time: 'Madame de Scudéry' might have been written by Dumas at a rare pitch of inspiration, but its air of sober authenticity is closer to Balzac.

Unfortunately, Hoffmann can also tangle himself and the reader in a web of mystification. Some of his tales are so full of absurdities that they make the plot of Verdi's *Trovatore* seem simple and elegant by comparison. (*Trovatore* seems to owe some of its more preposterous twists to Hoffmann's story 'The Deserted House', which ends in a splendid confusion of husbands lost and found, babies stolen by gypsies, etc.)

The chief interest of Hoffmann, in the present context, is the clear division in his stories between the healthy and the morbid. At his best, his stories are like a natural growth, like an oak tree in spring, with a Tolstoyan vitality. But when the element of the morbid enters into his work like a damp wind, immediately the stories are artificially twisted towards disaster.

The two elements should be clearly grasped, for they are fundamental to the study of imagination. All great literature has this treelike quality, the feel of a living organism, springing from the artist's firm and deep sense of life. Much great literature has the opposite quality too, the sense of being dominated by a single-minded obsession. But 'obsessed' literature cannot be great unless it also possesses the living-organism quality; for otherwise the obsessed artist is imposing his will on lifeless shadows. At his best, Dostoevsky has the organic, inevitable feeling; his most satisfying books – *Poor Folk, The House of the Dead, Crime and Punishment* – produce the impression of a man whose roots are in the earth. On the other hand, his worst books have all the bad qualities of Hoffmann (whose influence on Dostoevsky was great, particularly with a story called 'The Doubles'); such novels as *A Raw Youth* and *The Insulted and the Injured* develop into a confusion of character and incident. They lose the feeling of life, and one becomes aware of Dostoevsky the puppet master jerking the strings frantically.

GOGOL

Gogol's work contains the same opposing qualities. Gogol was another unhappy and sexually maladjusted man. (His only sexual experience was onanistic.) Today, it is hard to believe that Gogol was once regarded as the father of Russian realism. Gogol's world is real, but it has very little in common with the 'real' world; it is created, like Hoffmann's, out of a tremendous vitality of imagination. At its best it appears to be based on close observation – as in *Dead Souls, The Inspector, Taras Bulba*. At its worst, fantasy has no kind of anchor; it hardly rises above the level of a dream. 'The Nose' which many Russians find incredibly funny, is about a man who loses his nose and tries to track it down: the nose ends up driving a carriage and four around St Petersburg. Even allowing for the fact that noses are regarded as inherently funny in Russia, the story is as unsatisfactory as Poe's feeble attempt at humour in 'Loss of Breath'. This is because its absurdities are as arbitrary as those of Baron Munchausen or Lucian of Samosata. The same is true of 'Shponka and His Aunt', another of his famous 'humorous' stories.

Some of his best grotesque stories are marred by this quality of arbitrary fantasy. The famous 'Overcoat' begins as a piece of superb realism but ends in supernatural fantasy, with the little clerk haunting St Petersburg. 'Nevsky Prospect' has the same pattern. It beings by telling how a shy artist falls in love with a beautiful girl in the street, follows her home, and discovers that she is a prostitute; when she speaks, her voice is coarse and vulgar. Then the story turns into a bewildering dream-fantasy.

Gogol's most successful story, 'The Terrible Revenge', is a fine piece of rhetorical writing, describing the life of cossacks, the river Dnieper, the Russian countryside; its story of magicians and brave cossacks is entirely convincing for three quarters of its length; then abruptly, it dissolves into the usual mist of fantasy. It is as if Gogol had been telling some story and convincing his listener that he was telling the truth, and had then quite suddenly begun to lie; his manner becomes rambling and nervous; it is obvious he is trying to conceal something. (The story, incidentally, contains another reflection of Gogol's sexual peculiarities in the incest theme, which strikes a Freudian note in the Hofffmannesque atmosphere.)

The same objection applies to most of Gogol's 'supernatural' stories like 'Sorochinsty Fair' or 'Viy' (a tale of vampires). The language is beautiful – even translation cannot conceal it – the details are striking and full of life; and yet all is disordered, chaotic; you expect to see donkeys' heads and flowerpots upside down in the sky, as in Chagall's painting. Gogol's three volumes of stories – *Evenings Near Dikanka*, *Mirgorod* and *Arabesques* – seethe with life, and yet they are continually irritating. They keep bringing to mind a passage from Blake's novel *An Island in the Moon*: 'Then Mr. Inflammable Gass ran and shov'd his head into the fire and set his hair all in a flame, and ran about the room – No, no, he did not; I was only making a fool of you.'

Gogol is always making a fool of the reader in this way; but the worst of it is that it is not deliberate (as, for example, the nightmare fantasy of the Night Town chapter of *Ulysses*). Gogol is like a man subject to asthma; one minute he is telling a story soberly enough, the next he is writhing on the floor, choking. The wild imagination seizes him, and he can do nothing to resist the attack.

Admittedly there is no morbid fatalism in his work, as in Hoffmann's; but his women also fall into two classes: lifeless dolls and fearful vampires. Towards the end of his life, there were signs that Gogol was throwing off the effect of overheated fantasy. *Dead Souls* and *The Inspector* might almost be taken from life – or a caricature of life. Gogol's contemporaries mistook them for left-wing satires, until he shattered them all with his sermonising, fake-messianic volume *Selected Correspondence with Friends*. This was torn to pieces by all the critics, and thereafter Gogol abandoned himself to his religious mania, destroyed the second part of *Dead Souls*, went on a pilgrimage to the Holy Land, and ended by starving himself to death at the age of forty-three. The surviving fragment of the second part of *Dead Souls* shows that Gogol was trying to develop his tendency to portray the 'real' world rather than the world of fantasy; he makes an attempt to drop his method of exaggeration and caricature. It is generally agreed that this fragment is inferior to the first part so it may be that, after all, Gogol died at the right time. He was no realist; the practical world frightened him; this was why he never dared to approach women, and why his brief career as a professor of history was a failure. When his imagination ceased to be triumphantly self-justified, when he began to feel that he should establish contact with the 'real' world of religion and politics, he collapsed.

As a curiosity, it might be mentioned that Sergei Aksakov, the oldest of the great Russian writers of the nineteenth century, had an immense admiration for Gogol, and was one of Gogol's most indefatigable publicists. And yet it would be hard to name two writers less alike than Gogol and Aksakov. Aksakov was the first great Russian to write the treelike, organic novel, and his *Family Chronicle* and *Years of Childhood* are full of the spirit of the open air; without them, *War and Peace* could never have been written. Before Aksakov, Russian literature was episodic and dramatic, influenced by Scott and Byron; Aksakov changed it by producing three 'autobiographical' novels that are not in the least concerned with incident or drama but with 'truth to life'. And yet Aksakov, who could see little merit in Griboyedov and Pushkin, became the high priest of the Gogol cult. He was attracted by Gogol's realism, the use of Russian peasant material. Of the strange imaginative fever that inspired and finally killed Gogol he had little idea. How could he? Next to Izaak Walton, Aksakov must be the least neurotic writer of stature who ever lived.

GHOSTS AND THE SUPERNATURAL

Today, the devotee of science is seldom the believer in the supernatural. In the Middle Ages, they were almost the same thing. The twelfth-century chemist Theophilus the Monk could describe how to make gold from the ashes of basilisks, red copper, powdered human blood (from a redheaded man) and vinegar; yet the same treatise contains sober accounts of how to make glass and how to separate silver from gold with the use of sulphur. The pseudo Democritus describes how to make a crystal with white lead and glass, and then 'to this crystal add the urine of an ass, and after forty days you will find emeralds.' It is hard for us to grasp the state of mind in which these supernatural marvels were taken completely for granted, as if they were as well established as the theory of gravity or the composition of water. It comes home when one reads of the Buddha's 'early struggles for light' in the *Majjhima-nikaya*. Gautama tells the Brahmin Janussoni how he practised various disciplines to subdue his body; he starved himself, practised holding his breath, and invented penances. All this is usual enough in the records of asceticism. But he then goes on to say, 'Then Brahmin, I thought: Suppose now that on those nights that are notable . . . the fifteenth and eighth of the month – suppose I spend them in shrines of forest, park or tree, fearsome and hair-raising as they are . . . that I may behold for myself the panic fear and horror of it all.' He describes how every casual sound terrified him in the shrines, and how he used his will to subdue the 'panic fear and horror'.

125

We think of the Buddha as a symbol of the most rigorously pragmatic attitude to life, the man who found God an unnecessary hypothesis in considering the problem of how man can escape his suffering. And yet he appears to have taken ghosts sufficiently for granted to make use of them in his ascetic disciplines.[2]

Since the cosmology of the medieval church was replaced by the cosmology of science, the supernatural is no longer taken for granted. It is this that adds interest to the study of modern literature of the supernatural. And here one becomes aware that the belief in the supernatural is usually a form of compensation. This emerges clearly from consideration of Hoffmann and Gogol. Yet even here an important difference can be seen. Gogol was financially independent; he was the pampered son of a fond mother. His work is always unreal – particularly before *Dead Souls*. Hoffmann spent a large part of his life actively grappling with poverty and the dreariness of uncongenial work, and his work is always closer to reality than Gogol's; there is a fundamental sense of life and real people.

It may seem that talking about the degree of 'reality' in stories of the supernatural is a futile form of hair-splitting. Yet this is not really so, for the supernatural can be used to convey the artist's own sense of reality. I tried to illustrate this in analysing Lovecraft's *Shadow out of Time*, with its mixture of 'authentic: and 'inauthentic: imagination. Yet Lovecraft's imagination, even at its most adolescent, has a certain power; one can feel that it is rooted in deep emotions. Many modern tales of the supernatural seem inauthentic in every sense. This applies, for example, to most of the writing of Algernon Blackwood. It can be seen in 'Ancient Sorceries', an enormously long story that pays careful attention to the building up of atmosphere and obviously is intended as a *tour de force*, but only succeeds in being more feeble and irritating than anything in Lovecraft. Vezin, on holiday in France, stops overnight at a picturesque little town, likes the restful atmosphere, and decides to stay on. But the people keep reminding him of cats. He falls in love with the catlike daughter of the inn. The development of the story is tediously protracted. Eventually Vezin realises that the town is bewitched, that its inhabitants turn themselves into cats for a witches' sabbath, and that his ancestors had lived here and participated in the rites. The woman tries to persuade him to join in the witches' sabbath, but he manages to tear himself away and return to England. The story ends feebly.

As a two-page anecdote in a book on witchcraft, the story might be of interest to the social historian. Blackwood uses a ponderous machinery of sophistication to try to make it convincing, but the plot remains puerile and the story contains no 'meaning' beyond its plot. Henry James called 'The Turn of the Screw' 'a fairy tale pure and simple', but its subject – the deliberate corruption of innocence – gives it a weight and seriousness that Blackwood does not possess.

The consideration of *why* Blackwood's story is unsatisfactory again emphasises the difference between the authentic and inauthentic use of imagination. It is irrelevant here that it is long-winded and full of clichés. The important reason emerges if one asks the question: What if one were completely convinced by the story? What kind of world would it be in which a town can exist, marked on the map of France, easily reached by rail, in an ideal situation for holidaymakers, and yet full of lycanthropes? There is not enough subtlety about the idea; it is too much like declaring that black is white. When Hamlet tells Horatio that there are more things in heaven and earth than are dreamed of in his philosophy, he is attempting to *widen* the boundaries of Horatio's consciousness, to produce the authentic sense of awe and wonder. This sense can be evoked by works as different as Jeans's *Mysterious Universe*, Winwood Reade's *Martyrdom of Man* and Dostoevsky's *Brothers Karamazov*. It is even evoked by *The Shadow out of Time*. But Blackwood is making no attempt to widen the world of the reader's consciousness; he is trying to *substitute* a palpably unreal world. This kind of writing lacks force because it is too close to deceit.

In contrast, a fine example of the authentic use of imagination can be studied in Akutagawa's superb story 'The Dragon'. Ryunosuke Akutagawa, the Japanese writer who committed suicide in 1927 at the age of thirty-four, is best known for his story 'In a Grove', on which the film *Rashomon* was based. Another of his best stories, 'Kesa and Morito', is a powerful study in human pride and lust

127

that gives the reader a sense of being physically entangled in the feverish, neurotic relation between lovers who seem to will their own destruction. (Its story was used in the Japanese film *Gate of Hell*.)

'The Dragon' is about a practical joke which a priest with the disrespectful nickname Hanazo (Big-nose) decides to play on his fellow monks who live in a nearby temple. Beside an adjacent pond he puts up a notice that reads: 'On March third a dragon will ascend from this pond.' However, the joke is taken seriously, the people come even from distant provinces to be present at the dragon's ascension. On March the third, huge crowds, stretching as far as the eye can see, surround the pond. Hanazo watches gloomily. The morning goes by, and nothing happens. Hanazo begins to feel that he should have confessed that it is all a joke. Then a storm gathers and breaks over the pond. At that moment, a dark cloud seems to gather over the pond, a cloud that takes the shape of an enormous black dragon, and ascends with tremendous speed. Later, Hanazo does confess that it was all a joke, but no one will now believe him.

What is the point of Akutagawa's story? Is it that the human mind possesses powers it is unaware of? Or that people who want to be deceived will deceive themselves? It could be taken as a political allegory, of the same type as Mann's 'Mario and the Magician' (where the magician stands for the dictator and the audience for the gullible mob). Or it could be a study of the power of the human imagination ('faith can move mountains', etc.). Whatever the literal meaning of the story, its effect is the same as Hamlet's 'There are more things in heaven and earth, Horatio . . .' a widening of the reader's consciousness.

Unfortunately, too few writers on the supernatural have this attitude: so it is only possible to read most ghost stories in a spirit of derision. This is true, for example, of most of the stories in Montague Summers's *Supernatural Omnibus*. Evelyn Nesbit's 'Man Size in Marble' is typical. This is told by a painter who has gone to live in a cottage near a churchyard with his newly wedded wife. On either side of the altar are two marble figures of knights, and the legend attached to the place declares that they get up on All Saints' Eve and walk across to the cottage in which the painter lives. Before All Saints' Eve, the wife has presentiments of evil, and the painter broods on the legend. Finally, on the evening, he feels oppressed and goes out for a walk, in the course of which he enters the church and sees that the marble figures are missing. Their stone footprints lead to the cottage; he rushes in and finds his wife is dead. She holds a marble finger in her hand. The reader can guess what is going to happen from the first page of the story, and when the painter decides to go for a stroll on the fatal evening, leaving his wife alone, the plot creaks audibly. But the worst thing about it is that the reader can easily reconstruct the imaginative process that led to its composition; the sight of a marble figure in some churchyard, the schoolgirl *frisson* at the thought of how horrible it would be if it could move; finally, the completely obvious story constructed with a ruler and dividers. Like the Blackwood story, it comes very close to simply telling lies.

SHERIDAN LE FANU AND M. R. JAMES

Sheridan Le Fanu deserves to be compared with Hoffmann and Poe. His neglect in England is astonishing, for he is the only great writer on the supernatural that this country has ever produced.

Le Fanu's life follows the pattern that we have come to expect of writers of fantasy. When he was thirty (in 1844) he married an exceptional woman, and had fourteen years of happy married life. Then his wife died. Le Fanu withdrew into solitude in his house in Merrion Squre, Dublin, and spent the remaining fifteen years of his life writing his famous ghost stories and mystery novels. He wrote at night, sitting up in bed. He spent the day indoors, emerging in the later afternoon to wander round second-hand bookshops, looking for ghost stories. In his later years he refused to receive any visitors; even his friend Charles Lever was turned away from the house shortly before his death. Most of his work appeared in the *Dublin University Magazine*, which he edited for many years.

As might be expected from a man who had been happily married, there is no horror of women in Le Fanu's work. Nor can his stories be called 'romantic' in the sense that Hoffmann's or Gogol's can, though they have the same imaginative vitality.

Le Fanu's approach to his ghosts is sometimes in the spirit of the Society for Psychical Research: a clinical interest. We find this attitude in the excellent 'Narrative of the Ghost of a Hand', and in his best novel, *The House by the Churchyard*. At other times, his ghosts are in the folklore tradition: the kind that might be sung of in ballads. These are the type of 'Sir Dominick's Bargain', 'Schalken the Painter' and 'Madame Crowl's Ghost'. And there are the ghosts that are closer in spirit to Poe, or even Dostoevsky: the ghosts of the sick mind, like the evil monkey in the classic 'Green Tea', or the half-real spectre of conscience in 'The Familiar'. 'Carmilla' is probably the best vampire story ever written; unlike Bram Stoker's *Dracula* it is not unconsciously funny. Finally, Le Fanu was a skilful writer of tales of suspense: *The Room at the Dragon Volant, Wylder's Hand, Uncle Silas* and *The House by the Churchyard* are all classics of mystery writing.

All these were written in the small hours of the morning, by the light of two candles, in the silent house in Merrion Square. At times Le Fanu resembles Lovecraft in seeming to hope to frighten the reader to death. But Le Fanu is a better writer than Lovecraft, a more assured craftsman, and his spell is altogether more potent.

It is worth observing that his climaxes are usually of *physical* violence. *The House by the Churchyard* has a horrifying and grisly trepanning scene; *Uncle Silas* has a murder scene in which the wrong person gets murdered; *Wylder's Hand* ends with the barking of dogs at a black-ened twig sticking out of a bank – the twig proves to be the hand of the dead Wylder. In *The Room at the Dragon Volant* a young man is about to be buried alive under the influence of a drug that paralyses him but leaves him the full use of his senses. The final horror of 'Green Tea' (which some consider the most convincing ghost story ever written) is the suicide of the 'possessed' man, who cuts his throat with a razor and covers the floor with blood.

But Le Fanu is not an 'obsessed' writer; he is coolly in charge of his creation, he plans his effects, and he is not necessarily taken in by his own ghosts. He produces his impact on the reader by skilful and imaginative storytelling and climaxes of violence that often aim at the effects that are to be found in Zola. He has outgrown the desire to create ghosts and horrors as a gesture of rejection of the 'real world'. He knows the 'real world', he accepts it, he goes beyond it in his attempt to convey his sense of mystery and horror to the reader. His greatest horrors are psychological.

It is fitting that Le Fanu should have died like a character in one of his own stories. Towards the end he had a recurrent nightmare of being in an ancient, tottering house, and would wake up crying out with horror that it was about to fall on him. His doctor was treating him for heart disease. After Le Fanu's death, the doctor noticed the terrified expression on his face, and commented: 'I thought so – that house fell at last.'

One of Le Fanu's most fervent admirers was M. R. James, a Cambridge don who gained a limited fame with his *Ghost Stories of an Antiquary*. James is by no means as good as Le Fanu, but the reader of the *Ghost Stories of an Antiquary* will be again struck by the physical violence in them. James's ghosts are very likely to strangle their victims or to inflict some horrible disfigurement on them. What is most significant, however, is that they completely lack a centre of gravity. Poe's tales are all expressions of Poe's temperament; Lovecraft's all centre upon the same mythology. James's stories seem to be all over the place. They might almost have been written by several different men.

'Canon Alberic's Scrapbook' is about a man who comes into possession of a large folio scrapbook. On one of its pages is a picture of a monster. The man who sells it to him gives him a crucifix, which he advises him to wear. Later, the man removes the crucifix from his neck as he looks at the book; then he notices something at his elbow; it is the hand of the demon pictured in the book. He leaps out of his chair, and sees that it was standing behind him, its other hand poised over his head. Two servants rush into the room, and the monster (invisible to them) pushes past them.

In his most famous story 'Oh Whistle and I'll Come to You My Lad', a professor on holiday finds a whistle on the beach; when he blows it, he summons some kind of spirit into his bedroom. At the end of the story, he finally manages to see this spirit; it has a face of crumpled linen,

131

and seems to be attired in a sheet; when it attacks him, he faints.

'The Diary of Mr Poynter' is about a man who buys an old diary and finds a piece of material pinned to one of its pages; the cloth has a rippling pattern that looks like hair. He likes the pattern so much that he has a great deal of curtaining made with the same pattern, and hangs some of it in his bedroom. One evening, he dozes off to sleep in an armchair, and feels his hand touching something which he takes to be his spaniel. When he looks down, it is a human figure crouching at the side of his chair, its face completely covered by long, wavy hair. As he tries to rush from the room, the thing makes a feeble attempt to attack him, but he escapes.

There would be no point in detailing more of James's plots; he wrote only thirty stories, and most of these have physical ghosts or 'creatures'. Again, one observes that the quiet, retired writer, living in relative comfort – even luxury – feels the compulsion to create physical horrors, ghosts that, after all, could frighten no one but a nervous schoolboy. (Towards the end of his life, James wrote a few ghost stories for schoolboys; they are incredibly bad.) Adults continue to read James's stories, not because their horrors are convincing, but because James had a certain pedantic, scholarly cast of mind that somehow makes a delightful contrast with his ghosts and bogies. At his best, in 'Casting the Runes' or 'The Stalls of Barchester Cathedral', there is a gentle, ironic delicacy of touch that brings to mind – strangely enough – Max Beerbohm.

J. R. R. TOLKIEN

John Ronald Reuel Tolkien, an Oxford don, published his *The Lord of the Rings* (three volumes) in the mid-1950s. High claims were made for the work by noted critics. Richard Hughes compared it to Spenser's *Faerie Queene*, C. S. Lewis to Ariosto, Naomi Mitchison to Malory. A dissenting opinion came from a well-known novelist who dismissed the work as 'don's whimsy'.

At the present time, it is impossible to decide whether Tolkien has produced a classic. Although its admirers have insisted that the book is unique, and cannot be compared to anything else in English literature, its real forebears are the adventure novels of John Buchan and R. L. Stevenson. At its worst, it has touches of Enid Blyton, at its best, it is at least as good as *King Solomon's Mines*. Altogether, it must be admitted that it is a very remarkable work indeed; to be able to hold the reader's undivided interest for over a thousand pages is no small feat.

The Lord of the Rings is mostly a straightforward adventure story that takes place in a mythological land inhabited by dwarfs, elves, men, hobbits (half-size men) and various monsters. The tension of its plot depends on a simple conflict of good and evil, as accepted in fairy tales. An evil wizard named Sauron, dictator of a land called Mordor, wants to conquer all the surrounding countries.[3] To do this, he needs to regain a 'ring of power' that he lost in some previous war. The magical ring was stolen by one of his enemies, lost in a river, found by an unpleasant creature called Gollum, and eventually found its way into the hands of a hobbit named Frodo, the hero of the book. Like the ring of Nibelungs, this ring corrupts those into whose hands it falls. Luckily, the only thing that Frodo knows about it is that it makes him invisible when he puts it on his finger; this saves him from its power.

The book begins, in a manner recalling Enid Blyton, in the country of the hobbits, an idyllically peaceful place, where Frodo lives with his ring. Frodo's friend, the wizard Gandalf, discovers that the ring is Sauron's 'ring of power', and that Sauron is now actively searching for it. He warns Frodo to leave home before Sauron finds him, and Frodo finally sets out, taking with him his gardener Sam and two other hobbits. The adventures that follow are reminiscent of Buchan's *Thirty-Nine Steps*, where Hannay is hunted by his enemies all over England and Scotland.

Eventually, they decide that the ring must be destroyed, to prevent it from working any more evil. Unfortunately, it can only be destroyed in the same fire in which it was forged, and this is in the heart of the enemy's country. Frodo volunteers to take it, and a party of men, dwarfs and elves accompany him. They pass through various perils – encounters with evil magicians and various monsters – and finally Frodo manages to throw the ring into the fire, destroying the power of the evil wizard.

The above summary fails to do justice to the book's vitality. Anyone who has tried to read straight through

Buchan's Richard Hannay novels, or Haggard's Alan Quatermain series, will recall that the attention begins to flag towards the middle of the second or third volume. Tolkien gives the impression that he could have made the book three times as long, and still showed no sign of exhaustion.

As far as I know, no critic has so far tried to trace all the sources of *The Lord of the Rings*. Its resemblance to Wagner's *Ring* has already been remarked. Anyone interested in mythology will recognise bits of all kinds of legends and stories, from the Norse sagas to the Brothers Grimm. To say this is not to question Tolkien's originality, he uses mythology as Shakespeare used Holinshed. Occasionally, long quotations in elf language or dwarf language become a little tiresome. (Tolkien's runic characters look like Sanskrit.) But on the whole, its 'scholastic' framework (including a hundred pages of appendices on hobbit history, dwarf language, etc.) adds to the book's convincingness.

But the book undoubtedly owes most of its power and its fascination to its sense of evil. Sauron, although he never appears, broods over the entire book, and this keeps the tension high. At times, Tolkien brings Lovecraft to mind. 'Far, far below the deepest delvings of the Dwarves (sic), the world is gnawed by nameless things. Even Sauron knows them not. They are older than he. Now I have walked there, but I will bring no report to darken the light of day . . .' In fact, one is tempted to say that *The Lord of the Rings* is the kind of structure that Lovecraft always aimed for but never quite achieved. It succeeds in giving the impression of being a few pages from a much bigger mythology; as in Lovecraft's work, it is full of references to past ages and strange stories, so that the reader keeps wishing that Tolkien would write other books to explain himself. (As far as I know, Conan Doyle was the first to discover this technique of tantalising the reader; the Sherlock Holmes stories are full of references to cases that Dr Watson never got around to writing up.)

It could be said that this sense of evil is the *raison d'être* of the book; it is the main impression that remains in the mind when the book is finished. This is not the profound evil that William James talks about in *The Varieties of Religious Experience*, and that is evoked by some pages in

134

Dostoevsky, the ultimate sickness of the human soul facing the absence of God. It is the simple dualist evil of old mythologies, Ahriman, Rudra, Set, the dark principle. This is the kind of evil at which Blake jeers in *The Marriage of Heaven and Hell*, and that Nietzsche dismisses in *Beyond Good and Evil*. Nevertheless it is the kind that Lovecraft, Hoffmann and Gogol believed in, and Tolkien evokes it more convincingly – certainly more dramatically – than they did.

Although the novel is full of elves and dwarfs, its atmosphere is curiously realistic; it is closer to *The Seven Pillars of Wisdom* than *Alice in Wonderland*. The hardships and dangers of the journey are described with a precise eye for detail, and its battles and sieges have the same quality of imaginative accuracy. But when the book is examined more closely, it is seen that this is only an illusion of realism. There are several occasions when the hero escapes from danger, and the author makes no attempt to make the escape plausible. There are half a dozen occasions in the book when Sauron would have had the utmost ease in crushing his enemies and regaining the ring; Tolkien glosses these over. It is essential to the book's sense of evil that Sauron should be all-powerful, but it is also essential that the hero should escape. The situation is not unreminiscent of Ian Fleming's James Bond thrillers.

Finally, it should be noted that Tolkien, like James and Le Fanu, relies a great deal on physical violence to convey this sense of evil. The climax of the book is typical. Frodo has reached the cave in Mordor where the fire burns. Suddenly the power of the ring grips him, and he cannot throw it away. The evil Gollum, a former owner of the ring, has followed Frodo. He seizes Frodo's hand and bites off the finger that wears the ring. Then Gollum loses his balance and falls backward into the fire, with Frodo's ring finger still in his mouth.

THE GOTHIC NOVEL

The writers of supernatural fantasy have one point in common: all wish to create a notion of evil as a power existing *outside* man. This also implies a dualism in the nature of power itself. According to the Tolstoyan view, quoted at the beginning of this chapter, there is no such thing as good power or evil power. There is only power *for* good or evil, depending upon how human beings choose to use it. The notions of good power and evil power belong to the simple dualistic period of religion. An example of this can be seen in the vampire legend. Anyone who is killed by a vampire becomes a vampire. When the vampire is finally killed, by having a stake driven through his (or her) heart, the tales often describe the expression on the vampire's face as relaxing from its habitual evil into peace. (F. G. Loring's *The Tomb of Sarah* is a typical example: 'Over the face stole a great and solemn peace; the lips lost their crimson hue, the prominent sharp teeth sank back into the mouth, and for a moment we saw before us the pale, calm face of a . . . woman who smiled as she slept.') The vitality of the vampire is evil vitality, but it gives the damned soul no peace. In Nietzsche, as in Bergson or Shaw, there can be no 'evil vitality'. Tolkien's ring, on the other hand, confers a power that is *in itself* evil.

The need to write of this simple, dualistic evil seems to spring from rejection of the everyday world. At the same time, it indicates a refusal even to pay attention to the nature of the everyday world. (Yeats could 'reject' the world while nevertheless keeping a shrewd Irish eye on its business.) The kind of evil creatures envisaged by Hoffmann would posit a completely different world order from the one we recognise. This would not be simply an extension of our philosophy of 'heaven and earth', but a contradiction of what we actually know.

It would seem, then, that there is definitely a relationship between the creation of fantasy and the mental attitude of the recluse. It is more difficult to understand how the world of fantasy – Lovecraft's, for example – becomes involved with violent extremes of good and evil. Why did Lovecraft feel impelled to emphasise the omnipresent evil of the universe. World rejection may be comprehensible enough in any sensitive soul. Proust, for example, wanted to preserve a narrow universe in which there would be only love and friendship, excluding everything alien and hostile. But to create a personal world occupied largely by the alien and hostile is another matter. The cause may lie in the starvation of the affections. A strong capacity for affection, when starved, can turn into a self-destructive kind of malice. Turgeniev left some interesting recollections of his mother: as a young woman she adored her husband, who was indifferent to her and unfaithful; later, she became notorious for her cruelty to the serfs. This seems to be a simple case of frustrated affection turning into sadism. I have already pointed out the similarity of Lovecraft's attitude to that of Peter Kürten, the Düsseldorf sadist.

This can be further illustrated by considering some of the best-known 'Gothic' thrillers of the nineteenth century, comparing those written by women with those written by men. On the surface, there may not be much to choose between *The Mysteries of Udolpho, Frankenstein, The Monk* and *Dracula*. Considered a little more closely, it can immediately be seen that Mrs Radcliffe and Mary Shelley never go so 'far out' into gruesome and inhuman fantasy as Matthew Lewis and Bram Stoker. Mrs Radcliffe's interest was centred wholly on affairs of the heart, and all the 'supernatural' occurrences turn out to have a rational explanation. Mary Shelley started her novel with a terrifying vision of the biologist Victor Frankenstein waking up in the middle of the night to find his horrible creation looking down at him with 'yellow, watery but speculative eyes'. But in the actual writing, the novel soon ceased to be a horror story. Long before the end, it has turned into a tragedy of misunderstanding that evokes sympathy for the monster.

Lewis and Stoker, on the other hand, are not primarily interested in love, but in horrifying their readers. The spirit of both of them is not far from sadistic. The scene in *Dracula* where a mother searching for her murdered child is torn to pieces by werewolves could never have come from the pen of a woman, certainly not from Mary Shelley's.

Lewis's *The Monk*, the first best seller among Gothic novels, is sadistic in a more open way; that is to say, its sadism is closely connected with sex. Lewis himself was homosexual, and lived a life of constant emotional torment, finally dying, in appalling suffering, of yellow fever. The novel is about a saintly but proud abbot, who preserves his high puritanical ideal through strict seclusion. One of his favourite monks turns out to be a girl who is in love with him, and his downfall begins. Having seduced her, he conceives designs on another young girl, whom he succeeds in raping and then murdering. (He has already murdered her mother.) There is no attempt to explain away the supernatural elements; demons figure largely. Towards the end, Ambrosio is tortured by the Inquisition, and then seized by the Devil, who betrays him and drops him from a great height on to a sharp rock. Even so, Lewis is not willing to let the monk die yet; he makes him linger on for seven days, tormented by flies and thirst. (A recent English edition of the novel omits some of its nastier scenes, including his final seven days.)

The Monk was the ancestor of a long line of violent fantasies, including *Wuthering Heights*, Shelley's Gothic romances and Le Fanu's fourteen novels. No other Gothic novel ever achieved the same success, because no other united so many lurid elements – demonology, sex and sadism. Mrs Radcliffe had felt it essential that the virtuous heroine should escape and live happily ever after, Lewis gleefully allows her to be raped and murdered, thus inaugurating a type of fiction that has become an industry in our own day.

DE SADE'S *120 Days*

In *The Monk* can be seen the two lines of development of fantasy dealing with evil: the supernatural and the sexual. I have dealt so far only with the literature of supernatural evil. For these writers, evil is the destructive power outside man. The writers on sex have shown themselves more interested in the demonic powers inside man. Of these, one of the most interesting is the Marquis de Sade, whose most important work, *The 120 Days of Sodom*, was actually written ten years before *The Monk* (which came out in 1796), although it was not published until 1904.

De Sade's novel was composed in prison – according to his own claim, in thirty-seven days. It was written in minute handwriting on a roll of paper thirteen yards long by five inches wide. It was never finished (although the manuscript as it exists forms a bulky volume) and De Sade never saw the manuscript after he had been transferred from the Bastille to a lunatic asylum. He assumed that it had been destroyed when the Bastille was stormed. In fact, it had somehow found its way into Germany, and was eventually issued by Ivan Bloch, the authority on sexual aberration.

The 120 Days has the same kind of basic plot as the *Decameron* and *Heptameron*. Four libertines – typically, a duke, a bishop, a judge and a schoolfriend of the Duke's named Durcet – decide to shut themselves away for a hundred and twenty days, and in that time to indulge in every possible form of sexual excess. They take with them into their retirement four brothel madams – who are to act as major-domos – and an assorted crowd of young girls and young men – and their wives. The brothel madams recount long anecdotes of every sexual perversion they have encountered throughout crowded careers, and the four libertines perform the perversions themselves. It has been urged by some of its admirers that although the book may not be literature, it is the most comprehensive textbook of sexual perversion that exists. This is not entirely untrue, but no book was ever further from the spirit of a textbook.

A few words should be said about De Sade. He was born in 1740, and developed a taste for sexual excess. For instance he paid prostitutes to allow him to make shallow cuts on them, which he filled with hot sealing wax. Some of his exploits eventually landed him in prison. There he wrote the books for which he is most famous – *Justine, Juliette, Philosophy of the Boudoir* and *The 120 Days*. After the French Revolution, he tried hard to ingratiate himself with the revolutionaries – apparently hoping that the Revolution would lead to total abandonment of moral prejudices – and wrote a curious document urging the French to free themselves from the tyranny of God and morality now they had executed the king, the 'representative of God on earth'. In the same perverse spirit, Baudelaire was later to declare that he fought on the barricades only because he believed so enthusiastically in vice and torture.) In 1803, he was confined again, this time declared incurable; he died in 1814, having spent twenty-four years in jail.

It should be observed that most of De Sade's sadism was wishful thinking. As far as is known, he never killed anybody,[4] or even inflicted any particular harm on anyone (if superficial cuts and bruises are discounted). Compared with Peter Kürten or Albert Fish, he was merely an unskilled amateur. He was too much the philosopher and the intellectual to give himself undividedly to the violence he preached. And a great deal of the nastiness of his writings was an attempt to get his own back on 'society'. Today he would be placed on probation and treated by a psychiatrist, and would probably be welcomed by all the editors; in another fifty years his name would be as completely forgotten as that of Aleister Crowley, instead of being a synonym for torture.

The 120 Days is largely a work of reaction against morality. He intensifies his pleasure in the acts he describes by speaking of them as 'abominable', 'vicious', 'loathsome'. The standards he is offending are always present to his mind; he never develops a positive philosophy of sexual freedom (as Blake does, for example) because he never ceases to blaze with resentment against Mrs Grundy, and can express this resentment only by conjuring up scenes of pointless destruction. He is always on the defensive.

The 120 Days begins fairly quietly, with the brothel madams describing scenes that, except for their overabundance of detail, would not be out of place in Zola or in Kuprin's *The Pit*. The perversions become more and more startling – mainly because they soon lose all contact with sex. It would be easy to parody *The 120 Days*, beginning: 'Take two sheets of brown paper and the white of an egg . . .' De Sade completed thirty of his hundred and twenty days, and left a sketch summary of the rest. The unwritten part was to deal with the criminal passions, and included many recipes for murder. Some of them border on the comic – shooting people out of cannons, etc. – and much more is sheer nastiness, such as chaining a starving girl to a wall, placing a meal slightly out of her reach, giving her a large knife, and telling her that she must cut off her arm if she is to reach the meal. (De Sade overlooked the possibility that she might use the knife to reach the plate.)

It has been argued that most of De Sade is not pornography; it aims at disgusting and horrifying rather than at titillating. His defenders claim that this entitles his work to be considered as serious literature. But although *The 120 Days* may be anything but sexually stimulating, it is a pathological document that never rises to the status

140

of literature, even accidentally. Geoffrey Gorer's claim that the four libertines rank with the greatest characters in fiction cannot be taken seriously.

De Sade is the final argument against the 'power of darkness' school of fantasy. He exaggerates its tendencies until they can all be recognised. His sexual fantasy aims at creating 'evil'. He was too much of a rationalist to believe in black magic, or no doubt he would also have invoked the devil. He is a Gilles de Rais without religious faith, and therefore handicapped in feeling himself a sinner. He was intelligent, but his intelligence was crippled by his resentment, his feeling that he had been treated badly. But he often reasons acutely about sin and virtue; given enough time, or different circumstances, he might have ended by reasoning himself into genuine moral perception, of the sort possessed by Dostoevsky. But for the resentment that stunted his moral growth he might have developed like Stavrogin in *The Devils*. In 'Night Town', James Joyce caught all the essential qualities of De Sade – blasphemy, indecency and violence – and turned them into catharsis; they achieve an intensity that fuses them into literature. This intensity De Sade never achieved. Yet because he failed, he exposes the bankruptcy of the simple 'good-and-evil' morality. He wanted to 'do evil'; like Stavrogin, he only succeeded in making himself sick. With the exception of Lovecraft, no writer ever tried harder than De Sade to conjure up the powers of darkness; with the exception of Lovecraft, no writer made himself more absurd.

It can be seen that most of the writers I have dealt with in this volume suffer from a milder form of De Sade's naïve good-and-evil dualism. The sexual orgies of the puritanical spinster in Faulkner's *Light in August* follow the De Sade formula; so does the corncob perversion of *Sanctuary* and its rape fantasy. Joyce tries to settle his quarrel with Catholicism with an ecstasy of blasphemy and indecency in 'Night Town', and Beckett follows suit by making his characters in *Endgame* curse God. Greene also likes to associate sex with sin, and tries hard to convince the reader that the Devil exists because the world is sordid. The writers of supernatural fantasy declare that the Devil exists because the world is a haunted and cruel place. All are trying to deny the pragmatic position reached by

141

Tolstoy and Dostoevsky: that evil is only the absence of good, absence of love. Leonardo expressed the pragmatic position in his notebook: 'Evil is physical pain.' When examined closely, this is seen to contain a complete philosophical position. Leonardo is not *defining* evil as physical pain. The meaning of the statement would be clearer if it were expressed in the form 'Physical pain is evil', i.e., physical pain is the only evil that human beings can know. With its implications made explicit: that the value of life is such that nothing but physical pain can negate it. Everything is good except physical pain. This is the position of *The Brothers Karamazov*. (Ivan goes even further at one point and declares that everything is good, including pain, but his general concern with cruelty hardly bears this out.) It is also the general existentialist position, from Nietzsche to Sartre and Dürrenmatt.

CONCLUSION

This connection of the concept of evil with the imagination throws some light on the nature of imagination. De Sade wanted to create evil in reaction against his loss of freedom. Lovecraft achieved a catharsis from the oppressions of a mechanised civilisation through 'evil'. A man who is oppressed – psychologically or physically – has no freedom; freedom can be gained only be *objectifying* the oppression as evil. The moment the 'evil' has been objectified (expressed), a degree of freedom has been obtained.

Imagination is man's act of increasing his freedom. Its only enemy is the notion that man has no will. Its only limit is the conception of absolute freedom.

NOTES

1. Mr Patric Dickinson has pointed out to me the following quotation from Baudelaire: 'As for the ardour with which Poe often treats horrifying material, I have observed in a number of men that this was often the result of a very large fund of unused and vital energy, sometimes the result of an unyielding chastity and of deep feelings kept repressed.'

2. I am ignoring the possibility that the fear may have been a

fear of wild beasts or snakes, not of ghosts. Elsewhere in the *Nikaya*, Gautama describes plunging into a forest thicket that made his hair stand on end, and how he subdued the fear; in this place he is probably referring to the fear of wild beasts. I have used the account given in F. L. Woodward's *Some Sayings of the Buddha*.

3. It would seem at times that Tolkien has Hitler in mind. Sauron's chief agents are the 'black riders', called the Nazguls, which seems too close to Nazis to be coincidence.

4. Although he was the direct cause of the accidental death of two prostitutes, who took an overdose of Spanish fly; for this, he was sentenced to death, but reprieved.

Six

Sex and the Imagination

The most perfunctory study of *The 120 Days of Sodom* reveals that imagination is the source of all sexual perversion. Durcet even says as much at one point: 'One grows tired of the commonplace, the imagination becomes vexed, and the slenderness of our means, the weakness of our faculties, the corruption of our souls, leads us to these abominations.' De Sade has many other penetrating observations to make on the subject; for example, 'the idea of crime is able always to ignite the senses and lead us to lubricity'. This is not far from Zamiatin's observation that crime and freedom are always connected.

These ideas require some analysis: expressed in this way, they are too vague to be meaningful. After all, very few people feel led to lubricity by the crime reports in their morning paper, and any habitual criminal might feel that crime and the idea of losing his freedom are always connected.

To clarify this, it is necessary to refer to two episodes in Nietzsche's life. In a letter to Von Gersdorff, written when he was a student, Nietzsche tells how he climbed a hill and took shelter from a storm in a hut in which a man was killing two kids. 'The storm broke with a tremendous crash . . . and I had an indescribable sense of well-being and zest. . . . Lightning and tempest are different worlds, without morality. Pure will, without the confusion of intellect – how happy, how free.' The second occasion occurred when Nietzsche was a nursing orderly in the Franco-Prussian war. One evening, in a state of fatigue, he walked towards a small town near Strasbourg. He heard the sound of approaching hoofbeats, and watched his old regiment riding past. Again he felt the same exhilaration, at the thought that these men were riding towards the battle, and wrote to his sister: '. . . the strongest and highest will to life does not lie in the petty struggle to exist, but in the Will to war, the Will to Power'.

Although these two passages express only an aspect of

Nietzsche's philosophy, it is an aspect without which he cannot be understood. And De Sade's violent and blasphemous creation, the Duc de Blangis, was conceived in this Nietzschean spirit. (Blake also expressed it in the statement: 'Energy is eternal delight'.) Nietzsche's ecstasy of the tempest, 'pure will, without the confusions of intellect', becomes the Duke's sexual ecstasy.[1] It is no doubt true that there is an element of nonsense in Nietzsche's talk about immorality. It should not be forgotten, though, that the romantic temperament flinches from life and rejects it, that it tries to substitute for living experience a world of abstractions and imaginings. Nietzsche has overcome this extreme romanticism – still characteristic of German thought – and stands on the threshold of affirmation, a point at which distinctions are apt to be a little blurred. And De Sade, for all his silliness, is basically obsessed by the idea of 'men like gods'. He was a sensualist and a weakling, and his contemporaries were right to put him in jail. But he also had the makings of a poet's vision, and his position outside society produced an unusual depth of perception of the shortcomings of his contemporaries. His sufferings may have been deserved; but they sharpened his criticism of hypocrisy, pettiness and sheer feeble-mindedness. He wanted to create a figure like Milton's Devil (it is no accident that the tumescent duke is described as 'heaven-threatening'); but Milton's Satan is a puritan, who never does anything that would have struck his creator as disgusting or nasty. De Sade *wants* to horrify, to convince the world that he possesses a courage beyond its understanding. The jailers of his later years described him as a well-behaved and gentlemanly figure whose only shortcoming was 'a persistent desire for lewd conversation'. We can imagine him trying to shock his jailer: 'Now come, admit it – wouldn't you enjoy slicing a virgin into four pieces?' and then chuckling over his dinner as the horrified man rushed off to report it to his superiors.

De Sade, in short, was what Blake might have been if a persecution mania had arrested his development at the time of *The Marriage of Heaven and Hell*. He belongs to Sir Isaiah Berlin's 'hedgehog' category ('the hedgehog knows one thing, the fox knows many'); and the one thing he knew was that sex is obscurely connected with the 'god-

'like' in man. Everything else he knew was wrong – for example, that society and pettiness are identical, and that therefore crime, the revolt against society, is identical with the 'god-like'.

But the relation between sex and the imagination is not restricted to questions of sexual perversion. The two are so closely interwoven that it would almost be true to say that the sex life of human beings depends entirely on the imagination. In *Corydon* André Gide argues that it is only in the lower animals that sex is a physical matter, depending on the peculiar smell of the female in heat; therefore, it is only among animals that 'normal' sexuality can be regarded as part of the 'order of nature'. The imagination of most human beings may be conditioned to regard the male–female relationship as 'normal', but since the imagination is essentially free, this is no law of nature. Gide uses this argument to justify his own homosexuality. He regarded *Corydon* as one of his most important books; so far no critic has ever agreed with him. And yet Gide was right in his high estimate of the work, for he has stumbled on an idea whose implications for the psychology of imagination are immense. Human sexuality is full of paradoxes that can only be explained in terms of imagination. In *Doctor Faustus*, Mann pointed out that the words of the marriage ceremony, 'These two shall be one flesh', are nonsense. Sex depends on the strangeness, the separateness, of the other 'flesh'. 'Oneness' would be the destruction of the sexual impulse.

But what is the human faculty for perceiving 'strangeness'? Why does a certain picture arrest the attention when seen for the first time, and yet make no impact when it has hung on your wall for six months? What happens when you read a whole page of a book without 'taking it in'? The faculty for 'grasping' a picture or a page of prose might be called the attention. But attention is a simple matter, depending on an act of will (as when a schoolteacher calls 'Pay attention, please'). This ordinary attention is often inadequate to grasp the meaning of a picture or a piece of music; it is not 'open' enough to allow a full and wide impact of strangeness. The instantaneous act of grasping, that transcends the pedestrian 'attention', is the imagination. It is more active than attention; it is a kind of exploring of the object, as well as a withdrawal from it to see it better. And this same act of exploration and withdrawal is the basis of the strangeness of sex.

Yet although we might say that sex depends partly on the imagination, it would be equally true to say that the imagination, in sexual matters, is 'subsidised' by the sexual instinct. An irrational flow of vital energy stimulates the imagination; this flow might be described as the 'sexual shock', and it has much in common with the 'shock of recognition' that Edmund Wilson has described as being the response to authentic artistic power. The strength of the imagination is automatically magnified by the sexual impulse. This is the reason that so many works of literature depend upon a sexual development to hold the reader's attention; the imagination is 'subsidised'.

Like Gide, Tolstoy recognised this relationship of sex to imagination; unlike Gide, he was unwilling to acknowledge that, where sex is concerned, 'all things are lawful'. In *The Kreutzer Sonata* he attempts a compromise. The work is Tolstoy's sexual gospel – a curiously puritanical gospel. (It is difficult to understand why it was banned in Tsarist Russia.) Pozdnishev, a Russian gentleman, describes to a travelling companion how he came to murder his wife through jealousy, and declares that sex has become an indecent game played by moral imbeciles. The peasantry are saved from immortality by the hardness of their lives; for them, sex is closely connected with child-bearing. The aristocracy have nothing to do but cultivate their emotions and sensibilities, and this normally leads to sex. (His wife began a love affair with a young violinist, with whom she played Beethoven's Ninth Sonata.) Sex, Tolstoy thought, is not for pleasure, but for childbearing. In later life, he fought with his impulse to make love to his wife, and wrote stories in which sex is the source of all evil. Sex for pleasure is perversion, according to Tolstoy.

It is true, of course, that the imagination plays its part in all the basic human activities. Boswell records that Johnson ate like a pig, and preferred his meat strong and pungent, because he had starved so much as a young man. Here Johnson's privation (if Boswell is to be believed) led the imagination to connect itself with the idea of food. Then, as with De Sade, ordinary food was inadequate to satisfy the overstimulated imagination; Johnson had to wallow in food as De Sade wallowed in sex. (Lord

Chesterfield said that Johnson 'throws his meat anywhere but down his throat'.) In the same way, a sense of social underprivilege can produce an exaggerated preoccupation with social position(i.e., snobbery) as in the case of D. H. Lawrence. But a man starves without food, as he starves without money (the basis of social position). No man ever died from sexual starvation. Sex may mean the survival of the race, but it makes no difference to the survival of the individual. No doubt this is the reason that some instinct of survival has intensified the sexual impulse in men through the imagination, so that the sexual appetite is as strong as the need for food.

The power of the sexual impulse can be utilised like the cordite in a bullet, to drive the projectile of the imagination towards new insights. It provides no insight in itself – only the power. This distinction should be clearly understood. The power to project the imagination can come from many different sources. It may be connected with ill-health, and the sudden contrast of convalescence, as with Nietzsche and Pascal. Nietzsche conceived the idea of eternal recurrence in the exhilaration of convalescence, and wrote on a piece of paper 'Six thousand feet above men and time'. Dostoevsky had his sudden visions of the value of life in epileptic fits; and again, when he thought he was about to be executed. Lovecraft and the 'horror writers' use the emotion of fear as the 'cordite'. For the writers of fantasy, the driving force is wonder. Blake was right in emphasising the role of energy. The imagination is like an engine that can work on many different fuels; but it must be powered. And sex, properly used, is a fuel of high potency.

The Cloud of Unknowing uses the image of a spark flying upward to describe visionary insight. Some early religions used sex as the power to drive the 'spark'. Even in twentieth-century Russia, Rasputin was a member of a sect called the Khlysty, whose rites involved a dionysiac dance that ended in promiscuous sex. It seems that primitive people feel no conscience about associating religion and sex. It is only when notions of social morality begin to enter that sex is regarded as an ally of the Devil. Hence the dionysiac orgies of witches were associated with the Devil instead of God.

William Blake was one of the first writers of modern

Europe to revolt against the idea of sex as the Devil's province, and to attempt to restore it to its place as a fuel for visionary experience. There have since been four other European writers whose attitudes resemble Blake's; these are Maupassant, Wedekind, Artzybasheff and Lawrence. I propose to deal briefly with these in the remainder of this chapter.

MAUPASSANT

The name of Maupassant is associated with 'realism' and 'irony' rather than with sex. Yet every one of his important works, from the beginning to the end of his career, is dominated by sex. An enormous number of his two hundred and seventy short stories, as well as his six novels, are pivoted on sex. It would not be accurate to call Maupassant a sexual mystic. And yet the intensity of his love of life entitles him to be called a poet, if not a mystic, and sex plays a large part in his vision of 'life'.

This love of life is the source of Maupassant's greatness, and the source of his ultimate failure as an artist is his lack of intellect, of self-analysis. He is the most completely brainless of all the great authors. He accepted all experience without analysis, and his final judgments on life were shallow and pessimistic. But his immediate perceptions were of a very high quality indeed.

In his earliest work, Maupassant seems ashamed to reveal the importance he attaches to the sexual impulse; his long story, 'Boule de Suif', and his first novel, *Une Vie*, lean heavily on the realist tradition of Flaubert and Zola, and are full of 'irony and pity'. *A Woman's Life* (the usual English translation for *Une Vie*) is about an innocent and idealistic young girl who marries a man whom she takes for a Prince Charming. On the honeymoon, he reveals a pathological meanness, and soon after that she discovers that he is unfaithful. He is finally killed in the act of adultery by an outraged husband (who pushes the hut that conceals the lovers over a ravine). Jeanne now devotes her life to her son. He causes her as much pain as had his father, proving to be a profligate and a spendthrift. But when, at the end of the book, her son's child is brought home, Jeanne's servant makes the observation; 'Life is never so good or so bad as people think.'

Maupassant seems to take pleasure in emphasising that immorality is widespread. Even Jeanne's mother has had a love affair, which comes to light after her death. Maupassant himself was obsessed by sex. He lived for a time in a brothel, and contracted syphilis from one of his many casual pickups. But he was the son of a respectable family, and never ceased to be aware of 'moralist' opposition. (This is no doubt the reason that his early works play down sex and emphasise pity.) He is never a pagan immoralist, like Whitman. But as soon as he found his feet as a writer, he began to express his own peculiar amoral vision of the world. The vision has something in common with Hemingway's. Maupassant loves physical reality (he was an athlete, a fine swimmer, and a lover of boats). His world has much in common with the world of the Impressionists and Van Gogh. It is all light and colour and sheer joy in being alive. Sexual conquest is another of his chief sources of pleasure. He is keenly aware of violence and death, and knows that most human beings take little pleasure in being alive. His stories are full of portraits of meanness and pettiness. An early story, 'The Shepherd's Leap', contains all his characteristics in embryo. Its narrator, who is spending the summer in Normandy, tells the story of how the 'Shepherd's Leap' came by its name. The village had once been governed by a fanatical and puritanical young priest; on one occasion, he was so disgusted to discover a crowd of children watching a bitch in labour that he kicked the animal to death and killed all the puppies. One day in a storm, when about to take shelter in a shepherd's wheeled hut, he realised that a young couple were making love in the straw. He slammed the door, and pushed the hut downhill, to be smashed in the ravine. (This was, of course, the episode that Maupassant used again in *Une Vie*.)

Maupassant tells the story with typical 'detachment'; even in the horrible scene in which the dog is killed, there is no hint of disgust. He mentions that the young couple are still clasped together when their bodies are taken out of the wreck, 'in terror as in pleasure', hinting his delight in the act of physical love. And the description of the scenery leaves no doubt of his love of the countryside. So the only emotion that emerges from the story is pleasure. This combination of violence and delight gives many of his stories their curious effect of brutal loveliness, ruth-lessness and beauty.

And yet one feels that this detachment is not healthy. When Maupassant describes how an old Corsican woman trained her dog to rip out the throat of her son's murderer, or how an avaricious Norman peasant woman frightened a sick woman to death by pretending to be the Devil, or how a Normandy fisherman was so mean that he allowed a taut rope to sever his brother's arm rather than cut it and lose a net, the reader feels that Maupassant *ought* to feel horror and express it. Only a moral imbecile could refrain from feeling indignation when describing such episodes. Yet at other times, especially when writing of sex, Maupassant's 'detachment' obviously hides an attitude of approval. There sometimes seems to be more than a touch of De Sade about Maupassant. One suspects that his master was not Flaubert, but Laclos, the author of *Les Liaisons Dangereuses*, who described libertinage and moral dishonesty with ill-concealed delight. In one story, for example, Maupassant describes how a rake marries a beautiful imbecile girl for the sake of money; the girl's parents hope that marriage – and perhaps babies – will cure her. For the first few days after the marriage, she seems completely indifferent and unchanged. Then gradu-ally she develops an attitude of dog-like devotion to her husband, and it is obvious that she associates him with intense pleasure. Finally he gets bored and leaves her, and she sits at the window for years afterwards, waiting for him to reappear – still like a dog. One needs to know very little about Maupassant to recognise a wish-fulfilment fantasy in this story (he takes care to state that the girl is very beautiful although it seems more likely that, if she was a congenital imbecile, her lips would be loose and flabby, and she would probably dribble). It may be unjust to Maupassant to suppose that he took sadistic pleasure in the girl's betrayal, but it is at least certain that he was indifferent to it. (This was the period when George Moore could comment about one of Goya's nudes; 'What does it matter if a sixteen-year-old girl had to be debauched if the result is a masterpiece?')

The type of story that shocked Tolstoy – who did an excellent essay on Maupassant – is less harmful. Maupas-sant enjoyed writing about seduction. One of his most delightful stories 'That Pig Morin' tells how a linen draper named Morin was tempted to kiss a pretty girl on a train, and how she screamed, and he was arrested for assault. The editor of a local newspaper went to call on the girl to persuade her to drop the case, was charmed by her, and ended by sleeping with her. Maupassant's point is well made, that there are different ways of going about love-making, some of which lead to success, and others to disaster. Maupassant has many stories that end in seduction with no harm done. They are what used to be called 'typically French', although their attitude to sex is no more French than it is German or English; pleasure in seduction is not a national characteristic. (Musil in his *Man Without Qualities* has exactly the same attitude to seduction as Maupassant, and goes even further than Maupassant in including incest.) A mildly sadistic element enters into the pleasure Maupassant takes in cuckolded husbands.

In the novels, Maupassant's obsession with sex is unmistakable. *A Woman's Life* might be regarded as an indictment of the cruelty and immorality of men. But his next novel, *Bel-Ami*, describes how an amiable scoundrel rises to prosperity through sheer luck and his love of women, and it would be blindness to regard it as a disapproving portrait. 'Our handsome friend' is a scoundrel in a purely Shavian sense.

Mont-Oriol is the last of Maupassant's major novels; the remaining three betray his breakdown. It centres around the seduction of a young married woman at a French watering place. The subplot of the novel deals with the intrigues that centre around the new bath that is established at Enval; this reveals Maupassant in an unfamiliar light, as a writer of high comedy. But the main plot of the novel can be simply summarised: Christiane, the young married woman, is pursued by Paul, a friend of her brother, and finally submits to him. This happens halfway through the book. Then Paul slowly loses interest in her, although she is carrying his child; after the birth of the child, Christiane also loses interest in Paul, having learned the Byronic lesson that 'Love is of man's life a thing apart; 'Tis woman's whole existence'. The basic feeling of the book is Maupassant's healthy male conceit; he enjoys describing the seduction.

Maupassant's last three novels are uneven in quality.

Pierre and Jean is the first that is simply a long-winded bore. Again, it deals with one of Maupassant's favourite themes: the lucky and the unlucky. Pierre and Jean are two brothers. Jean is lighthearted, happy-go-lucky, and his mother's favourite; Pierre, the elder, is brooding and serious-minded. Then an old friend of the family dies and leaves Jean a large legacy. Pierre suspects that the man was his mother's lover and Jean's real father. Finally, he discovers this to be true, and violently accuses his mother, trying, like Hamlet, to make her feel her guilt. But nothing much happens; Jean gets engaged to the pretty widow with whom they are both in love, and Pierre goes to sea. Jean and his mother are relieved to see him go. The book has no real point. Maupassant had already used its theme in a short story (where it is more successful). He dwells at preposterous length on the mother's guilt; it seems curious that Maupassant should make such a mountain out of a molehill of immorality when so many of his other stories have made molehills out of mountains. Pierre's jealousy and his mental torments are too protracted to hold the reader's attention. Having written about Pierre's discovery of his mother's guilt, it is obvious that Maupassant has no idea of how to finish his story; moreover, he has no idea of his attitude to his material. This is the dullest of all Maupassant's works.

Notre Coeur shows a momentary return of the author's powers. It is told with his usual economy and vividness of style, and engages the reader's attention from the beginning. But it is a decadent world Maupassant describes with open approval. André Mariolle is a rich bachelor, who allows himself to be taken to the salon of the beautiful Michele de Burne. He is determined not to be captivated by her, but is soon in love. Maupassant exercises all his usual ingenuity in keeping the reader waiting for the seduction scene which, of course, happens ultimately. Mariolle now becomes the woman's slave and lapdog; the situation of *Mont-Oriol* is reversed; it is the woman who has the whip hand. Mariolle consoles himself somewhat by seducing a pretty servant girl, and tries hard to become master of himself again. But at a signal from Michele, he rushes back to her feet. So the book ends. It seems to be the beginning of a defeat complex in Maupassant, completely unlike the attitude of *Bel-Ami*. The difference is

153

as striking as that between Scott Fitzgerald's *This Side of Paradise* and *Tender Is the Night*. All the optimism has evaporated, and Maupassant tries to make a virtue of despair.

After *Pierre et Jean*, Maupassant's last novel, *As Strong as Death*, is the weakest of the series. Oliver Bertin is a rich and successful painter, who has had for many years a love affair with Anne, Countess de Guilleroy. In a flashback revealing all his old power, Maupassant tells how the liaison began, how they became lovers, although the Countess was a virtuous wife, and Bertin was no seducer. The remainder of the book tells how Bertin comes to realise that he has fallen in love with his mistress's daughter, Annette. But Maupassant has none of the delicacy that makes Thackeray's treatment of a similar theme in *Henry Esmond* so successful. Bertin's sleepless nights and orgies of self-pity are as boring as Pierre's in the earlier novel. The book might have been turned into a success if Maupassant had attempted to show the complexities involved in winning Annette's affections; but he does nothing of the sort; Bertin loves gloomily and despairingly, and no one is sorry when he gets himself killed in a street accident at the end. The book reveals the utter bankruptcy of Maupassant's seduction complex. And it does it badly.[2]

The reason for Maupassant's breakdown was approaching insanity due to syphilis, and probably complicated by alcoholic poisoning. This can be seen clearly in the horror story 'The Horla', in which a man is haunted by some kind of invisible monster. But even without syphilis, the seeds of madness were already present in Maupassant's mental make-up, in the Weltanschauung of a man who could declare that cruelty and violent death are as much the order of nature as love and beauty. Morality, after all, is a direction that we give to the world, a kind of grain that we profess to see in the wood of experience. Without some such conviction, there can be no evolution of the personality, for there is no sense of purpose on which the will can take its stand. Maupassant's early works are full of a sense of meaning, but it has not been put there by Maupassant; it is simply a reflection of a supremely healthy living organism. Like Van Gogh, he is affirming without knowing why, affirming in spite of misery and death. But Maupassant never used his brain, he never tried to gain permanent possession of this knowledge by turning it into ideas and convictions. So when his sickness robbed him of it, he had nothing; there was nothing he could do in his work but imitate the old gestures. Again one is reminded of Hemingway.

Maupassant ended by becoming completely insane, and committing suicide. In the ten years of his creative life, he had written more than most writers achieve in a long life. He wrote very quickly, and this is the right way to read him. Critics who carefully analyse one of his short stories – say *The Necklace* – and then solemnly declare it as a masterpiece are doing him an injustice. Taken on their own, none of his short stories are great. They should be swallowed in dozens, like oysters; this is the only way to get the true Maupassant flavour. The impression that emerges then is of incredible vitality, the 'great health' that Nietzsche spoke about when creating *Zarathustra*. And an important part of this health is Maupassant's immense delight in sex: Maupassant treated sexual experiences like oysters.

WEDEKIND

Wedekind's Christian names, ironically enough, were Benjamin Franklin, but he preferred to shorten this to Frank. He was born in 1864 in Hanover, and died in 1918, so that his literary career is roughly contemporaneous with Ibsen, Björnson, Brieux and Strindberg. Consequently, his name is seldom mentioned in England or America, except as an afterthought to Ibsen and Strindberg.[3] This is unfair; Wedekind is also a 'sexual philosopher', and his nearest literary relative is Nietzsche.

Wedekind was born of a theatrical family – his mother was an actress and his father a doctor, a domineering, violent man. He grew up in Switzerland, preferred a wandering life, was fascinated by circuses (one of his mistresses was an acrobat) and criminals, and worked as a journalist and an advertising manager before he became an actor and producer of his own drama. At the age of thirty-five he spent some time in prison, having been charged with insulting royalty in some political poems published in a satirical magazine. The remainder of his life was not particularly happy. Some of his plays were a success, but he was constantly being charged with indecency. A sketch of his life story gives the impression that, like Poe, he was born unlucky. His family was noted for eccentricity and internal feuds (Gerhart Hauptmann is said to have portrayed their quarrels in his early play *The Peace Festival*). One of his brothers committed suicide. Wedekind himself was lame from birth. In his work as a cabaret artist, singing his own cynical political ballads to tunes of his own, he anticipated the Weill-Brecht collaboration of twenty-five years later. His fame was brief; when he died in 1918, he was prematurely old, and considered out of date by the new German Expressionists. (Wedekind is usually regarded as a Symbolist, like the later Strindberg.)

The earliest scandal associated with Wedekind's name followed the first performance of his drama *The Awakening of Spring*, when he was only twenty-seven. This play deals with the sex lives of adolescents, and already states Wedekind's main contention – that the most important impulse in human life is the erotic impulse, and that our society is based on the suppression of this fact. If Wedekind had known Barbusse's *L'Enfer*, he would have approved of the scene in which someone tells about the rape and murder of a little girl, and the respectable bourgeois listeners lick their lips and try to conceal their excitement. *The Awakening of Spring* owes its technique of short scenes to Büchner's *Wozzeck*. Wedekind is concerned to try to present the sexual torments of adolescence with complete honesty. His hero, Melchior, is a brilliant schoolboy, who is conversant with 'the facts of life'. His friend Moritz and the schoolgirl Wendla are less well-informed. Melchior writes an account of human sexuality and gives it to his friend, who conceals it in some schoolbooks. Moritz commits suicide because he is about to fail his exams, and Melchior's sex notes are found in his books. It is also discovered that the fourteen-year-old Wendla is pregnant, and that Melchior is responsible. Wendla dies, from an abortion. The last scene of the play is wholly symbolistic. Melchior meets his friend Moritz in a graveyard, but Moritz is carrying his head under his arm. A muffled stranger appears, who tries to dissuade Melchior from joining Moritz among the dead. (Moritz insists that death is one long holiday.) Finally, Melchior and the stranger go off together, leaving Moritz to return to the grave. The stranger was probably supposed to symbolise life, or experience.

The play is not Wedekind's best, but it succeeds in being honest about adolescent sexuality. There is, for example, a remarkable scene where Melchior and Wendla meet in the woods. (This is before she becomes Melchior's mistress.) They talk about virtue and morality, and Wendla says that she often daydreams that she is a poor beggar child who is beaten by her cruel father. (She admits that she has never been beaten in her life.) She gives Moritz a switch and begs him to beat her. He refuses, then throws away the switch and beats her with his fists; she runs away, crying. It required a great deal of courage, in 1891, to evoke sado-masochism with such intensity. The result was that the play was banned for fourteen years.

Wedekind's most popular work, the one-act play *The Chamber Singer* (which Hugo Weisgall used for his opera *The Tenor*), is not one of his important works. It is about an interior decorator who becomes a huge success as a tenor, and is swamped by success – particularly by the women who fling themselves at him, dazzled by the vision of his Tristan and other operatic heroes. A great composer, old and neglected, tries to get an interview with Gerardo, and before the end of the play, he manages to tell the singer that the tragedy of the artist is that he has no private life; he is a slave to art and the public. The two men are incarnations of different aspects of Wedekind, and express his favourite theme: the inescapable failure of communication between an artist and the public. The old composer is unsuccessful, the tenor successful for the wrong reasons.[4]

A short story called 'The Burning of Egliswyl' contains the essence of Wedekind.[5] It is told by a young peasant who is serving a jail sentence for arson. At the age of nineteen, an attractive young girl named Susan seduced him – or persuaded him to seduce her. The discovery of his sexuality was followed by a series of affairs. Other girls are jealous of Susan, and try to steal her lover; he is happy enough to offer his services to all who require them. He relates his 'conquests' with detachment: 'I felt how warm she was. She was as solid as if she had been fed for the butcher. If she had been a three-year-old heifer I'd have given twenty napoleons for her. We went home arm in arm. When the clock struck one, there was a knock outside her window . . .' When the farmer's fifty-three-year-old wife discovers that he goes out at night, she threatens to tell her husband. He pushes her back into the stable, makes love to her, and then blackmails her into keeping quiet about his nightly escapades with other women. Then he falls in love with a chambermaid named Marie, and spends a great deal of time courting her. Finally, she becomes his mistress. One day she tells him how he can get up to her room after dark. He goes to her at midnight, but finds that, for some reason, he is impotent. This drives him half insane, and he sets fire to the village. 'I howled and shrieked like an animal in a slaughterhouse. And all I could see was flames.' He is arrested, and has periods of insanity, during which he has to be kept in a straitjacket.

The story is so elliptical in parts as to admit of several interpretations. Why did the peasant become impotent; why did he go mad? Possibly Wedekind was intentionally obscure. He aimed at conveying the feeling that sex is a dangerous vortex, a power behind the comprehension of most human beings. Too much explanation might have ruined this effect. In the image of the burning village and the madman 'shrieking like an animal in a slaughterhouse', Wedekind has achieved an unforgettable symbol of the power of sex. It is like Ramakrishna's vision of the Divine Mother who contains in herself all creation and all destruction. Wedekind implies that sex is a destructive force only because men are too small to understand its power; he seems to be driven by a compulsion to reveal to men that we are all enslaved by this elemental force, no matter how much we try to hide it with hypocrisy or talk about 'the tender passion'. For Wedekind, it is the biggest joke of all to talk about 'the tender passion'; he sees sex as something more like the hydrogen bomb.

This becomes unmistakably apparent in his most interesting work, the two plays about 'Lulu', *Earth Spirit* and *Pandora's Box*. On these, Alban Berg based his greatest work, the opera *Lulu*. The plot of the Lulu plays (which, for convenience, I will here treat as one play) is so complicated that only the briefest summary can be offered. Lulu is Wedekind's incarnation of the sex urge, the eternal feminine; she answers to many different names, including Eve. Although she leaves behind her a trail of total destruction, she is no *femme fatale*; on the contrary, she is completely innocent, and is herself finally a victim. (She has many of the characteristics of Shaw's Ann Whitfield in *Man and Superman*.) Like *The Awakening of Spring*, the Lulu plays were promptly banned.

Lulu is a foundling who is trained to steal by an old beggar. The beggar, who poses as her father, makes her his mistress when she is only a child. One day, Lulu is about to steal the watch of a newspaper editor, Dr Schön, who catches her in the act. Instead of calling the police, he takes her home, befriends her, and of course sleeps with her. She is his mistress for some years, until he finds her an old husband named Goll. Goll is jealous, and when one day he finds his wife in a compromising position with a painter, he collapses in rage, and dies of heart failure. Lulu then marries the painter, who sees in her an incarnation of the eternal woman. Lulu continues to see as much as she can of her original benefactor, Dr Schön, who finds her presence embarrassing: he has got himself engaged to a young girl and is afraid that someone will discover his intrigue with Lulu and ruin his engagement. He decides to talk to the painter, tell him a few home truths about his wife, and advise him to keep Lulu at home. The painter is shattered by the revelations about his wife. He believed she was an orphan. Now he learns that the disgusting old beggar who calls is actually her father (even Schön does not know that the beggar was Lulu's lover), that Lulu is not an angel of purity; he shoots himself.

Lulu now goes on the stage, and plots how to make Dr Schön marry her. She is acting in a play for which Schön's son Alva composed the music. Alva is also in love with her. One night, Schön is foolish enough to come to the theatre with his fiancée. Lulu has a fainting fit on stage and has to be carried off to her dressing room. Schön follows her there in a rage, certain that she is shamming because she refuses to dance in front of his fiancée. Now Lulu uses all her charm and vitality; Schön finds it impossible to resist. At her dictation, he writes a letter to his fiancée, breaking with her, and marries Lulu.

Schön is the only man Lulu has ever loved. And yet Lulu is easily bored, and she still has crowds of admirers, including a lovesick schoolboy, a lesbian countess, and Schön's son. Alva continues to be fascinated by her even

159

when Lulu admits to him that she poisoned his mother. Schön is frantically jealous of her. There is a comedy episode, in which Lulu makes various lovers hide behind curtains as more lovers arrive. Schön sees his own son making love to her, and threatens her with a revolver. Lulu replies coolly: 'If men have killed themselves for my sake, that does not lower my value . . . You betrayed your best friends with me . . . I have never pretended to be other than I was taken for. And no one ever took me for anything but what I am.' (This is an interesting admission, for everyone takes her for something quite different.) As Schön is about to shoot her, she manages to get the revolver and shoot him. Schön, as he dies, tells his son: 'Don't let her escape. You will be the next.'

Lulu's arrest for murder ends *Earth Spirit*. Between this, and the beginning of *Pandora's Box*, Lulu spends ten years in prison. She is finally rescued through a plot. The lesbian countess, who is devoted to her, has deliberately contracted cholera, given it to Lulu in prison, and then helped Lulu to escape from the prison hospital. An athlete who wants to marry her is driven away when Lulu pretends to be a ravaged cholera victim. As soon as Lulu is left alone with Alva, she radiates beauty and health again. They sing a love duet and she becomes Alva's mistress on the same settee on which Alva's father had died.

The remainder of the play shows Lulu's downfall; instead of being the seductress, she is now the victim. She escapes to Paris with Alva, and a white slave trafficker tries to force her to enter a brothel.[6] She flies to London, and moves to Whitechapel, where she becomes a prostitute to support Alva and the old beggar. The lesbian countess turns up too. Her last customer is Jack the Ripper, who murders her and the countess, who tries to protect her.

The above description may make the plot appear complicated; the two plays are in fact more complicated. Yet the figure of Lulu dominates and unifies them. The prologue declares that Lulu was created to 'bring evil, to attract, to seduce, to poison, to murder so that it cannot be felt'. In spite of this, Lulu's most striking quality is her innocence and good faith. She personifies the fire in 'The Burning of Egliswyl'; it is not her fault if moths find her irresistible. Alva tells her: 'With your divine gifts, you turn

160

all those around you into criminals without being aware of it.' Again there is the same connection between crime, sex and freedom. But only Alva, the artist, is aware of her true nature. And, contrary to Schön's prediction, Alva survives her. Wedekind obviously identified himself with Alva (as did Alban Berg in his opera).

Wedekind wrote many more studies of women, as well as of the artist; none of these need be examined at length in this context. Effie, in *Castle Wetterstein*, also makes prostitution her career, and dies at the hand of a pervert. The heroine of *Franziska* is a kind of female Faust who experiments compulsively with sex; strangely enough, Wedekind permits her a happy ending in domestic love. In *King Nicolo*, Wedekind treats the artist as a fallen king whose majesty is inalienable, even though he has to become the court jester. (Here, no doubt Wedekind was hitting back at the charge of *lèse-majesté* that had landed him in jail; it was written immediately after his release.) In his best comedy, *The Marquis of Keith*, Wedekind writes with humorous approval of a confidence swindler.[7] At the end of the play, the swindler's plans having collapsed, his successful rival offers him the choice between a revolver and a small sum of money; he grins and takes the money. Here, as in *The Awakening of Spring*, Wedekind implies that life is the greatest value of all, and that only a fool would commit suicide.

Altogether, Wedekind's work is unique. As an artist, he may lack the warmth and humanity of D. H. Lawrence, but his sexual vision is in every way clearer. No other European writer has paid such homage to the sexual urge. He exalts it, not as the 'solar plexus' or 'the dark forces', but as the most naked expression of the powerhouse, the force of life. Spiritually, Wedekind is Nietzsche's twin brother; neither can be understood without the other.

ARTZYBASHEFF

Artzybasheff's *Sanine* has a unique distinction; no other famous novel has been slighted so consistently. Prince Mirsky dismisses Artzybasheff as 'a curious and on the whole regrettable episode in the history of Russian literature'. Artzybasheff came to notice for the first time at the age of twenty-six with a short story about a life of 'search for truth' followed by a meaningless death. His *Tales of the Revolution* (the unsuccessful 1905 revolution, of course) pleased the radical public. The Russia of the last Tsar was a decadent, disillusioned country, dominated by the strange figure of Rasputin. Its most popular writer was the pessimistic Andreyev (although Gorki made a close second). The symbolist Briussov was Russia's foremost poet. A new religious mysticism was rising, inspired by Dostoevsky. Rozanov, Dostoevsky's greatest disciple, wrote conservative articles over his own name, and radical articles over a *nom de plume*, declaring that politics was nonsense anyway. Merezhkovsky wrote novels about warring antitheses – Christianity and paganism, the spirit of the flesh, and so on – and was the idol of the avant-garde.

Artzybasheff specialised in descriptions of murder, rape and suicide in *Tales of the Revolution*. (Eisenstein's film caught faithfully his atmosphere in describing the Potemkin mutiny.) His novel *Sanine* had been rejected in 1903, the publishers feeling that it was too philosophical, and perhaps indecent. After the revolution, *Sanine* appealed to the mood of cynicism and disaster, and the book swept Russia. There was already a tendency to sexual promiscuity among students in the capitals; *Sanine* extended it to every corner of Russia.

The book is by no means as badly written as many of its critics make out; it is nearly as readable as Maupassant. The young student Sanine returns to his provincial town and the company of his mother and sister. He has taken part in some revolutionary activities; but unlike most of his contemporaries, he is healthy-minded and indifferent to moral taboos. His indifference often reminds the reader of Dostoevsky's Stavrogin, but Sanine loves life and takes it for granted. The plot of the book is devised to demonstrate the effectiveness of Sanine's good-natured, laissez-faire attitude to life. His beautiful sister Lida has two suitors, a shy doctor and a brutal army officer, Sarudin, who seduces her. When she discovers she is pregnant, she is about to commit suicide, but Sanine dissuades her, convinces her that things are not so bad after all, and persuades the shy doctor to marry her. Later, Sarudin calls at their house to show off his ex-mistress to a friend, and Sanine orders him to leave the house. Sarudin challenges

Sanine to a duel, but Sanine regards these military ideals of 'honour' as outdated, and refuses. Later, he meets Sarudin in a public garden, and Sarudin tries to provoke him to a duel by attacking him with a riding crop. Sanine promptly knocks him down and blacks his eye. Sarudin goes almost insane at the humiliation of being struck publicly by a man who coolly refuses to fight him, and commits suicide.

There are many other characters in the book, and several sub-plots. There is a gloomy student named Yuri, who spends a lot of time brooding on whether life is worth living. Yuri falls in love with a girl named Sina, who returns the feeling. Instead of marrying the girl, Yuri broods on the futility of human life and commits suicide. Again, it is the healthy-minded Sanine who actually seduces Sina. After Yuri's death, Sanine is asked to say a few words by his grave. He comments: 'Another fool less in the world,' and horrifies everyone.

There are two more deaths in the book; a consumptive student, Semenov, dies in hospital, and Sanine's healthy indifference to death becomes apparent. And a Jewish revolutionary, Soloveitchik, feels that life is futile and commits suicide. He is an idealist who is drawn to the Christian idea that this world is a vale of sorrow and should be renounced. Sanine tells Soloveitchik a story that perfectly illustrates his Nietzschean attitude. He had a Christian friend called Lande who showed an amazing capacity for self-sacrifice. (Lande had already turned up in Artzybasheff's Tolstoyan first story.) One day a fellow student hit Sanine when Lande was standing nearby. Sanine looked at Lande, and felt ashamed to hit back; he turned and walked away. But later he began to feel that the 'moral victory' was false; he had gratified the belligerent student. Sanine chose the next opportunity for a quarrel, and thrashed the student until he became unconscious. Lande was displeased, but Sanine felt a great deal better. Soloveitchik assures Sanine he is wrong and that Lande was right. He ends the conversation by asking Sanine whether a man who finds no joy in living should commit suicide. Sanine replies unconcernedly: 'You are already dead. The best place for you is the grave,' and leaves him to commit suicide.

At the end of the book, Sanine leaves the town –

pursued by the moral fury of his fellow townspeople – and catches the train. He tires of the foul, smoky atmosphere of the train and, as the dawn rises over the steppe, jumps off, leaving his belongings behind, and stands there enjoying the dawn on the open fields.

It will be seen that *Sanine* is a somewhat exaggerated translation of Nietzsche and Blake into terms of fiction. It is not entirely true, however, to the spirit of Nietzsche. Sanine's last thought as he jumps off the train is: What a vile thing man is. To get away . . . And the amoralism of the book may seem a little overdone. There are even traces of an incest theme between Sanine and his sister. The seduction of Sina by Sanine must be one of the most unconvincing seduction scenes in literature; it takes place in a small boat, and its purpose is obviously to prove that Sanine has no qualms about sex, while his friend Yuri is working himself into a mood of suicidal despair about whether he should take Sina's virginity.

Artzybasheff's vision of sex lacks the intensity of Wedekind's, and his novel is not quite successful in making its points. These points were: visionary affirmation of life at all costs, condemnation of suicide, rejection of social codes of morality and 'honour', and a Blakeian delight in sex as a basis for affirmation. Artzybasheff had begun as a disciple of Tolstoy; *Sanine* was his declaration of independence. But he seemed to be unsure of where his amoralism was leading him. The condemnation of suicide disappears in his later novels, and *The Breaking Point* seems to imply that suicide is the only honest reaction to life. It is about an epidemic of suicides that destroys all the élite in a small town, and its hero, Naumov, talks about 'destroying in man the superstition of life'. From Nietzsche, Artzybasheff seems to have turned to Schopenhauer – a curious evolution. He continued to treat sexual problems with the same attitude of biological eroticism (that gives him so much in common with Wedekind), in novels and plays: *The Millionaire, Jealousy* and *The Law of the Savage*. The Bolsheviks expelled him from Russia in 1923, and he died four years later an embittered man whose vogue had passed. On the whole, his finest novel is *Sanine*, which deserves a place as a minor classic; in it, he achieves a sense of the open air, of healthy optimism, that had been absent from Russian literature since Aksakov.

D. H. LAWRENCE

Lawrence's sexual mysticism is completely unlike that of the other writers I have dealt with in this chapter; it is altogether more personal. Wedekind, like Blake, seemed to conceive sex as a thing in itself, a power beyond human personality. For Lawrence, it can never be separated from human personality. Lawrence's tragedy is similar to Maupassant's. He was no thinker; he never tried to raise his vision of life to an analytical level. But the advantage of intellect is that it can at least place concepts beyond the reach of fluctuating human emotions, separate the pure from the impure, the permanent from the fortuitous. Like Maupassant, Lawrence became sick and embittered, and his original vision darkened. *Lady Chatterley's Lover* is only an ugly parody of his early vision of sex. His complete reliance on his own emotions and instincts gave him no yardstick to measure change of attitude. His novels are supposed to express a basically optimistic viewpoint; but the works of his last eight years are pervaded by an atmosphere of gloom and futility that can be paralleled only by the later Artzybasheff or Andreyev.

In many ways, Lawrence's best work is similar to Maupassant's in its sensation of impressionism, of love of nature; it differs from Maupassant's in its love of people. But Lawrence's love of people is also his weakness, for in his later work it turns to a negative distaste. His work is dominated by personality in a way that the work of Maupassant and Wedekind is not. It contains always two extremes, and the reader can never cease to be aware of them: the instinctive life affirmation of a poet, and the torments and complications of human relationships. Shaw admitted that he had tried to read *Sons and Lovers* but had been unable to finish it. No one who knows Shaw's work can be surprised at this; he must have found it all too personal, lacking in the attempt at objective communication.

In his preoccupation with personal relationships, Lawrence is related to the Aldous Huxley of *Point Counter Point*, or to the novels of Angus Wilson. He is not above his characters, detached from them, moving them around like pieces on a chessboard; he is down among them, reacting to them as a human being reacts to other human beings – with affection, irritation, boredom, interest. The consequence is that the reader seldom feels himself in the hands of a detached artist; the sensation of reading Lawrence's novels is more akin to listening to Lawrence gossip about his characters. To admire Lawrence's writing, it is necessary to like Lawrence personally, or at least to tolerate his personality. There is probably no other important novelist of whom this is so true, with the possible exception of Henry James. Graham Hough, in his book on Lawrence, writing of 'The Princess', says:

There is something repellent about the treatment of this story, as about the treatment of similar themes elsewhere in Lawrence. I believe it is an impurity of motive, perceptible, but hard to pin down. Lawrence is often implicated in his stories in the wrong way; and he often overcomes the difficulty by putting himself or a representative of himself into the fiction. This is not the most refined artistic method, but as often as not it works . . . But it is hard to get rid of the feeling that the author, not only his character, also wants to revenge himself on all cold white women, especially if they are rich; and it is this suspicion of a suppressed sexual malice in the tale . . . that makes it offensive.

This feeling of revenge and malice is, unfortunately, present in a great deal of Lawrence's fiction. Lawrence had not learned Nietzsche's lesson of 'passing by' the things he hates and concentrating on the things he loves.

It is this involvement with personality that continually wrecks Lawrence's artistic intentions. Sex, and to a lesser degree, nature, are his symbols of freedom. Civilisation and the family are frequently his symbols of enslavement. Much of his work plays with these two symbols. Simple examples are 'Daughters of the Vicar' and 'The Virgin and the Gypsy'. In both these stories, a 'respectable' middle-class young lady is stifled in her artificial social background, and turns for sexual release to the simple male of a lower social class, in one case a miner, in the other a gypsy. But at this point Lawrence's imagination always fails him; he obviously has no idea of what happens next. For this reason, most of his stories dealing with the contrast of primitive and artificial are left unfinished, and the reader is left in the air.

Lawrence's failure can be seen by comparing his novels with Wells's *History of Mr Polly*. Wells is also concerned about freedom; for him also society and the family are symbols of enslavement. But when Mr Polly kicks free of his wife and his unsuccessful shop, he finds an idyllic life in the country at the Potwell Inn, working as odd-job man. This was certainly not Wells's idea of ultimate freedom, but he convinces the reader that Mr Polly has solved his own problem of freedom. When Lawrence writes of men or women who seek freedom, he can never convince the reader that they have found it. Aaron Sisson in *Aaron's Rod* feels an increasing dissatisfaction with his family and, like Mr Polly, walks off one day to live his own life. Then the book degenerates into a malicious satire on the English living abroad; Aaron meets the 'prophetic writer' Lilly – Lawrence himself – whose idea of solving Aaron's problems is to advise Aaron to submit completely to his domination. Aaron refuses, and the book peters out, with nothing solved and no progress made.

Lawrence's 'nirvana' was usually a sexual relationship; but Lawrence knew from personal experience that even the most satisfying marriage is no bed of roses. So when the sexual relationships that bring freedom are at last achieved, there is always a further vista of conflict. Lawrence could never conceive freedom as idyllic relaxation at a country inn. He was a compulsive traveller and quarreller.

An example to the point is the long story 'The Fox'. This is about two young women who run a chicken farm; one is thin, sharp and bespectacled, the other robust, warm and slow. It is not difficult to guess which one Lawrence dislikes. A young soldier comes to work on the farm and falls in love with March, the robust girl. Banford, her partner, opposes the match. At the end of the story, the soldier chops down a tree which 'accidentally' falls on Banford and kills her. Now the lovers should be ideally happy. But Lawrence cannot write about happiness; the lovers are still in conflict – Lawrence's usual war of the sexes – at the end of the story. They decide to go to Canada where the soldier feels that everything will be all right. 'If only we could go soon,' he says, in the last sentence of the story. But the reader has the feeling that going to Canada will solve nothing, and that Lawrence knows it too.

His finest short story, 'The Prussian Officer', shows the same uncertainty of purpose. Basically, its theme is the same as that of the story Sanine told Soloveitchik about fighting the student – never submit to indignity from other men, always fight back. A young soldier has a sadistic officer, whose sadism is stimulated by the homosexual attraction he feels for the youth (who is his batman). The officer devises a series of humiliations for the batman. The reader shares the author's loathing of the officer, and hopes that the soldier will revolt. He does, strangling the officer. He has achieved a kind of freedom. What now? Again, Lawrence shirks the issue; the soldier dies of thirst after hiding in the woods.

One feels sometimes that Lawrence evokes death to conceal his artistic uncertainty. It is a convenient way of wiping the slate clean of the problems of personality. In one of his poems, he writes:

> And be, oh be
> A sun to me
> Not a weary, importunate
> Personality.

He tries to devise all kinds of methods by which his characters can escape their weary importunate personalities. In one of his silliest tales, a woman allows herself to be sacrificed by a tribe of Indians because she finds in their primitive reliance on instinct an escape from her own personality. Another woman finds that lying in the sun awakens in her the life of the instincts. On the whole he disapproves of the Wordsworthian solution – the peace of nature. This is illustrated in one of his most curious stories, 'The Man Who Loved Islands'. The moral of this tale was supposed to be that man should not try to escape his fellow human beings. His island-lover buys three islands, one after the other. The first is too big, and he gets tired of the complications that arise from his servants and keeping the place in repair. The second island is smaller, but there are still too many complications. So he buys the third island, a mere rock in the sea, and has a small concrete house built on it, where he lives alone. Soon he finds even the sheep on this island distracting, and has them taken off. The winter comes, and the story ends with a masterly evocation of the silence, and the snow falling into the black sea. By this time,

Lawrence implies, his anti-social islander is almost an imbecile.

But the story does not have the effect Lawrence intended. His description of the third island is one of the most moving and poetic pieces of writing in all his work. Whether he likes it or not, the effect is Wordsworthian. Instead of being a tract against solitude, the story is a poem to solitude. And it leaves an impression that Lawrence failed to investigate one of the most important sources of freedom.

The chief instrument of 'escape from personality' is, of course, sex, and Lawrence applies this indiscriminately. It serves for Jesus as well as Lady Chatterley. Lawrence's basic weakness is revealed in his short novel *The Man Who Died*, in which Jesus comes back from the dead, realises the error of his ways, the futility of being a world-betterer, and finds fulfilment in a sexual relation. Lawrence had no faith in Jesus's idea of universal love; it was a vision that meant nothing to him. Jesus had to be corrected and acknowledge that sexual love is the ultimate solution for man, and that no man has a right to try to be more than man. But there is too much disgust in Lawrence for him to be convincing. Even at the end of the novel, when Jesus steals a boat, Lawrence comments: 'The oars were yet warm with the unpleasant warmth of the hands of the slaves.'

This element of disgust is important in Lawrence's work, but it would be unfair to pretend that it is always present. He overcomes it mainly when he is writing about the English countryside, or about his home county of Nottinghamshire. The story 'Love Among the Haystacks' is one of the few entirely delightful tales in his output. Its theme, as usual, is the need for freedom. There are two brothers, farmer's sons, and they are both in love with a pretty governess at the vicarage. She prefers the younger brother. On the same night that the younger brother first sleeps with the governess in a haystack, the elder sleeps with the wife of a shifty tramp, and asks her to marry him. And at the end of the story Lawrence overcomes his usual inability to end satisfactorily with the brief statement: 'Geoffrey and Lydia kept faith, one with the other,' which, strangely enough, is more convincing than his usual truncated endings. In this story, as in his early novel

The White Peacock, Lawrence seems free from the disgust and malice that disfigures so much of his later work.

But in the final analysis, Lawrence cannot be judged a great writer. He was too small a man to be a satisfactory instrument of the vision that sometimes possessed him. At the moments when his work seems to be on the point of rising to a great, impersonal vision, the angry and petty Lawrence intrudes with some obsession about social position or intellectual women. And Lawrence was a very bad satirist. His hatred is never, like Swift's or Voltaire's, cleansing and exhilarating.

His lack of detachment brings to mind another writer with whom, at first glance, he has nothing whatever in common – Frederick Rolfe, 'Baron Corvo'. Lawrence, rather surprisingly, reviewed Rolfe's *Hadrian the Seventh* sympathetically, saying that although it was caviar, at least it came from the belly of a live fish. Rolfe's chief fault as a writer is his malice and self-pity, which are always obtruding. Rolfe specialises in scathing descriptions of his characters, most of whom he hates. He seems not to realise that he is committing an artistic sin when, in a third-person narrative, he describes a character as, for instance, 'a mealy-mouthed, unctuous, knock-kneed, button-eyed dwarf of a man'. Lawrence could sympathise with him: they both found it impossible to stop irritation and disgust from bubbling over into the narrative. The malice and wish fulfilment of *Lady Chatterley's Lover* are not at all unlike the malice and wish fulfilment of Rolfe's *Desire and Pursuit of the Whole*.

The difference, of course, is that Lawrence was also a genuine poet and mystic and Rolfe, at best, was only a sentimentalist. Lawrence was both Jekyll and Hyde, and the Hyde half might have been a reincarnation of Frederick Rolfe.

It is too late now to allot blame, but it seems plausible that when the delicate child called Bert Lawrence was spoiled by his mother, and encouraged to become imperious, fretful and self-pitying, England lost a visionary novelist to compare with Dostoevsky.

CONCLUSION

When one considers the power and importance of the sexual impulse in human beings, it seems strange that so few 'visionary' writers have emphasised it. When one has mentioned Blake and the four writers dealt with in the present chapter, the list is almost exhausted. The reason for this may be that the 'visionary' writer begins with an attitude of world-rejection. He tends to be an 'outsider'. Sexual experience depends upon having a reasonable personal relationship to the opposite sex. To be obsessed by one's dead mother, like Poe, or to be too shy to approach women, like Gogol, is obviously not conducive to a positive, least of all a visionary, attitude towards sex. Yeats was one of the few visionary types who finally came to regard sex as the most important human impulse, and it took him a lifetime of self-unification to arrive at that point. The 'healthy' writers on sex – Rabelais, Casanova, Robert Burns, Synge – are too objective to bother about visionary ultimates. Besides which, the 'secular visionary' is a fairly new phenomenon, and most religious visionaries of the past seem to accept the Pauline view of sex as a necessary evil.

And yet it may be that the vision of Wedekind and Lawrence will play a more important part in the future. The sexual taboos of the nineteenth century are in process of vanishing, and an increasing number of writers seem to recognise the gap left in man's imaginative life by the decay of religion. A century earlier, Lawrence might have become a Swedenborgian (as Balzac did). A century hence, the writer who is inclined to mystical religion might automatically become a Lawrencian. Wedekind and Lawrence barely touched the fringes of the sexual impulse; in many ways, Blake went further than either. There may be writers of the future who will go further still, regarding the sexual impulse as one of the world's strangest and greatest mysteries, and an immense untapped source of power for the human spirit. The work of Shaw often foreshadows this, particularly the two evolutionary plays, *Man and Superman* and *Back to Methuselah*. In the speech of Eve that I have already quoted, sex and the imagination are specifically connected, united by the concept of evolution.

It has become apparent in the course of this book that the imagination does not operate *in vacuo*; it is intimately connected to the psychological impulses and problems of individual writers. Sometimes these problems are wholly personal, with no kind of general significance. But what of the general problems, the problems expressed in such words as 'freedom' and 'evolution'? What is their relation to the imagination?

NOTES

1. 'Frightful cries, atrocious blasphemies, sprang from the Duke's swollen breast, flames seemed to dart from his eyes, he foamed at the mouth, he whinnied like a stallion; you'd have taken him for the very god of Lust.' *The 120 Days*: Introduction.

2. To understand how well it *can* be done, one should read Arthur Schnitzler's short novel *Casanova's Homecoming* – preferably after reading the six volumes of Casanova's memoirs. Casanova takes the same gleeful delight as Maupassant in describing his conquests. But the memoirs are incomplete, and end while Casanova is still young and successful. Schnitzler tells how Casanova, as an old man, calls on an ex-mistress, and falls in love with her niece. But the niece prefers an army officer. Casanova finally discovers a means of persuading the officer to allow him, Casanova, to take his place in the niece's bed. The ruse is successful; Casanova spends the night with the girl. But when she sees him in the morning, she is horrified and disgusted, and Casanova realises that he is an old and wrinkled libertine. Outside the girl's window, he fights the young officer and kills him, then returns to Venice, where he sinks to the level of a spy. The book is an overwhelming postscript to the famous *Memoirs*.

3. Wedekind quarrelled with Strindberg in Paris and later lived with Strindberg's second wife, Frieda.

4. Weisgall brings this out cleverly in his brilliant opera; the only heroic and tuneful aria is the one in which Gerardo tells his servants how to fold clothes. 'Packing clothes is quite an art,' he sings, with the lyricism that Tristan brings to the love duet.

5. This story is contained in a volume called *Feuerwerk* (1905) which has a famous preface 'On the Erotic'. The preface, however, is of less interest than one might suppose; it is Wedekind's attempt to justify himself in the eyes of the bourgeoisie. So instead of containing an attempt to explain his sexual mysticism, it speaks of the social importance of sexual frankness. It has the characteristic phrase 'flesh has its own spirit', and

speaks of the discussion of sex as a 'gymnastic of the spirit'. It would hardly seem out of place as an introduction to *Mrs Warren's Profession* or Ibsen's *Ghosts*.

6. Wedekind wrote another play, *Dance of Death*, about this white slave trafficker, Casti-piani, that ends in his suicide.

7. Wedekind based his character on a forger of paintings named Willy Gretor, whom he characteristically admired.

Seven

The Need for Polarities

It is necessary at this point to try to define more precisely the function of imagination.

In its usual connotation, as I said earlier, imagination means the power of creating images of something not actually present. If I concentrate hard enough, I can create an image of my friend Bill sitting in the empty chair opposite my typewriter. If I happen to be leading a frustrating and unhappy life, and I spend my time conjuring up heroic daydreams, like Thurber's Walter Mitty or Wells's Hoop Driver, the result may be a complete dislocation from 'everyday reality'. In so far as it obstructs my natural evolution as a social being, this dislocation will be dangerous, and a marxist critic will rightly refer to it as 'escapism'.

But it is obvious that the function of the imagination is not restricted to compensating for frustrations. 'Escapism' is an accurate description when there is no connection between the image and 'everyday life'; and even then there is room for argument about what constitutes a connection. For in the ordinary way, the function of imagination is to foresee the future and to enlarge the present consciousness. The imagination may 'see' a very long way indeed, until its vision has no kind of connection with the everyday life of the subject. Heinrich Schliemann was a wholesale merchant who dreamed all his early life of Troy. In his late forties he gave up business and went to look for the ruins of Troy – and found them, nine buried cities, one on top of the other. It would seem, then, that the only way of judging between Schliemann and Walter Mitty is to apply the pragmatic test; and this is always a half measure.

It is more interesting to ignore definitions and consider the workings of the imagination. Although it may be true to say that too much imagination makes for inefficiency in practical affairs, the opposite may be equally true. Everyone has noticed the power of the imagination over the body. You may be tired in the evening; you try to grapple with a volume of philosophy, or even a crossword puzzle, and your eyes refuse to stay open; no matter how hard you try to bully your body into staying awake, you drift towards sleep. On the other hand, you pick up a book that touches the imagination, and six hours later you realise that it is after midnight and you are willing to read on for another hour. The body may be difficult to bully into submission, but it is easily charmed by the imagination. And when 'charmed', its efficiency is increased in every way.

The explanation would seem to be that the imagination is the detonator of the will. When connected with a purpose – which is necessary in the future – it can arouse the will. The more distant the purpose, the greater the power of the imagination. The need to solve a crossword puzzle is too immediate, its implications are too narrow, its connection with the evolution of the individual too limited.

The imagination, then, is a machine that must work on fuel; its fuel may be any spontaneously generated energy: fear, love, lust, jealousy, wonder, ambition. The difference in quality of imagination between a great artist and the 'ordinary man' is that the artist has learned to generate large quantities of fuel, and to use them to drive the imagination. If I merely imagine that my friend Bill is sitting opposite me, I am using the ordinary, conscious energy of the brain to maintain the image. When I cease to use it, the image will fade instantly; it has no life of its own. On the other hand, if I am sexually frustrated, I may conjure up an erotic scene that has enough reality to induce sexual excitement. Stories of the desert fathers, who deliberately repressed the sexual impulse, reveal that sexual images often possess a power that seems independent of will – to such an extent that many believed they were being tempted by demons in the shape of real women. In the same way, many artists have complained that their characters seem to develop a will of their own. (Pirandello's story 'A Character in Distress' is a good example.)

Even more to the point is the curious story of Shelley that is frequently told in connection with the genesis of *Frankenstein*. Shelley and Mary Shelley, Byron and Poli-

175

dori, all decided to write ghost stories. Mary was the only one who finished her task. But one evening when they were discussing ghosts, and Byron was reciting lines of 'Christabel', Shelley uttered a shriek and rushed out of the house. Later, he explained that he had been staring at Mary when he had remembered an old story about a woman who had eyes instead of nipples; the image was so powerful that he mistook it for reality.

In none of these cases need it be assumed that the imagination actually took on a life of its own. But the imagination fuelled by the energy of fear, or by sexual energy, may work at an intensity that is unknown to the ordinary conscious image-making imagination. Drivers of old cars who change to a new, fast car have similarly recorded the sensation that the car is running away with them.

The fundamental and undeniable fact about the imagination is that its purpose is to intensify the life in man. Left to itself, life makes for stasis, just as the process of nature makes for equilibrium, as a rolling stone finally comes to rest. On a long train journey, the traveller first of all watches the passing scene and reflects on it; then he merely observes passively; finally, unless a stimulus is applied, he probably falls asleep – even passive consciousness disappears. These are the three states of consciousness familiar to most of us: the body's consciousness, which is maintained in sleep, the ordinary observant consciousness, and the reflective consciousness. This reflective consciousness is already close to the imagination, for you may forget to observe and become lost in reflection, which is a type of imagination, fuelled by intellectual curiosity. But man also aims at possessing a fourth type of consciousness, which is far wider than ordinary reflection. Reflection is like a train that runs on two narrow rails; it has to be reflection about something and that 'something' is normally immediate experience. So reflection runs on railway lines that stretch from the past into the future.

But the fourth type of consciousness aims at another type of extension, a third dimension of awareness of other times and other places. Its instrument is memory, which has stored up all kinds of knowledge in the brain cells. This knowledge is dead unless it is illuminated by consciousness. In a sense, it might be said that every human brain possesses *all knowledge*; for as well as its actual memories, it also possesses powers of reason that can relate these memories and produce new pieces of knowledge. A simple illustration is given in Plato's *Meno*, where Socrates proves that an ignorant slave already has a knowledge of geometry by persuading him to reason out a geometrical problem.

Yet it would be more accurate to say that each brain has a *capacity* for all knowledge, rather than the possession of it. Wells's comments at the beginning of the *Experiment in Autobiography* are profoundly perceptive. If we ask why men would rather sit and bite their nails than turn their attention inward and convert some of their immense store of potential knowledge into actual knowledge, the answer is that men are only accustomed to bother about the knowledge that they require for survival. And Wells suggests that a new type of man is appearing, who wants a third dimension of imaginative consciousness for its own sake, not for his survival. This type of man, as Wells points out, demands imaginative consciousness – as distinguished from observational and reflective consciousness – as his *sine qua non*.

In *The Doors of Perception*, Aldous Huxley makes some speculations about the problems of consciousness that are very much to the point here. A problem that must strike anyone who reflects about the imagination is, *why* are human beings confined to their grey, two-dimensional world of the present? With the immense riches of the human brain, with the immense capacity for pleasure of the human body, why are even the greatest men so disappointingly ungodlike? When we read Wells, for example, we plunge into an intellectual and imaginative vortex of incredible energy. Then when we turn to his life, we find a short, fat man with a cockney accent and a habit of flying into petty rages. Why are even the greatest men so firmly anchored in mediocrity? The Catholic may explain it by referring to original sin, and by implying that, since Adam's fall, man has been serving a prison sentence. Convicts cannot expect many privileges. There are others who feel that this view – even with redemption thrown in – is pessimistic. Man may be, in a figurative sense, in prison, but he has also been given a large bunch of keys and several files. There was an age when scientists were condemned on the grounds that it was blasphemous to look too closely into God's secrets. Since then, man has advanced in many different ways, his stature has increased perceptibly, and there is no sign that God has set any limits. On the contrary, the scientist, the psychologist, the artist who creates new areas of consciousness, may feel strongly that he is serving some 'higher power'. And yet, with everything on his side, man seems confined to littleness. It is as if he possessed an enormous powerhouse which refuses to produce more than the faintest trickle of electricity.

Aldous Huxley has some interesting suggestions to make. The effect of taking mescalin was apparently to make his 'powerhouse' work at full efficiency for a short time. The consciousness expanded, the world became more beautiful and real than he had ever seen it. But this sense of widened consciousness was accompanied by a blissful lassitude; he felt no desire to do anything but stare at the incredibly beautiful physical world.

It might be said that mescalin had affected Huxley's perceptions rather than his imagination, but this is hardly borne out by much of what he writes: 'Confronted by a chair which looked like the Last Judgement – or, to be more accurate, by a Last Judgement which, after a long time . . . I recognised as a chair . . .' This widened perception of significances is the third dimension of consciousness.

Huxley then quotes Bergson's idea that

the function of the brain and nervous system and sense organs is . . . *eliminative* and not productive. Each person is at each moment capable of remembering all that has ever happened to him and of perceiving everything that is happening everywhere in the universe. The function of the brain and nervous system is to protect us from being overwhelmed and confused by this mass of largely useless and irrelevant knowledge, by shutting out most of what we should otherwise perceive . . .

But the purpose of human beings is to survive, and this universal consciousness would not help survival. So the brain contains a reducing valve to protect us from too much awareness.

This seems a plausible answer to the question of the limitation of human consciousness. Man's energy must be used for survival and for practical purposes. Man may possess the equipment to become a god, but he does not possess the energy to make use of the equipment.

At this stage, it should be added that the picture of the imagination as a 'machine, is not entirely accurate. The workings of the imagination are not in the least like the workings of a simple engine. There are times when the sensation of the working of imagination is more like inflating a series of balloons to raise some heavy object. One by one, the balloons expand, each one tied to the body; finally, slowly, they begin to lift the body clear of the ground. There is a definite sense of power flooding different compartments, like switching on the light in various rooms of a house. Consciousness 'expands', the power of the will suddenly seems boundless.

The definition of the imagination – as the third dimension of consciousness – would seem to be broader than the 'escapist' definition. The imagination, like the reasoning faculty, is an *extension* of the powers for survival. All animals need reason to stay alive, but no animal *needs* Boole's symbolic logic, or Planck's quantum theory. The kind of recreation of the past in which Proust spent twenty years of his life is quite simply a luxury. And yet Proust, no doubt, would have agreed with Wells: that without this luxury he had no desire to stay alive.

Unfortunately, Proust's glimpses of the past were brief and infrequent. To achieve a few moments in which the past relived in him, he had to spend many years in a disciplined re-examination of his life. Instead of that third dimension of consciousness for which he craved he had to put up with the second dimension – the rigid railway line from past to future.

And yet men at least possess memory in abundance. There are many animals that possess almost no memory, no continuity on a conscious level. There are also living creatures – the simplest living organisms and the plant world – that do not even possess the 'first dimension' of consciousness – conscious existence in the present. They live in the non-dimensional world of unconscious life.

This suggests a speculation that has at least the virtue of unifying the theory of imagination. Wells had already hinted that he suspected the 'men of imagination' were a new species, or at least an important variation on the old

179

species, as distinct as the first amphibians from the fishes that preceded them. Is it not possible that such men as Wells and Proust are on the brink of a new stage in human evolution? There can be no possible doubt that the imagination is almost synonymous with freedom – as synonymous, at least, as 'air' and 'wind'. Imagination is man's attempt to break out of the prison of his body to possess an extension beyond the present. But if imagination is meaningless unless defined in terms of freedom, freedom is also meaningless unless defined in terms of evolution. Under pain or repression, we may think of freedom simply as a desirable state, like breathing. But once we cease to measure freedom in this negative way, it becomes a question of evolution. Freedom is either freedom *from* something or freedom *for* something; it cannot exist statically.

But there can certainly be no doubt that the general notion of evolution is always connected with the imagination. Anyone who has ever conceived a large work of construction or creation recognises the sense of freedom that comes with grandiose plans. Can we doubt that one of Zola's greatest moments was the hour when he conceived the Rougon-Macquart cycle? Or that Newton experienced his deepest satisfaction when disconnected fragments of mathematics and physical observation began to cohere into the material of the *Principia*? This activity of planning a large work is not in itself an exercise of the imagination, but it *is* a preparation for a long journey away from the physical actuality of the present, and therefore a kind of practice for inhabiting a new field of consciousness.

The followers of Flaubert believed that 'the artist' has no business with 'convictions' or general ideas. Writers as unlike as Maupassant, Henry James, George Moore and James Joyce subscribed to this dictum. Admitted, these writers did not insist that an artist should have no direction; they believed that 'life' can provide all the direction an artist needs. The classic argument on the theme developed between Henry James and H. G. Wells as a result of the publication of Wells's satire *Boon*,[1] James protesting that all the artist needs is an 'appetite for life'. *Finnegans Wake* reveals the bankruptcy of this belief; stuffed with curiosity about history, philosophy and human beings, it is a mausoleum of 'life', a collection of materials for a great novel that was never written. Like freedom, the 'appetite for life' cannot exist without direction. It should be noted that Joyce, Maupassant and James all emerged from a prisonlike adolescence with a ravenous appetite for 'life' and freedom; like prisoners, they were inclined to believe that 'life' and freedom can have a static and independent existence. The results of this view can be seen in their later works. James's favourite theme is the tragedy of the undirected 'appetite for life'; in his early novels – *Roderick Hudson, The Portrait of a Lady* – he shows young people with a zest for living but no idea of what to do with it; in his own later work, the same need for evolution was forced to express itself in the language, which becomes increasingly involved. Joyce's case is identical, and I have already spoken of Maupassant's failure to develop. The point about these writers is that one cannot imagine how they could have continued to write if they had lived. Their 'amoralism' precluded the possibility of a development in the realm of ideas. But the need for some kind of development is obsessive in an artist. It comes easiest to the writer who finds it natural to express ideas – Dostoevsky, Mann, Hesse, Shaw. Other artists content themselves with merely reflecting their personal development in their work – usually either an increasing mellowness (as in Shakespeare) or defeatism (Maupassant, Fitzgerald). This type of artist tends to take his work rather casually, and concentrate on living. But the serious artist who strives for development but tries to avoid ideas or convictions is usually forced to allow his style to carry the full weight of his craving for evolutionary complexity. The later Joyce, James and Meredith all have their fervent admirers; but for some reason, posterity usually seems to feel that the size of the kernel hardly justifies the effort required to crack the nut.

My conclusion is that artistic development is associated with certain 'evolutionary preoccupation'. No artist can develop without increasing his self-knowledge; but self-knowledge supposes a certain preoccupation with the meaning of human life and the destiny of man. A definite set of beliefs – Methodist Christianity, for example – may only be a hindrance to development; but it is no more so than Beckett's refusal to think at all. Shaw says somewhere that all intelligent men must be preoccupied with either religion, politics or sex. (He seems to attribute T. E. Lawrence's tragedy to his refusal to come to grips with any of them.) It is hard to see how an artist could hope to achieve any degree of self-knowledge without being deeply concerned with at least one of the three.

'ILLUSION' AND 'REALITY'

Throughout this book, I have spoken of 'reality' in inverted commas, to indicate that I am speaking of 'everyday reality', not of the reality of the mystics, or Kant's noumenal reality. But obviously this use of the word is as dubious as calling somebody 'imaginative' when you mean they tell lies.

Reality, illusion, imagination; these fundamentals need more precise definition. We use the words vaguely, but their meaning *seems* concrete, and this seems to justify the vagueness. If we say that a small shopkeeper is unsuccessful because he is out of touch with reality, the meaning is clear enough; we are speaking about commercial realities and the psychology of the modern consumer. If we say that a man is unsuccessful in love because he has too many illusions about women, the meaning is again clear; here the reality is a knowledge of feminine psychology. But in both these cases, 'reality' is bound up with a defined and restricted purpose: either to sell goods, or to make a woman (or women) happy. On the other hand, consider Ramakrishna's comment to his disciples; that the best way of overcoming the sexual illusion is to consider that women are 'really' made up of disagreeable things like blood, bone and gristle. Is this the reality of women? Obviously not.

Goncharov illustrates the conflict between these common conceptions of illusion and reality in his amusing early novel *The Usual Story*, in which an idealistic young man comes to St Petersburg to make his fortune, and has a series of disillusionments. The character of the young idealist is contrasted with that of his uncle, a down-to-earth realist, who tells him to forget the poetry and concentrate on success. The young man's idealism is revealed in his tendency to fall repeatedly in love. His love affairs are usually unhappy, but when he falls in love with a pretty widow, as idealistic as he is, and they become lovers, they enjoy a long period of bliss before he discovers that her perpetual chatter about poetry and the spirit bores him. Then he abandons her, and retires to the country, shattered by his various contacts with 'reality', but eventually returns to St Petersburg, marries for money, and becomes a commercial success. Goncharov emphasises that the 'successful' young man is in every way a less interesting person than the young idealist. He also points out that the wife of the practical uncle is deeply unsatisfied with her husband. Goncharov's novel is a practical demonstration of the meaning of the words 'illusion' and 'reality' as we use them in everyday life; both are shown to be ultimately unsatisfactory. Goncharov implies that the most desirable type of man would combine the best characteristics of both uncle and nephew. Idealism need not mean incompetence.

The difficulty of drawing a line between 'illusion' and 'reality' can be seen even more clearly by considering the nature of sexual relations. Flaubert remarks contemptuously that Emma Bovary's husband soon began to treat sex as a kind of dessert after his dinner. According to the usual interpretation, Charles Bovary was in the grip of sexual illusions when he courted Emma, and soon discovered that the 'reality' of sex is something far less exciting; and Emma's tragedy was her inability to accept 'reality', her need to live in the imagination. But is dullness synonymous with reality? The so-called 'sexual illusions' are part of man's evolutionary appetite. The excitement of sex is the instinctive craving to increase the complexity and intensity of life. When Charles Bovary first saw Emma, he was dimly aware of her as the prototype of all women, and therefore of the implications of her womanhood, of her involvement in the evolutionary process. If intimate knowledge of her personality and her body destroyed this instinctive awareness, then he had certainly not moved towards reality but away from it.

It is natural that this broader awareness should fade, and give way to a narrower and more solidly defined consciousness. It was also natural that Emma should need more love affairs, to attempt to restore her own broader awareness. Many highly imaginative people seem to require a multiplicity of sexual experience for this reason. (H. G. Wells is an example.) But the need for multiple

183

experience is in itself a failure of the imagination. To recognise this is to move towards a more precise definition of imagination, and to recognise that the relation of imagination to experience is identical with the relation of logic to 'facts'. Socrates showed that the slave already possessed the 'facts' necessary to understand Pythagoras's theorem, but had not used his logical faculty to relate them. H. G. Wells must certainly have possessed the experience necessary for a profound understanding of women, and yet failed to relate it with his imagination.

For the sake of definition, the area covered by mathematics could be called 'the logical field'. The experienced mathematician becomes aware of various 'facts' in this field, annd learns how to relate them to one other. In the same way, a literary critic requires a knowledge of different 'facts' in the literary field, and an ability to relate them, to see connections between them. The faculty for relating these facts is not unlike the logical faculty, although it probably contains a larger element of 'feeling' than the faculty required by a mathematician.

But when we come to the field of experience, the 'logical faculty' is no longer the right instrument for relating the 'facts'. To begin with, the facts are too complex to be defined like the pieces on a chessboard. A cynic might say, for example: 'All women are alike.' One immediately has to ask: 'What do you mean by "women" and what do you mean by "alike"?' Modern mathematics has shown that the premises of mathematics are not as solid and as obvious as Euclid and Archimedes thought. But the 'premises' underlying any general statement about experience are infinitely more vague. And just as one and one are two, whether we understand the foundations of mathematics or not, so we are able to apply general rules to our everyday experience even though we have no understanding of the foundations of life. But attempts to generalise about experience are far more treacherous than attempts to generalise about numbers – or about books and writers – and the ordinary logical faculty is of very limited value indeed. The ability to make accurate generalisations about the 'field of experience' depends on a faculty that might be called intuition, but which can more correctly be called imagination.

An example might make this clearer. Goncharov's

young idealist had a tendency to fall in love with every pretty girl. This tendency finally vanished under the impact of a great deal of experience. But the experience only had the effect of strengthening the imagination so that it could *anticipate* the same experiences with authority. Hence the man would not merely be able to say: 'I know exactly what it would be like to seduce this pretty but rather empty-headed girl,' but to be able to create the experience in anticipation.

This faculty might be called 'imagination', but it might equally well be called a grip on reality.

The imagination, then, is merely another tool of the human mind, like reason, its purpose being to work with reason in the task of correlating the 'facts' of experience. It can never, of course, be a genuine substitute for experience. No amount of imagination – even aided by reading – could give a young man the same experience as his first love affair. But life evolves by means of developing 'short cuts'. Man has achieved civilisation by replacing real experiences by symbols, by words, and then by learning to replace whole groups of symbols and the relations between them by formulae. The 'modern neurosis' would seem to be due to a tendency to lose contact with the reality underlying the formula. Nevertheless, the 'formularising' is indispensable.

SUMMARY

It is necessary at this point to attempt to make some general statements about the purpose and methods of literature, and this involves summarising and restating the arguments of earlier chapters.

We judge literature primarily by the pleasure it gives. Although this pleasure can often be explained, it can never be ultimately defined. We can say that we enjoy Jane Austen because of her sense of humour, and because her books are somehow 'orderly', well defined. But this does not even begin to explain her charm and genuis. Jane Austen never 'says' anything important, never expresses any great ideas. Literary critics can therefore only attempt to express their own pleasure in reading her, and hope to communicate this pleasure to their readers. Hence, literary criticism has nothing in common with, let us say, a scientist's criticism of another scientist's theory. It never has well-defined premises.

On the other hand, there is a kind of criticism of literature that is more concerned with ideas. Most readers of Dostoevsky will agree that *The House of the Dead* is somehow more 'pure' Dostoevsky than *The Brothers Karamazov*, in the sense that it is full of that indefinable vitality of a young man of genius who is just discovering the nature of his own genius. It is a warmer, more alive book. And yet no one would claim that *The House of the Dead* is a greater novel than *The Brothers Karamazov*. Although the latter novel lacks the instinctive sureness of touch of the earlier work, its conception is in every way greater. *The House of the Dead* is like a small, well-built house. *Karamazov* is like a gigantic, half-finished, badly built palace. In judging it the greater book, we are admitting that literary standards are not everything. The greatness of the ideas of *Karamazov* outweighs the careless writing, poor construction and long-windedness.

If standards we apply to Dostoevsky were applied to literature in general, most literature would have to be dismissed. Ideas about human destiny could not be applied to *Emma, Mr Midshipman Easy, Annals of the Parish* or *The Old Wives' Tale*. It is right that we should judge these books by their indefinable vitality, by a kind of 'smell' about them, rather than by their ideas.

But this notion of 'literary criticism' has led to the problems that I spoke of at the beginning of this book. Because no work of literature can be judged solely by its ideas, a literary mystique has developed. Literature has no need of general ideas; it is a pouring of words onto paper in the hope of catching the indefinable 'smell' of real literature. If a writer appears to be incomprehensible, it may be because these mystical intentions are dictating a new form. If whole pages of Beckett, Kerouac or Robbe-Grillet are apparently meaningless, it is the business of the literary critic to study them until they 'communicate', and then to convey his enthusiasm to a wider audience. A more analytical attitude would ignore the basic premise of literary criticism – that the meaning of a work is inexpressible except in the work itself.

But is it true that literature has no general purpose? If it is true, then no one has any right to pass judgment on an unreadable book; the writer has a right to reply that artists are not all supposed to be marching in step to the same goal.

But here it is necessary to attempt a more general analysis of literature and the imagination. It is true that men live from day to day, and make few attempts at a general assessment of the value of their struggle. This is because the events of everyday life absorb most of the attention, and because of the 'valve' in the human brain that limits man's consciousness to the present. But man never ceases to be aware of the pressures of *pro* and *contra* in his life. He attempts to establish his life on an even keel, to establish a norm from which he can measure fortune and misfortune. Every minute of the day makes demands on his energy, and therefore on his sense of values (since he has to judge whether it is worth expending the energy). To counteract the worries and anxieties, there are various pleasures and relaxations. Spiritually speaking, man is a kind of bladder floating underwater, responding to all the pressures around him, expanding or contracting according to the value judgments that he has to make at every moment.

All literature has one feature in common – it attempts to step back from the flux of the present and to make some broader generalisations about 'life'. It may step back from the life of individuals, and show a large cross section of human existence, many people suffering and loving and dying, as in *War and Peace* or the novels of Kazantzakis. It may do the same thing in a less ambitious way, as in *The Old Wives' Tale* or Priestley's play *Time and the Conways*. It may only describe the life and problems of a single individual, as in *Wilhelm Meister*, Keller's *Green Henry*, James's *Roderick Hudson*. Finally, it may take a detached, warmly interested attitude, as in Trollope or Jane Austen, with the underlying assumption that there is no question of judging life in general, but only of accepting the ambitions and love affairs of the central character as the book's sufficient *raison d'être*.

But even in this last type of book, a certain value judgment about life is implied. No one would suggest that Trollope is a romantic pessimist, even though no writer is less concerned with the problems of human destiny than Trollope; there is an undeniable attitude of 'acceptance' underlying his work, even if Trollope has no great insight into good or evil. There is no writer, no matter how limited, whose work does not possess some implied value judgment on life and human destiny.

It is my contention that these value judgments are the mainspring of the imagination; they are, in fact, so closely connected with it as to be almost synonymous with imagination. Of every work of art, we can ask the question: what kind of world would this be if the events of this book were completely typical of it? 'World' here means not merely the physical order of nature, but the relation of man and 'human destiny' to nature. If this question were asked about the majority of stories of supernatural evil, the answer would be that man is a small, helpless creature, stranded in a terrifying universe, his relation to this universe being essentially the relation of a child to an adult – one of dependence, and recognition of superiority. This attitude is a long way from the Pascalian sense of awe and terror in the face of the universe – in fact, it is the reverse of it. Pascal, like many 'free thinkers' of the nineteenth century, could say with Eliot's Gerontion: 'I have no ghosts.' Though he may be a mere insect in a terrifying universe, Pascalian man is adult, fully responsible, strangely dignified by his nescience, a 'thinking reed'. Pascalian man (and one might equally well say Nietzschean man or Dostoevskian man) is closer to the gods, and therefore more aware of the ungodlike element in himself, of his closeness to the beetle. 'Man' in the supernatural tales – whether by M. R. James, Tolkien, Bram Stoker – is protected from the world of malignant spirits by bourgeois ordinariness. His position in the universe may not be a very great one, but at least it is secure.

In most science fiction, man is still the unimportant childish creature of the ghost story, except that his creators now take a slightly more optimistic view of his capacities. In the ghost story, the man who is bold enough to explore the unknown often goes mad, or meets a nasty end. In the science story, he is likely to get back to earth unscathed. But he is still very much man, not Pascal's thinking reed, poised between god and worm. The powers he possesses are not spiritual powers. But the imagination is activated by the clash between known and unknown, the way in which the unknown world impinges on the known.

The imagination works on this basis of polarities. It now becomes apparent why so much modern literature would appear to have reached a crisis of imagination. Some writers, such as Gide and Huxley, openly confess that they have little power of imaginative invention. (The thin, muddy trickle of *Les Faux Monnayeurs* was the work of many years, and even then Gide had to abandon the novel abruptly instead of finishing it.) The heroes of Huxley and Gide are inactive neurotics, confined to their narrow world of self-doubt and reason. When Huxley introduces murder into *Point Counter Point* it seems arbitrary and casual, not an organic part of the book's central problem. This is because Huxley's polarities are not sufficiently far apart to activate the imagination; 'passion and reason, self-division's cause', he explains in the epigraph to the book, and the human passions and the human reason are both too claustrophobically limited, too far from the universal, to make an impressive clash.

Some kind of moral judgment on the world must, then, be inherent in all works of literature, the writer's accepted view of man and the universe – which is to say that, in some sense, every work of fiction that has ever been written is somehow obscurely concerned with the problem of how men should live. The judgment may be overt, as in *Candide* or *Rasselas*, both openly concerned with man's dubious position in the universe. It may occur only at the end of a work, as in *Epitaph for a Small Winner*, the work of the great Brazilian writer Joaquim de Assis, who feels that his hero is a 'small winner' in the game of life because he has left no children to whom he can pass on the misery of human existence. In this case, as in all classic tragedy, the polarities are the hopeless desires of man and the indifference of the universe. But the most important condition for the function of imagination has been observed – the great gap has been fixed.

This generalisation leaves one important fact unexplained. There are many writers, particularly among the great novelists of the nineteenth century, who seem to work on a 'humanistic' level, with no great polarities of good or evil, triumph or tragedy, and yet who reveal a considerable inventive power. Dickens, Thackeray and Balzac are arguably among them (I am leaving out of account the mystical side of Balzac revealed in *Seraphita*,

Louis Lambert and *Le Peau de Chagrin*); Trollope and Dumas most certainly are.

The interest here lies in the 'unseen' pole of which the writers may be completely unaware, the instinctive faculty of 'affirmation'. The negative pole of the world is always visible, since man is far more capable of pain than of pleasure. Most pleasures are brief and easily forgotten; on the other hand, human life seems to be largely a matter of obstacles, always culminating in death, and frequently in a great deal of pain. It is easy to be fully conscious of 'evil'; any philosopher of minimal talent can produce a hundred reasons why life is not worth living. The power of the urge to live is an altogether different matter. It requires either enormous strength to become aware of it, or one of those freak mystical insights that certain men seem to experience. A powerhouse exists in the subconscious regions of the mind. Occasionally we may become aware of it in some moment of relief from anxiety or of sudden joy. But for the most part, it seems to communicate the urge to life in a curiously stealthy manner, on a level where we fail to notice it. A man like Dostoevsky, about to be executed, sees it without disguise, and spends the rest of his life trying to explain to human beings that they have no idea what life is. He does so by a curious method; from the gentle melancholy of his early work, his books develop an increasingly gloomy picture of human existence. There are brief flashes of mystical affirmation, but these are only hints. His purpose seems to be to communicate to his readers the inexpressible value of life by deliberately trying to produce a kind of 'soul sickness' in them, and relying on this sickness to evoke a sense of values, in the same way that his near-execution revealed his own values. His own imaginative powers increase as he becomes more deeply aware of the polarities, the visible pole of human misery and futility and the invisible strength of the powerhouse.

It might be said, then, that the ultimate aim of all imaginative literature is to teach men 'what life is'. In *La Nausée*, Sartre points out that 'nature' has an aggressive way with the human consciousness, which is analogous to the way a bellicose man thrusts his face close to the face of a person he is threatening. It tends to hypnotise, to jam the 'prehensive powers'. Art is the most primitive human device for enabling the consciousness to retaliate; it attempts to thrust nature to arm's length. Like science, it works on the principle of hypothesis and proof; it suggests 'general theorems' about life (i.e., spirit is good, nature evil; 'you can't win'; 'as for living, our servants will do that for us,' etc.) and then tries to create works of art that will 'demonstrate' the idea.

All this means that the Flaubert–Joyce attitude to literature is untenable. Literature need not have a 'message', in the sense that a problem play has, but neither is its purpose simply to hold a mirror up to nature. The passive attitude to literature is ultimately as untenable as total pessimism. No matter how detached and uncommitted an artist pretends to be, he is involved in a world whose 'direction' is as positive as the current of a river. It is impossible to exercise the imagination and not to be involved in this current, in man's need for a supra-personal purpose, in the evolutionary drive.

THE NEED FOR AN EXISTENTIAL CRITICISM

In *After Strange Gods*, published in 1934, T. S. Eliot suggested that literary criticism should be supplemented by a criticism of a moral or theological nature. No one ever followed up this remark (except perhaps Mr Eliot), but its importance as a suggestion is becoming increasingly apparent. The quarter of a century that has elapsed since then has produced many obscure works on which the critics seemed too modest to comment. When *Finnegans Wake* appeared, no one said boldly that Joyce had totally wasted the twenty years he had devoted to it, in the way that a man wastes the time he spends engraving the Lord's Prayer on a pinhead. When Beckett's plays were presented in London, and his latest novels published, the bewilderment of the critics was interesting to watch. One noted young theatre critic devoted a long review of *Endgame* to a parody of the play; but he took care not to say that it was nonsense. The poetry and novels of the 'Beat Generation' have been handled gingerly and sometimes contemptuously; but no one has bothered to try to define the notion of freedom underlying Kerouac's work and to question its validity. Robbe-Grillet's novels have been called unreadable, but no one has asked whether the idea of the completely 'detached' novel has any meaning, or whether there is not a basic self-contradiction in the whole attempt. This is because we have become used to reading books as 'works of literature', and questioning only the impact they make on the sensibilities. This attitude has led us also to accept paintings that are made by throwing paint at the canvas, and music that is written according to a mathematical formula. No one has yet suggested that this is analogous to a physicist accepting symbols and figures tossed at random onto a sheet of paper as a mathematical treatise.

Existentialism has been defined as the attempt to apply the mathematical intellect to the raw stuff of living experience. It might also be called an attempt to create a new science – a science of living. Existential criticism is therefore the attempt to judge works of art by the contribution they make to the science of living, to judge them by standards of *meaning* as well as impact. It can never replace literary criticism, which concerns itself with the general artistic 'satisfactoriness' of a work. But neither can literary criticism do without existential criticism, except at the most rudimentary levels. In examining, for example, the work of Hemingway or Eliot or D. H. Lawrence or Aldous Huxley, literary criticism must confine itself to the comment that their later work shows a sad falling off in quality. Since it concerns itself only with artistic quality, it can make no comment on the reasons for the change.

It might be suggested that this contrast of literary criticism with existential criticism is only another expression of the old form-versus-content controversy, with art-for-art's sake at one extreme and 'engaged' realism at the other. This would be to translate the whole matter to a superficial level. It is true that, in earlier ages, there was no need for an existential criticism, just as there was no need for existentialism. When Christian standards were taken seriously by most people, any work of art was automatically scrutinised for its 'values'. Existential criticism, like existential philosophy, is a creation of an age of spiritual flux; the need for it began when Rashkolnikov enunciated the proposition: All things are lawful. (But Goethe, Byron and Schiller had already experimented with the same idea.)

Eliot's *After Strange Gods* is a determined attempt to create an existential criticism. Unfortunately it failed, because Mr Eliot is not a thinker; his absolute refusal to discuss the basis of his religious convictions in public is sometimes reminiscent of a Victorian maiden refusing to talk about her underwear. Thus *After Strange Gods* attempts to discuss its authors – Lawrence, Hopkins, Hardy, Joyce, and others – from the basis of a deliberately mystifying dogmatism.

Nevertheless, the intention is clear; and the book is undeniably a work of existential criticism. It fails because it accepts a ready-made set of 'absolute values', or rather, because it refuses to discuss the values as well as the authors to whom they are applied.

All this is not to suggest that 'existential criticism' can make dogmatic statements about the reasons for the failure of a work of literature. But it can recognise the necessity for understanding the reasons. It can state, for example, that there is a serious contradiction in the work of T. E. Hulme, the early Hulme being a Bergsonian and an evolutionist, the later Hulme a believer in original sin and the completely static quality of human beings. The same division can be found in the work of Eliot; his early work is animated by his dislike of the morally 'static' nature of modern society and therefore by a desire for a 'change' in human nature; the more recent plays are based upon the orthodox Anglican position, and therefore on the belief in the unchangeableness of human nature. Since Mr Eliot has come to contradict his own early premises, it is not surprising that his later work should appear to be curiously inconclusive.

In writing elsewhere about Hemingway, I have suggested that the falling off in his post-1930 novels was due to his failure to develop his early concern with what I then termed 'Outsider problems'. There was a certain simplification here, for these problems are not confined to 'Outsiders' (i.e., to oversensitive social misfits). But these problems are certainly the concern of existential criticism – if, in fact, they were a contributory reason to Hemingway's decline as a serious artist. The early Hemingway wrote about the contrast between man's need for a sense of purpose and love, and the indifference (or cruelty) of nature. In *A Farewell to Arms* he adopted a stoic position, and then preferred to write about the 'compensations' of life – big-game hunting, deep-sea fishing, sex and alcohol. Like Eliot, Hemingway's later work often reads like self-parody.

Mathematicians know that most theorems and propositions are susceptible of several proofs, and that some proofs are 'beautiful' and some are clumsy. A mathematician who cared only whether a proof was beautiful or ugly would be the counterpart of the purely literary critic. The existential critic is concerned less with the beauty of the proof than with what it is proving.

Art is an equation in which there are two terms: the artist and his material. The 'material' is a complex matter of the world he lives in, the tradition he works in, the social forces that enter his daily life.

There are three possible attitudes to this equation. The first is the most prevalent in our time: both terms are fixed. The artist is the sensitive observer, and can be no more than honest; the times are the outcome of the current of history, and are beyond the reach of individual approval or disapproval. Therefore, the artist can only work honestly with the material he has been given, and prove his worth by expressing his 'sense of his own age'.

The second attitude is typical of the communist countries. The times can be changed, and the artist can play his small part in the change. His business is to communicate to the people, to play his small part in bringing about the utopia of the future. He must, of course, be an optimist.

This attitude is sometimes too quickly condemned in Western countries. Although it may not be desirable as an ultimate philosophy of art, it is often preferable to the gloomy subjectivism or sterile experimentalism of 'free artists'. Soviet literature and music has produced a great deal of 'popularist' trash; it has also produced many first-rate novels and operas. Social optimism may occasionally be a shallow and inadequate philosophy for the artist, but it is usually preferable to nihilism.

The third possible attitude is potentially the most fruitful; it is the artist's belief that both he *and his times* can be changed. Such an artist would combine the metaphysician with the social reformer. Kazantzakis is a modern example of the artist preoccupied by self-change; the proof of his genius lies in his accomplishment of the apparently impossible: the writing of a great epic poem. When most modern writers seem to be agreed that the chaos of time can be expressed only in some experimental, chaotic form like Pound's *Cantos*, Joyce's *Ulysses*, Sartre's *Roads to Freedom*, Kazantzakis ignores the impossibility of creating a modern heroic epic, and simply creates one. This could only have been done by a man who was accustomed to trying to change himself as well as the world, who believed that the artist is far more than a mere observer.

This is the problem of our time: to destroy the idea of man as a 'static observer', both in philosophy and art. All imaginative creation is involved with the three absolutes: freedom, evolution, religion.

NOTE

1. A full account of which is given in Vincent Brome's *Six Studies in Quarrelling*. A briefer account can be found in Cyril Connolly's *Enemies of Promise*. James's replies are, in many ways, of more interest than Wells's attack.

Note to Appendices

The following three appendices have all appeared at different times in the *London Magazine*, which I wish to thank for permission to reprint them. The article on Huxley, which has been considerably lengthened and rewritten, provides a convenient summary of the methods of existential criticism.

I have grouped together these three writers – Huxley, Dürrenmatt and Kazantzakis – because I feel they all begin from the same position of total amoralism ('All things are lawful'), and all make a genuine attempt to *create* a system of values. In this sense, they are more 'positive' than any other writers dealt with in this book. Kazantzakis, of course, is dead; it also seems unlikely that Mr Huxley will now make any major alterations in the position he has expounded so brilliantly over the past quarter of a century. Dürrenmatt, however, seems to me a different case; he has started from a position as 'existential' as Nietzsche's, and has already advanced far beyond Camus and Sartre as a creator of positive values. Because he seems to me to be a most important herald for the future, I have placed him at the end of this book.

Appendix One

Existential Criticism
and the Work of Aldous Huxley

Some of what I say may seem destructive, and to indicate an anti-Huxley bias. It may be as well, therefore, to emphasise two important facts about Huxley. One is that for the past twenty years his voice has stood for sanity and human dignity in a world that becomes increasingly like a nightmare. The other is that no one can have even the briefest contact with Huxley without becoming strongly aware of a gentleness and humility which indicate plainly that for him discipline and asceticism are not just abstract words. (A poet of the 1930s once described him to me as 'almost saint-like'.)

Bertrand Russell has stated that his aim in philosophy has always been 'to understand the world'. The most immediate difference between existential philosophising and abstract philosophy can be explained in this way: if Russell achieved his aim, and solved every problem of philosophy (as he understands it), he would have achieved a vision that would be a sort of glorified version of Newton's *Principia*. He would have solved the universe like a huge crossword puzzle. If an existential philosopher achieved his aim, the first problem he would understand would be the problem of human suffering, of man's relation to God (or to nothingness, if the followers of Sartre are right).

For the most central facts in the mind of the existential thinker are death and degeneration, the human capacity for self-delusion, the problem of human suffering and human happiness. He does not, like Hume, ask whether our senses are to be trusted when they tell us there is a tree in the quadrangle. He asks whether our emotions are to be trusted when they tell us that life is worth living, or not worth living.

The basic concept of existentialism is that of *the stature of man*. This sounds simple enough, as one pronounces the words. It would still sound simple if one changed it to 'the greatness of man' or 'the insignificance of man'. This is only because we have got used to accepting the problem as the province of the scientist. We would listen with perfect gravity to a discussion between, say, Sir Julian Huxley, the Astronomer Royal and Professor Jung on 'man's place in nature'. The existentialist would deny that any scientist is qualified to talk in general terms about 'man' as if 'science' was somehow in possession of 'the facts'. The existential philosopher would begin a discussion on the station of man by stating that there are times when he feels a worm, and that this problem is far more important than how long man has inhabited the earth.

Art is naturally concerned with man in his existential aspect, not in his scientific aspect. For the scientist, questions about man's stature and significance, suffering and power, are not really scientific questions; consequently, he is inclined to regard art as an inferior recreation. Unfortunately, the artist has come to accept the scientist's view of himself. The result, I contend, is that art in the twentieth century – literary art in particular – has ceased to take itself seriously as the primary instrument of existential philosophy. It has ceased to regard itself as an instrument for probing questions of human significance. *Art is the science of human destiny*. Science is the attempt to discern the order that underlies the chaos of nature; art is the attempt to discern the order that underlies the chaos of man. At its best, it evokes unifying emotions; it makes the reader see the world momentarily as a unity.

But first and foremost, art and existentialism are identified in this: they deal with the question of man's stature: is he a god or a worm?

Huxley's first publication was a volume of verse. In the earliest poetry, one detects the influence of Shelley; but already, in some of these poems, the Shelleyan poet gives up his attempt to see the world in 'poetic terms', and observes coldly its lack of dignity. This is the first and most important step in Huxley's development. Shelley was the romantic idealist, driven by a sense of the greatness of the human spirit. For him, there were moments when an appalling grandeur seemed to burst through man, when he felt that man could never be defeated by time or misery. Huxley found he could not sustain the burden of this idealism, and he pitched it off in favour of naturalism. Describing a conversation on top of a bus:

> 'Conservation of energy,' you say,
> But I burn, I tell you, I burn . . .

A long mythological poem, *Leda*, gives him an excuse for dwelling at length on one of his favourite subjects, seduction. Every one of Huxley's major novels, and many of his stories, contains a seduction or a rape. This is worth observing because of Huxley's ambivalent attitude to sex. Some critics have remarked on Huxley's 'Swiftian loathing' of the body; but sex – particularly the idea of the violation of innocence – fascinates him almost as much as it fascinated that other intellectual philosopher of the boudoir, De Sade. In the early Huxley, there is a certain attempt to 'disinfect' this interest in rape and seduction by writing of mythological subjects. Hence *Leda* and the translation of Malarmé's *L'Après-Midi d'un Faune*, the story 'Cynthia' in which the rape of Selene by Pan is re-enacted, and many shorter poems on such subjects as 'Nero and Sporus'.

In the poems, it seems that Huxley has reluctantly abandoned the poet's faith in the greatness of human feelings, but there is still a certain greatness in the intellectual honesty that replaces it. And there is a seductive literary charm and grace.

Huxley's first volume of stories follows, *Limbo*. Once again, we are aware of the two worlds. There is the world of human charm and grace, in a story like 'The Bookshop' (which Charles Lamb would have enjoyed); but the satirist creeps up in 'The Farcical History of Richard Greenow', the story of an 'intellectual' who changes into a sentimental female novelist by night. I would be inclined to rate 'Richard Greenow' as Huxley's finest single literary achievement; except in its final pages, it comes very close to perfection. There is a certain autobiographical element, and it is told without self-destructive irony.

This gentleness is also there in the first novel, *Crome Yellow*, which shows the influence of Peacock. The autobiographical element is focussed in Denis Stone, the young poet who goes to stay at Crome; but the irony has entered. The irony lies in the contrast between the Shelleyan world of Denis's poetry and his ineffectuality in love and worldly matters. The ineffectual idealist had been a familiar character in nineteenth-century Russian fiction (Turgeniev's Rudin, for example); but Huxley adds an element of mockery – apparently by way of self-protection. What is most important is that Denis scores no kind of triumph in the novel It is not about a man floundering and *then* gaining self-confidence.

This is a point worth underlining. Denis is the central figure; Huxley takes a great deal of trouble to enlist the reader's sympathy for him. The reader obligingly identifies himself with Denis. He would like to see him cut a better figure; he would like to see him get the girl and gain a little more self-respect. At the end of the book, Denis is still a shy, oversensitive poet, who can never get anything he really wants. But unlike other poetic failures in literature – Werther, Oblomov, Julien Sorel, Axel – Denis does not seem to enjoy his creator's sympathy; he gets a raw deal from every angle. Huxley's readers might have been forgiven for being puzzled. They were used to oversensitive heroes; most of them had read their Proust, their *Sinister Street*, their *Portrait of the Artist as a Young Man*. But Proust, Mackenzie and Joyce had taken care to indicate that the weakness of their characters was also a kind of strength (just as Shaw, in *Candida*, had expressed his feeling of the poet's ultimate triumph – after his failure in love – with the words 'But they do not know the secret in the poet's heart'). Huxley seems to be saying: If you are sensitive, there is no alternative to being unheroic and ineffectual. Denis is his first incarnation of the Chinless Intelligent hero.

There is, of course, an element in *Crome Yellow* that can be best understood in relation to the mood of postwar Bloomsbury. Lytton Strachey had created a mood for a whole generation when he wrote in a frankly personal and prejudiced manner about some eminent Victorians (1918). But this cannot be held wholly responsible for Huxley's switch from idealism to satire. Besides, Huxley brought to it a wholly new feeling of metaphysics; his satire is not historical, like Strachey's, but philosophical.

There are some interesting developments in his next novel, *Antic Hay* (1923). Once again, the central character is shy and oversensitive, and consequently frustrated in his emotional life. But Huxley is not yet ready to make his

200

meanings unequivocal, so Gumbril also receives the satirical treatment. From the opening chapter, you would suppose that the book is going to be a piece of objective and lighthearted satire, by a more intelligent Noël Coward. Gumbril buys a blond beard from a theatrical costumier, wears a coat with padded shoulders, and fortified by these aids to self-respect, goes into the world in search of heroic adventure. And heroism will include Getting the Girl – sexual conquest.

The blond beard is successful. His first appearance in it leads him into someone's bed. Later, the beard helps him to get the girl he is actually in love with. And when he wishes to seduce her, he removes the beard, and the seduction still goes forward without a hitch. Unfortunately, fate is still lying in wait with a sandbag. The girl deserts him because she is afraid of happiness, and he is left alone again, still oversensitive and frustrated. Moral: even if the sensitive man overcomes his ineffectuality, Fate will sneak up on him and get him from another angle. He can't win.

But this blond beard symbol has not yet yielded up its full significance. It is not simply a symbol of self-confidence. There is a section in a long poem, 'Soles Occidere et Redire Possunt', that elucidates it:

> 'Misery,' he said, 'to have no chin,
> Nothing but brains and sex and taste,
> Only omissively to sin,
> Weakly kind and cowardly chaste.
> But when the war is over,
> I will go to the East and plant
> Tea and rubber, and make much money,
> I will eat the black sweat of niggers
> And flagellate them with whips.
> I shall be enormously myself,
> Incarnate Chin.'

The first stanza paints the typical Huxley hero, the chinless, intelligent man. In the second, he dons the blond beard, he becomes Incarnate Chin. Yet he does so by an act of self-delusion, by convincing himself that he is God's gift to Africa. One is immediately reminded of Sartre's story, 'L'Enfance d'un Chef', in which another chinless, intelligent man conquers his oversensitivity by becoming a fanatical anti-semite. He refuses to bear the burden of

201

his sensitivity – the faculty that raises him above other men – and deliberately stupefies himself This is bad faith, another fundamental concept of existentialism. Huxley's implication is that Gumbril's histrionics in the blond beard are also an act of bad faith.

We might recall an axiom of another existential philosopher, Nietzsche: 'The great man is the play-actor of his own ideals' (*Beyond Good and Evil*). The existentialist problem is the problem of oversensitivity. It is self-analysis, knowledge, the 'tree of good and evil'. It makes the ancient hero impossible – the modern hero is Hamlet, Faust, Dostoevsky's Beetle Man who is contemptuous and envious of the man of action who 'lowers his head and charges like a bull'. (Huxley, like Dostoevsky, takes pleasure in comparing men to insects; Gumbril states: 'I glory in the name of earwig'). *Antic Hay* might be subtitled: *How Not to Be a Hamlet*. The solution that is briefly examined and rejected in this novel is: wear a blond beard.

But is it absolutely necessary that Not Being a Hamlet involves self-deception? Nietzsche obviously thought so. Play-acting is self-deception (presumably). In that case, living up to an ideal is also bad faith? This is implied in Huxley's rejection of Shelley in his early poetry. He found the Shelley ideal too difficult to live up to, and rejected it; to accept would have been bad faith.

But what, in that case, would be good faith? It would be simple, instinctive life, unreflective vitality. And this kind of instinctive living is impossible for the Hamlet, whose consciousness of the pleasure of living is diluted by reason. There is no turning back.

There is, perhaps, a possible solution, but it is not one that Huxley ever considers seriously. There are two ways of compensating for dilution. If your coffee is too weak, you can either add less water or use a stronger coffee. Huxley never ceases to jeer at the people who accept the first of these alternatives, the men incapable of reason; or – worse still – the men who abnegate reason and choose emotion. If one has reason, one must use it, even if the self-analysis dilutes one's consciousness until it is almost tasteless, until the appetite for life is enfeebled. But at this point one becomes aware of Huxley's most dangerous weakness: a certain frivolity, an ambiguity about his feelings. For he *might* choose the second alternative to intensify the will, to rise to heroic efforts of feeling and analysis, even if its implications seem tragic – as in Nietzsche or Kazantzakis. But Huxley is too much the epicurean, too addicted to posing, to accept this answer to the problem he postulates. He is the satirist, not the saint. He will jeer at stupidity, but he has no inclination to be a martyr for 'truth'. Not yet, anyway.

His ambiguous attitude to his own work becomes apparent in his next novel, *Those Barren Leaves*. This shows a sad falling off in quality from *Antic Hay*. Huxley is now content to be the pet of Bloomsbury, the witty essayist, the cultured scourge of intellectual shams and lukewarm eroticism. The book is a leisurely, self-satisfied piece of work, a boring feat of social comedy and intellectual agility that is probably the most effete thing Huxley ever wrote. In *Antic Hay* he had satirised the overcultured Mr Mercaptan with his devotion to Crébillon *fils* and his witty little essays published in a highbrow weekly; *Those Barren Leaves* might have been written by Mercaptan.

Point Counter Point (1928) is a return to seriousness, but it shows some of Huxley's worst mannerisms making inroads in his work. Manifestly influenced by Gide's *Les Faux Monnayeurs* (as the opening of *Antic Hay* was influenced by *Ulysses*), it tackles the Hamlet problem, the problem of bad faith, as honestly as Huxley is capable of attacking it. He is at last in the open, with no pretence at lighthearted satire. There are three major characters in it: Philip Quarles (Huxley's mouthpiece), Rampion – a portrait of D. H. Lawrence, and Spandrell, apparently inspired by Stavrogin in Dostoevsky's *Devils*, a man without motive or conviction, clever, rich and bored. Spandrell illustrates Huxley's usual ambiguity of attitude, for in an essay on Baudelaire, published at the same time as *Point Counter Point*, there is a violent condemnation of Dostoevsky, with special reference to Stavrogin.

Philip's marriage is menaced by his own dehydrated intellectuality, and by Everard Webley, the leader of the League of British Fascists. (This showed remarkable anticipation on Huxley's part; in 1928, Hitler was still an unknown agitator, and Mosley a young socialist.) Webley is in love with Philip's wife. On this level, the novel contains the usual Huxley antinomies: Chinless Intellect versus Big-chinned Bad Faith. But Rampion-Lawrence

203

appears as a type of man preferable to either. Philip reflects:

Being with Rampion rather depresses me; for he makes me see what a great gulf separates the knowledge of the obvious from the actual living of it. And oh! the difficulties of crossing the gulf. [Note here one of Huxley's most irritating mannerisms – the habit of old-maidish exclamation and apostrophe.] I perceive now that the real charm of the intellectual life . . . is its easiness. It's the substitution of simple intellectual schemata for the complexes of reality . . . it's much easier to be an intellectual child or a lunatic than a harmonious adult man.

This, then, is the aim of Huxley's work: to create a picture of the 'harmonious, adult man', Gumbril's Complete Man. But it would seem as if Rampion was included rather as a compliment to Lawrence than as a tenable solution of the problem of the Complete Man. Rampion is rather a bore (as Lawrence himself found him on reading the novel). There may even be an element of dishonesty in the portrait, for Huxley has created a far more scathing, and rather more convincing, picture of Lawrence, as Kingham in *Two or Three Graces*. At one point in the novel, Rampion attacks Shelley for bad faith – for being a 'bloodless white worm' of idealism (Huxley has a talent for disgusting images), who lost contact with Mother Earth. But Back-to-Nature Rampion does not seem Mother Earth's answer to Shelley's failure. Huxley obviously wanted to portray the nature-god type of artist – the type that Thomas Mann thought Goethe and Tolstoy represented – but his artistry failed to rise to the occasion. Rampion resembles Tolstoy in expressing a dislike of Beethoven – in this case, the third movement of Opus 132 – but the effect he produces is a kind of undergraduate cantankerousness. Rampion is too unreflective to be heroic – like his original.

In his soliloquy on the 'harmonious adult man', Philip has touched on another existentialist problem: that of authentic and inauthentic existence. Inauthentic existence is almost another name for bad faith, but with this difference: bad faith is a form of *deliberate* self-deception, inauthentic existence may be simply a mistake. A man has not committed bad faith until 'knowing the good, he chooses the bad'. When a man discovers that he is half

204

living instead of living, he has achieved a degree of self-knowledge that demands that he dismantle his life and personality and start building again from the bottom. Philip is living an inauthentic existence, and he knows it; it worries him. He actually tries at one point in the book, to commit 'bad faith' by seducing a plump and silly woman whom he doesn't really want, merely to feel himself 'the conqueror', the seducer. This doesn't work either.

Spandrell, the other major character in the book, is also intelligent enough to perceive that he is living an inauthentic existence, a life of seductions, boredoms, witty conversation – worthless and stupid. He tells himself that he is different from his loquacious companions in one important respect – he is capable of action. To prove this to himself, he murders Everard Webley, the fascist leader. This proves his point, but it doesn't make the action seem morally significant. He has so far lost touch with the springs of his own vitality that he is like a man without a compass in a desert. Instead of setting out to disicpline himself to recover his 'compass', he prefers to commit suicide.

Point Counter Point is superficial, bloodless, observed. It intellectualises in preference to attempting to enter into, to participate, to feel. It satirises with the precision of a butcher cutting up a pig, but there is something disgusting in the massacre of all the characters. Worst of all, it shows Huxley's faults growing like ivy.

These are worth speaking about in some detail. To begin with there is his habit of exclamation and apostrophe. This gives his prose a feminine, effete quality, which later prevents one from taking his religious philosophising seriously. More important is the ruminative habit, the essayistic manner. He is too fond of telling the reader at great length what his characters are feeling. Added to this is a stylistic trick: padding out his work with repetition. This is partly necessitated by the long digressions, for Huxley assumes (rightly) that the reader has forgotten what he said when he started to digress, and repeats it, usually with the transparent trick of pretending that his character is doing the repeating. This is a typical example from one of his earliest stories, 'Eupompus Gave Splendour to Art by Numbers':

205

'I have made a discovery,' said Emberlin as I entered his room. 'What about?' I asked.

'A discovery,' he replied, 'about *Discoveries*.' He radiated an unconcealed satisfaction; the conversation had evidently gone exactly as he had intended it to go. He had made his phrase, and repeated it lovingly – 'A discovery about *Discoveries*.'

The only effect of these repetitions is to hold up the flow of the story. An unkind critic once suggested that Huxley disguised his essays as novels, and padded them shamelessly, because a novel sells better than a volume of essays. There may be some truth in this assertion. In a few cases, Huxley might argue that the repetition is stylistically necessary; but this is not often so. I open the volume of his short stories at random, and find on the first page:

'My dear boy,' he kept repeating, 'it *is* a pleasure to see you. My dear boy . . .'
Jacobsen limply abandoned his forearm and waited in patience.
'I can never be grateful enough,' Mr Petherton went on – 'never grateful enough to you for having taken all this trouble to come and see a decrepit old man – for that's what I am now, that's what I am, believe me!'

One begins to suspect that, like Dumas, Huxley was being paid by the line. The habit never left him:

In their little house on the common, how beautifully the Claxtons lived, how spiritually! Even the cat was a vegetarian – at any rate officially – even the cat . . .

As the twenties drew to an end, the slow-motion habit seemed to grow on Huxley. The opening of *Point Counter Point* is typical:

'You won't be late?' There was anxiety in Marjorie Carling's voice, there was something like entreaty.
'No, I won't be late,' said Walter, unhappily and guiltily certain that he would be. Her voice annoyed him. It drawled a little, it was too refined – even in misery.
'Not later than midnight.' She might have reminded him of the time when he never went out in the evenings without her. She might have done so; but she wouldn't; it was against her principles; she didn't want to force his love in any way . . .

And so on, with infinitely slow uncoiling. (Shaw has a brilliant parody of the various methods of padding in the article in which he rewrites the last scene of *Macbeth* as a chapter of a novel by Bennett; 'He was going to fail after

206

all then. The day was going against him. His men were not really fighting . . .')

A final example of the slow-motion style. This is from the beginning of a short novel *After the Fireworks*:

'Late as usual. Late.' Judd's voice was censorious. The words fell sharp, like beak-blows. 'As though I were a nut,' Miles Fanning thought resentfully, 'and he were a woodpecker. And yet he's devotion itself, he'd do anything for me. Which is why, I suppose, he feels entitled to crack my shell every time he sees me.' And he came to the conclusion, as he had so often come before, that he didn't really like Colin Judd at all. 'My oldest friend, whom I quite definitely don't like. Still . . .' Still, Judd was an asset, Judd was worth it.

'Here are your letters,' the sharp voice continued.

Later on, the same story has a fine example of Huxley's trick of ruminating. Miles Fanning comments: 'A world without goodness – it'd be Paradise'. Then for five long paragraphs, Huxley analyses the thoughts and feelings of his characters at length – for about a thousand words. Finally, he gets back to the point he left from: 'He had been, for some obscure reason, suddenly depressed by his own last words. "A world without goodness – it'd be Paradise." ' Here, Huxley has no alternative but to repeat the sentence, since he has held up the action by two pages of rumination, and can hardly expect the reader to remember what Fanning's last words were.

After the Fireworks provides several more examples of Huxleys weakness as a creative writer. It is a very long story – more than a hundred pages – whose essentials could be compressed into a thousand words. A famous novelist, fifty years of age, receives a fan letter from a pretty girl of twenty-one. He meets her, takes her out for meals, and she ends by becoming his mistress. Then he gets tired of her, she is upset by his coldness, and ends by leaving him for a less intelligent but more faithful young man.

The story bears the signs of being a wish-fulfilment fantasy, rather like Rolfe's *Desire and Pursuit of the Whole*. It seems to have no more 'point' than Hemingway's similar exercise in sexual self-aggrandisement in *Across the River and Into the Trees*. It is interesting to note the way that Huxley handles the scenes in which Fanning and Pamela become acquainted. Fanning is supposed to be a

207

fountain of witty and sophisticated conversation. His remark about a world without goodness is a fair sample of his 'sophistication'. The 'witty conversation' consists in endless intellectual theorising, which progresses by Huxley's usual essayistic method – association of ideas. To speak of Huxley's 'wit' is rather misleading; there is very little in his writing that reminds one of Oscar Wilde or Sydney Smith. He takes no trouble to conceal the processes of thought by which he arrives at his *bon mots* – on the contrary, he takes pleasure in showing the reader every single step of his thought progressions, complete with references to painters and musicians one is unlikely to have heard of, and quotations in foreign languages. Once one gets used to his habit of thought, one can recognise the *bon mot* in the distance; he signals it as a bad boxer signals a punch. It is not unlike Chesterton's habit of paradox that makes his later writing so monotonously predictable. The consequence of all this is that the reader simply cannot believe that Fanning is sexually attractive to Pamela, and the final seduction seems downright incredible. The reader seems to hear Fanning's highly cultured monologues in a fluting, sexless voice that trips skilfully through quotations in Italian and Latin. Nothing could be more conducive to dissipating a young girl's infatuation. At times, the Huxleyan 'wit' becomes as ponderous and stylised as the 'conceits' of Elizabethan poetry, involving long metaphors and far-fetched comparisons. Philip Quarles is right; in some indefinable way, Huxley is quite out of touch with reality and this story contains all his faults in capsule form.

The problem is that Huxley would regard it as bad faith to stop intellectualising, and yet while he intellectualises, he delays indefinitely the act of starting to create. This paradox is revealed clearly in the volume of essays that followed *Point Counter Point – Do What You Will* – where Huxley seems determined to escape the limitations of his intellectualism. In an essay on Swift, he attacks Swift for his maniacal loathing of the body and its functions. In *Francis and Gregory*, he compares St Francis unfavourably with Rasputin, emphasising Rasputin's Whitmanesque love of the body. In the essay on Baudelaire already mentioned, he praises Robert Burns and attacks Dostoevsky as a kind of emotional masturbator who created

208

characters without bodies. He criticises Pascal for allowing his religion to be influenced by his sickness.

The strange thing is that Huxley's novels contain all the faults he condemned – the distaste for the body and its functions, the fear of positive belief, the dilettantism, the bodiless characters which he condemns in Dostoevsky. He also has a sick man's hatred of illness (he was bedridden for a part of his childhood, and was almost blind for many years). At the end of *After the Fireworks*, Pamela's infatuation for Fanning finally dissolves when he is ill, and she has to nurse him. The notion that two people might be drawn closer together by such an experience never seems to enter Huxley's mind. His own appetite for life is so easily undermined by the sight of illness that he cannot imagine that healthy people might find illness less disgusting. This is the very essence of Huxley's failure as an artist. He is so firmly entrenched in his own weaknesses that he can never escape them, even in imagination, or create a character who is free from them. In this respect, he resembles Graham Greene.

In 1931 there was an amusing and instructive exchange between Huxley and Ernest Hemingway, which shows two quite different kinds of conceit at loggerheads. In an essay called 'Foreheads Villainous Low', Huxley criticised Hemingway:

In *A Farewell to Arms*, Mr Ernest Hemingway ventures once, to name an Old Master. There is a phrase, quite admirably expressive (for Mr Hemingway is a most subtle and sensitive writer), a single phrase, no more, about the 'bitter nail-holes' of Mantegna's Christs: then quickly, quickly, appalled by his own temerity, the author passes on (as Mrs Caskell might hastily have passed on, if she had somehow been betrayed into mentioning a water-closet), passes on shamefacedly to speak of the Lower Things.'

Huxley went on to say that once upon a time the stupid tried to be thought educated; now the snobbery was inverted, and the educated wanted to appear stupid. It seems unbelievable that Huxley, who was an enthusiastic admirer of Lawrence, should be unable to sense the merit of *A Farewell to Arms*, with its technique of detachment and understatement. Or at least, if he *did* sense it, that he should be unable to see that references to Mantegna could only weaken a book like *A Farewell to Arms*.[1]

Hemingway replied to these criticisms in *Death in the Afternoon*, which shares with *Green Hills of Africa* the distinction of being his worst book, full of fake simplicity, fake toughness and fake wisdom. Hemingway came back with violent counter-charges that were as unfair to Huxley as Huxley had been to him, declaring that a writer who spices his books with culture must be a faker who wants to show off. He talked gravely about the writer's responsibility to create people, not characters, and offered other generalisations to prove that, for all his casualness, he was a serious artist. But just as Huxley had missed the real quality of the best Hemingway – which uses detachment to convey intense love of the physical world in spite of its brutality – so Hemingway seems to have had no awareness of the quality that makes 'Richard Greenow' and *Antic Hay* minor masterpieces. This failure of understanding is a revelation of the weaknesses of both. The very qualities that caused Huxley's deterioration – intellectuality and affectation – are the qualities Hemingway despises; the qualities that caused Hemingway's deterioration – conceit, intellectual laziness – are the qualities that Huxley despises. A combination of Huxley and Hemingway would probably be a very great writer. As it is, the two writers are mirrors each faithfully reflecting the fatal weakness of the other.

Huxley's worst qualities – the self-satisfied intellectuality of *Those Barren Leaves* and the desire to be regarded as Bloomsbury's brilliant *enfant terrible* – disappear after 1930; but the long-winded style remains, the unrealistic treatment of sex remains, and, worst of all, the 'weakness premise' remains. He cannot believe that human strength can exist, or conceive it imaginatively. His boring portrait of old John Bidlake, the painter (based on Augustus John?) in *Point Counter Point*, proves this; this character is always identified by a Huxleyan leitmotif, a 'booming Rabelaisian laugh'. (These leitmotifs are a sign of Huxley's uninventiveness, and recur in all his novels, another aspect of his tendency to repeat himself.)

The usual ambiguity and self-division are apparent in *Brave New World* (1931). Intellectually, the book is an exposure of the communist-humanist fallacy that man is

210

perfectible and needs only better social conditions; Huxley argues for imagination and poetry. But the central character is once again the Chinless Intelligent man. The book deserves high praise: it is brilliant, amusing, penetrating, intelligent. But it is also negative. The existential problem – How not to be a Hamlet – is still unanswered. The book is an argument against mere reason and common sense. Enlightened sexual relationships are exposed as boring and meaningless. A high standard of education makes for mediocrity. The book argues for 'inner direction', for the personal against impersonal, for the poetry of Shakespeare against the economics of Marx. Yet though Huxley is so expert at exposing the meaningless and boring, the unvital and futile, he has no creative power to express the vital, the heroic. In making his Chinless Intelligent man the hero of the book and the rebel against the ethics of the brave new world, Huxley seems to be setting the seal of his approval on his weaknesses, as if saying 'Keep your neuroses and obsessions; without them, you would be a mediocrity like the others'. If this is so, then Huxley has abandoned all attempt to solve the problem of the 'harmonious' man.

I have commented that the earlier Huxley seemed sneakingly ashamed of himself for not being more serious, for not being willing to be a 'martyr for truth'. After his orgy of satire in *Brave New World*, Huxley seemed to experience a revulsion for the old intellectual dilettante who had written *Those Barren Leaves*. *Point Counter Point* seems to have been modelled on Gide, and *Brave New World* on Zamiatin; his next major novel seems to be inspired by Proust. (Characteristically, there is a sneering reference to Proust in its early pages.) *Eyeless in Gaza* is Huxley's major attempt to find an ideal to live by, to abandon the old universal scepticism and commit himself to a faith. However, the Proustian influence seems to have been only a starting point, which led him to play tricks with the time sequence of the chapters. It also serves to emphasise the main theme of the book – the need for the 'timeless' reality. The main character is once again the over-sensitive modest man. Like Philip Quarles, he keeps a journal. But unlike any previous Huxley hero, he is interested in religion, in mysticism, and in the problem of man's responsibility to other men. The plot of the book is largely the mixture as before: weakness, vanity, self-delusion. There is a character called Gerry Watchett who is Huxley's usual cad – vulgar, handsome, treacherous and highly successful in love. There is the usual high percentage of seductions and rapes – all of them curiously unrealistic. At the end of the book, the hero goes to a pacifist meeting where he knows he will be beaten up. A carping critic might object that, in view of Huxley's scrambling of time in the rest of the book, there is a certain inconsistency in finishing the book on this note of heroism. However, in spite of all the usual Huxley faults, the book is certainly an attempt to be serious and positive. It is a pity that the author's good intentions are hindered by his compulsion to portray all his characters either as unpleasant or as weak and miserable.

Eyeless in Gaza was followed by an excellent critical book, *Ends and Means*, in which the religious and political conclusions of the novel are stated with more force and persuasiveness. Again, it affords striking evidence of how positive and creative Huxley could be when merely *thinking* about problems. The volume is an attempt to 'relate the problems of domestic and international politics of war and economics ... to a theory of the ultimate nature of reality'. Huxley's view of the ultimate nature of reality corresponds with that of the *Bhagavad Gita* and the Christian mystics, and is present in everything he has written since 1936. In a certain sense, Huxley had ended his spiritual pilgrimage when he decided that there is an absolute spiritual reality, and that man's sole business is to know it, vitally and immediately.

And yet, creatively speaking, he was as far as ever from his absolute. Just as *Brave New World* had been a reversion to the manner of *Antic Hay*, and *Eyeless in Gaza* to that of *Point Counter Point*, so his new novel *After Many a Summer* was a reversion to *Crome Yellow*.

The novel is set in California. An English 'belle-lettrist' (i.e., a literary dilettante), Jeremy Pordage, has gone to California to edit some papers for an unpleasant million-aire named Stoyte, who lives in an imitation castle with his pretty young mistress Virginia and a suave Casanova of a doctor, Obispo. Huxley's mouthpiece – there has to be one in every book – is an Englishman named Propter, who spends a great deal of his time talking about God and

Reality. In many ways, *After Many a Summer* is one of Huxley's best books – provided, that is, you accept the convention of a discussion novel, varied with light comedy, satire and sex. Jeremy Pordage is one of Huxley's alter egos, bookish, shy and well-meaning. Obispo is as silly as most of Huxley's diabolists; he is perhaps the most embarrassing of Huxley's alter egos, the amoral amorist whose electric fingers are guaranteed to make any girl writhe with sexual ecstasy. ('Dr Obispo had engineered her escape into an erotic epilepsy more excruciatingly intense than anything she had known before or even imagined possible.') The reader becomes aware that Huxley's idea of sex is strangely adolescent, as idealistically unreal as – though less detailed than – a schoolboy's accounts of his sexual conquests. Obispo is a cruel, coarse lovemaker, with no finesse, a man without emotions, who treats sex purely as a physical exercise, but in this exercise he has a devilish skill that can play on a girl's body as if it were a harp, rousing it to an insanity of lust . . . And so on. Huxley's sex scenes have the air of having been written by a fourteen-year-old virgin with a vivid imagination.

The main conflict of the book between the saintly Propter and the selfish millionaire (who is, however, by no means wholly bad – only stupid), provides *After Many a Summer* with its main interest, and is superbly done. But Propter has long chunks of discourse that might have been lifted straight out of any of Huxley's later books. Moreover, there is something very subtly unsatisfying about all his talk about 'absolute reality', no matter how much one sympathises basically. The same thing is wrong with all the religious ideas of the later Huxley, as expressed in *The Perennial Philosophy* and *Grey Eminence*. For all his attempts to escape his limitations, Huxley is still a kind of Manichee, a man who will never feel a Whitmanesque acceptance of the world. He cannot control his dislike. As Propter inveighs against the selfishness of industrialists and the stupidity of dictators, one continues to feel that this is still the world-hater of *Point Counter Point*, the man whose influence in the twenties had turned Lawrence into a clumsy and malicious satirist. There is something wrong. He is still not Holy Huxley. His knowledge of 'the way' of Brahman is curiously dehydrated, bodiless. The knowledge that Hemingway possesses so abundantly – of the goodness of physical reality – is missing.

And yet *After Many a Summer* remains a splendid book. This is partly due to the presence of Jeremy Pordage, who represents the best side of Huxley, the love of literature and of the past, the Huxley who is a not-too-distant relation of Charles Lamb. One suspects that the Huxley who began to develop with *Those Barren Leaves* was an appalling mistake, a series of attempts to graft onto this original Huxley various misconceived alter egos: the ruthless satirist Huxley, Huxley the castigator of morals, Huxley the saint, Huxley the professor.

This becomes more apparent in the book that followed *After Many a Summer – Grey Eminence*, a study of Father Joseph of Paris, the spiritual adviser of Richelieu. Here Huxley shows himself to be a born historian; some of his evocations of the Thirty Years War are more moving and exciting than anything in the novels. On the whole, it is probable that *Grey Eminence* is Huxley's best book. It allows opportunity for the expression of all his best qualities – the sharp intellect, the love of the past – and for none of the bad ones: malice, the sexual obsession, cleverness for its own sake.

The superiority of the essayist Huxley becomes more obvious when one compares his later novels with the works of non-fiction. Each novel is followed by a non-fiction book: *Time Must Have a Stop* (1944) by *The Perennial Philosophy*, *Ape and Essence* (1948) by *The Devils of Loudun*, *The Genius and the Goddess* by *Adonis and the Alphabet* (called in America *Tomorrow and Tomorrow and Tomorrow*). *Time Must Have a Stop* is another reversion to the early Huxley, with the shy schoolboy hero who spends his time in an agony of embarrassment. (One wonders why it is that Huxley is drawn back so persistently to memories of childhood and adolescent humiliation.) It actually borrows one episode from *Antic Hay* (the play scene with the prostitute) and involves the new hero in it. It has some excellent and lively scenes and embodies Huxley's ideas on what happens after death – one of the characters dies, and is shown going through a process that owes something to the Tibetan *Bardo Thodol*. It has the usual proportion of highly unpleasant people, the usual unreal scenes of seduction (always involving agonies of lust), the usual 'weakness premise' about the hero, and the expected lectures on the absolute. It might be added, though, that during the course of the book, the hero is shown growing up, and has become slightly less weak by the end.

The Perennial Philosophy is an anthology of mysticism, connected with commentaries by Huxley. It *ought* to be in every way a satisfying volume – for anyone who is interested in religion – yet for some reason it is strangely cloying and irritating. This may be for the reason I have tried to suggest – that Huxley becomes a little too much the parson in his pulpit. It may also be due to a suspicion on the part of the reader that Huxley's knowledge of these states of mystical ecstasy and affirmation is all very theoretical. In spite of Huxley's intentions, *The Perennial Philosophy* is not a religious book, only a book *about* religion.

The short novel *Ape and Essence* is entirely pessimistic; it shows the society of the future reduced to murderous barbarism. It is generally agreed to be a very bad book. (If it had appeared more modestly, in a volume of short stories, judgment on it might have been less harsh.) Its non-fiction counterpart is *Brave New World Revisited*, which was not published until 1960; this is an equally gloomy account of the problems of overpopulation, brainwashing, and various other evils of our civilisation. The section called 'What can be done?' has no solution to offer, except (perhaps the only one possible) that we can be 'educated to freedom'.

The Devils of Loudun, which followed *Ape and Essence*, is a pendant to *Grey Eminence*, and is very nearly as good. The 'demonic possession' of the Loudun nuns had been briefly mentioned in the earlier book, together with a short account of the trial and execution of the priest Urbain Grandier. Huxley takes his usual delight in describing the sexual escapades of Grandier, the 'goat in a biretta', and a feeling of frustrated sexuality hangs over the book like a fog. In spite of this, the book has some of Huxley's best pages.

This was followed in 1954 by *The Doors of Perception*, Huxley's account of his mescalin experiments, which contains the interesting admission:

215

I am and . . . always have been a poor visualiser. Words, even the pregnant words of poets, do not evoke pictures in my mind . . . When I recall something, the memory does not present itself to me as a vividly seen event or object. By an effort of will, I can evoke a not very vivid image of what happened yesterday afternoon, of how the Lungarno used to look before the bridges were destroyed, of the Bayswater Road when the only buses were green and tiny and drawn by aged horses . . . But such images have little substance, and absolutely no autonomous life of their own. They stand to real, perceived objects in the same relation as Homer's ghost stood to . . . men of flesh and blood . . . To those in whom the faculty of visualisation is strong my inner world must seem curiously drab, limited and uninteresting.

All this can easily be guessed from Huxley's novels. It is what makes them basically unsatisfying. Huxley's world lacks life, lacks atmosphere, lacks vitality, lacks the smell and colour and feel of the real world.

Huxley argues that mescalin should become generally available to the public, and that it would probably replace alcohol and tobacco as a stimulant. It would also help to combat the problem of the 'civilisation neurosis' that causes so many of our social problems – particularly crime and suicide. This seems a reasonable argument, and yet it has raised strong resistance, particularly from the churches and from some of Mr Huxley's 'fellow seekers' (like Arthur Koestler). The objection is that 'divine insight' induced by drugs is a very different thing from divine insight produced by long ascetic discipline. There is an obvious element of truth in this. The 'visionary experience' in itself is nothing, what matters is the ability of the perceiving mind to grasp its significance and to relate it back to 'everyday experience'. Huxley, in a sense, was the ideal subject for the mescalin experiments, having spent a lifetime in a barren intellectual discipline. The consequence is that his two books about mescalin, *The Doors of Perception* and *Heaven and Hell*, contain some fascinating psychological insights. But for minds with no kind of discipline, the mescalin experience might well be as meaningless as getting drunk or having casual sex. Worse still – as some subsequent investigators have pointed out – it may intensify all the morbid elements in the mind, and plunge the mescalin taker into hell instead of heaven. It is obvious, from accounts by less disciplined and talented

216

writers, that the significance of the mescalin vision depends entirely upon the taker.

At the time of writing (1961), Huxley's most recent novel is *The Genius and the Goddess*, which is really no more than a long short story. The central incident of the book occurs when Maartens, a famous scientist, is dying from a self-induced illness, and his wife Katy is also exhausted and miserable, so that she cannot 're-charge his batteries' from her own vitality. Then, accidentally, she becomes the mistress of her husband's handsome young assistant; her vitality is restored, and she is able to save her husband from death. The Huxley sex mystique has now begun to bear a distinct resemblance to the ideas of D. H. Lawrence.

Besides telling the love story of John Rivers and Katy Maartens, *The Genius and the Goddess* is also another sermon on the ills of our civilisation, and on how we all ought to try harder to be holy. In one of his least convincing moments, Huxley confides to the reader that the fat Negro servant is 'well along the road to saint-hood': Beulah's goodness is about as convincing as Spandrell's wickedness.

But in some ways, *The Genius and the Goddess* is an immense advance on anything Huxley has written before. It is a comparatively healthy and breezy story; the portrait of Katy's daughter, the morbid poetess Ruth, is altogether delightful. It may have been the release of the mescalin experiment that gave the novel its unusual vitality, its almost good-humoured tone. Huxley has written nothing so relaxed and human since 'Richard Greenow'. With less sermonising, and a less catastrophic ending, the book might have been Huxley's masterpiece.

To try to summarise: each of Huxley's books has been a move towards a synthesis. He has come a very long way indeed, from the shallow frivolity of *Those Barren Leaves* to the attempt at a moral synthesis in *The Genius and the Goddess* (whose main lesson – condemnation of the egotistic intellectual Maartens – is also a condemnation of the early Huxley). His early self-portraits, in Denis Stone and Theodore Gumbril, show fundamentally decent young men who are too preoccupied with their own worries and embarrasments. The later books show these young men developing into socially responsible individuals with a certain grasp of religious 'fundamentals'.

217

This is as far as 'literary criticism' can go – to consider the artist's aims, and how far he has achieved them. It is by considering the general 'unsatisfactoriness' of all Huxley's work that literary criticism attempts to expand into existential criticism. One reason for this sense of 'something lacking' I have already suggested: Huxley's attitude to the physical world, which is never far from that of Sartre in *La Nausée*. It takes very little to disgust him. One has only to compare the deathbed scenes in *Point Counter Point* or *Eyeless in Gaza* with Tolstoy's death of Count Bezukhov in *War and Peace* or Trollope's death of the bishop in *Barchester Towers*, to realise that Huxley is always too near the borderline of 'nausea'. And yet to have a dim appreciation of the physical world is not necessarily a disadvantage to a writer, as we can see in the case of Dostoevsky. Unfortunately, although he is serious, Huxley never takes himself *that* seriously. He can never escape a tendency to do intellectual cartwheels and handstands; he can never escape from his own frivolity.

When I was writing the first version of this article, I was also engaged on a book that attempted to define the 'weakness premise' in a great deal of modern literature, and the general 'unheroic hypothesis' that is exemplified in Huxley's writing. I had some correspondence with him on the subject of the hero, which he has given me permission to quote.

The study of literature and art is surely a very indirect and inadequate way of studying the total human situation, if only because many of the most significant aspects of that situation simply don't lend themselves to treatment in literature. For example, how can anyone write a play, poem or novel about the pressure of population on resources?

This paragraph shows Huxley's typical later preoccupation with social problems. The obverse side of the coin is his unwillingness to admit that the writer's task may be to speak about the human will rather than about the problems of civilisation. When I suggested that his heroes never learn to act, he replied by retorting that some of the literature of the 'Angry Young Men' showed the same deficiency, adding that '*Look Back in Anger* is surely far more negative than anything I have been guilty of; for it is merely the story of a neurotic who wallows in his neurosis and refuses to come to terms with the kind of universe wc have been born into.' On the general problem of the 'hero', he commented:

Perhaps the decline of the hero in a large-scale social context is the obscure realisation of the fact that such a hero is merely a substitute for good government, a man who makes up by his good qualities and improvised actions for deficiencies in a social order.

Another paragraph is even more important in grasping Huxley's general attitude to writing:

I don't feel that the hero becomes heroic in passing from self-analysis to belief. He becomes heroic in using intelligence and love to do good in minutely organised particulars – and doing good, let it be remembered, to people each of whom is unique and has his or her particular need to have love and the fruits of intelligence applied in a specific and unique way. This is the kind of hero I hope some day to be able to portray.

This is certainly consistent with the type of hero Huxley tried to create in *Time Must Have a Stop* (in the figure of the Italian pacifist), or in Mr Propter in *After Many a Summer* – perhaps even in the Negro Beulah in *The Genius and the Goddess*. But it is significant that these characters are *not* the 'heroes' of the books in which they appear – they are incidental. The problem of the hero is the problem of the 'Complete Man' posed in *Antic Hay* or the 'harmonious adult man' posed in *Point Counter Point*. It is interesting to reflect that, in 1928, Huxley published his sketch of the 'harmonious adult man' (Rampion) in *Point Counter Point*, and at the same time declared his preference for the 'lovers of the body' (Burns, Rabelais, Rasputin) in *Do What You Will*. (The title itself is a tribute to Blake, another glorifier of the physical world.) And yet ten years later, his 'new hero' was the talkative Mr Propter, who is more the type of the Christian saint than of the Nietzschean superman. The flaw in all of Huxley's heroes, from Denis Stone to Sebastian Barnack (in *Time Must Have a Stop*) is excess of self analysis, *the dilution of the vital forces by thought*. To create a satisfactory hero, this balance would have to be righted. Yet Huxley's attack on Hemingway in 1931 shows that he has no intention of righting it by dealing with the problem of *increasing the vitality*. The physical world remains absent from his books, except in a rather dim way, seen through an intellectual prism. (One of the consequences of this lack of contact with the physical is his overestimate of the power of sex.) Finally, there is an artificial resolution of the problem in *Eyeless in Gaza*, where Anthony Beavis accepts mysticism and pacifism. Huxley seems unaware of how close he has come to Marjorie Carling of *Point Counter Point*, whom he satirised for allowing religion to comfort her for her broken love life. The need for a different attitude to physical reality – something closer to that of Burns – is forgotten; instead, man must turn away from this disappointing physical world (which was never much more than dust and ashes) and strive for unity with the absolute. Self-respect will come from doing good; the split personality will be united by intuitive experience of the Godhead.

Huxley's work makes one aware of the hopeless inadequacy of 'literary criticism', the need for standards that get at 'fundamentals'. This is one of the highest compliments that can be paid to a writer.

NOTE

1. I have not been able to locate this reference to Mantegna in *A Farewell to Arms*, and as Hemingway was apparently unable to remember writing it, I am inclined to believe that Huxley was thinking of some other book.

Appendix Two

Nikos Kazantzakis

Five of Kazantzakis' major works have been published in translation in England, and even more in America, and yet his name remains almost totally unknown. This is a curious situation, which may be due in part to the fact that Kazantzakis wrote in Greek, and that modern readers do not expect to come upon an important Greek writer. Even his name was a discouraging sound: if he had written in Russian and been called Kazantzovsky, his works would no doubt be as universally known and admired as Sholokov's. There is something of tragedy in this. Readers who are familiar with his life and works have no doubt that here is a writer who can stand with the nineteenth-century giants, with Tolstoy, Dostoevsky, Nietzsche (with all of whom he has affinities). Yet he made very little money from his writing, and the *Columbia Dictionary of Modern European Literaure* does not even mention him.

When writing about Kazantzakis, it is difficult to avoid the over-coloured words associated with Nietzsche and Dostoevsky, 'suffering giant', 'spiritual torment', etc. They were appropriate enough in the nineteenth century, but seem out of place in our own. The truth is that Kazantzakis was a man of the nineteenth century; he is too much the primitive for the age of Freud and Joyce. An extraordinary incident in his life illustrates this. In May 1922, when he was thirty-nine, Kazantzakis was living in Vienna. He had passed through two important periods: an early period of total romanticism, strongly influenced by D'Annunzio and Nietzsche, and then a period of Christian asceticism when Christ became his ideal symbol. Then he discovered the Buddha, and began to practise total renunciation, at the same time writing an immense verse drama on Gautama. (This was eventually published in 1956.) One evening in the theatre Kazantzakis fell into conversation with a most attractive woman who was sitting next to him. They left the theatre together and walked the streets until late, discussing ideas. Finally, Kazantzakis invited her back to his room. She explained that she could not come immediately, but would come the following evening. The next morning, Kazantzakis woke to find that his lips had swelled and the flesh of his face was becoming bloated. He wrote to the woman, asking her to come the next day instead. However his flesh was even more swollen on the next day, and his lower lip began to run with a yellow liquid. The meeting had to be indefinitely postponed. Some weeks later, Kazantzakis attended the theatre, his face swathed in bandages. He was approached by a stranger who asked him if he would mind answering a question. Kazantzakis agreed. The man asked what role eroticism played in his life. Kazantzakis was shocked. The man then introduced himself as Wilhelm Stekel, the psychiatrist, and he asked Kazantzakis to call and see him the next day. Kazantzakis did so, and ended by telling Stekel the story of the woman in the theatre. Stekel was delighted: he told Kazantzakis that he was suffering from 'saint's disease', a malady common in the Middle Ages, but almost totally unknown today. When the desert ascetics of the Middle Ages could no longer resist the temptations of sex, and set out for the cities, very often their bodies would break out in horrible running sores, their faces become bloated, and a yellow liquid would drop from the sores. Thus was the subconscious resisting sin (which the saints supposed to be a punishment from God). Kazantzakis had also been obsessed for years by the ideal of total asceticism, and had left his wife for this reason. As soon as he left Vienna, the sores disappeared.

The anecdote reveals a great deal about Kazantzakis, his strength and his weakness, and the impression is verified by his works. In the primitive simplicity of his approach to life and 'salvation', he was not a man of our time. Photographs show a heavily built man with a Nietzschean moustache and sensuous lips. He fought tremendous battles with himself, but one cannot help feeling that he was like an impatient man trying to open a door the wrong way under the impression that it is jammed. All his work creates an impression of seething, violent torment; and yet one wonders whether he was not doing things the hard way out of ignorance. He was a non-stop traveller, rushing from one end of the world to the other as if possessed. In the same way, he was a non-stop 'mental traveller' (and the violent and bloody images of Blake's poem of that title fit in singularly well with the whole mood of Kazantzakis). From German romanticism, through Christian asceticism (he spent six months in a monastery, trying to see 'the vision of God', but gave it up), through Buddhism and communism, to the final phase (which lasted a quarter of a century) of great artistic creation, with such works as his *Odyssey* (a seven-hundred-page epic poem), *Zorba the Greek, Christ Recrucified, Freedom and Death* and *The Last Temptation*.

Shortly after the Vienna phase of 1922, Kazantzakis went to Berlin, where he wrote a 'credo' called *The Saviours of God* (subtitled *Ascetic Exercises*), and fell in with a group of young Communists. He studied Lenin, and conceived a great admiration for his personality; typically, this was his way of becoming a Communist. Later, he attended a cultural congress in Moscow, and then journeyed from end to end of the Soviet Union on a free railway ticket provided by the Communists. But in his usual protean way, he was outgrowing Lenin as his ideal figure. His basic philosophy was always closer to Gide's: the necessity of never being attached to any external 'truths', of continually contradicting oneself and returning over one's tracks. Although this philosophy never led Kazantzakis to the same lengths of weakness and fickleness for its own sake as with Gide, it produced a certain inner confusion in his greatest work.

Having abandoned Nietzsche, Christ, St Francis, Gautama and Lenin, Kazantzakis now turned to Odysseus, and began the epic poem in which Odysseus leaves Ithaca for the second time and goes in search of 'God', or a meaning for human existence. Like all books about men who travel in search of meaning – Hesse's novels, for example – his *Odyssey, A Modern Sequel*, is ultimately unsatisfactory. But its sheer creative greatness cannot be denied. The goal may be a failure, but the journey is probably the greatest in modern literature.

It is impossible to offer an adequate summary of the poem here. (There is an excellent book about it by the author's friend Prevelakis, *Kazantzakis and His Odyssey*, which has been published in America and which, one hopes, will be published eventually in England.) It begins when Odysseus sheaths his sword after killing the suitors.

He finds life in Ithaca a bore, and decides to set out again on his travels. He renounces human happiness, in the form of Nausicaa, marries her to his son Telemachus, and then leaves Ithaca for the last time. He takes five companions, selecting them for their different qualities. He sails to Sparta and steals Helen of Troy again from Menelaus; the violation of hospitality (which involves killing a guard) symbolises his Nietzschean rejection of 'morality'. In Crete (the home of Kazantzakis) he takes part in a sexual orgy, and ends by setting fire to the palace. He deserts Helen and goes on to Egypt. There he takes part in a workers' revolt, and comes close to being executed. He dances in front of the king in a horrifying god-mask. Pharaoh sets him free. He decides to found the ideal city-state at the source of the Nile. After battles with a Negro tribe, he has a vision of God on a mountain, and then builds the Ideal City. It is barely completed when an earthquake destroys it. Odysseus experiences total despair at the destruction of all his companions, but now feels that he is fully aware of the illusory nature of the world. He rejects the temptation to suicide and travels on. In subsequent books he meets figures who are thinly disguised versions of Gautama, Don Quixote and Christ. In Don Quixote he 'salutes a madness equal to my own', but rejects his vision, as he has rejected Gautama's. Odysseus is ultimately the life-affirmer, the lover of the earth. He makes his final voyage towards the South Pole in a boat, and the last three books are occupied with a description of this voyage, ending with an impressive evocation of the snowy wastes (for which Kazantzakis drew on his memories of Russia's tundra regions). Odysseus climbs onto an iceberg, where the spirits of his old companions join him and he finally dies. The ending is as noisy as the end of a Wagner opera and as rhetorical as the last scene of *Faust* but it does not give one the impression that Odysseus has found what he set out to find.

Such a summary can do no justice to the poem (which has been superbly translated into English by Kimon Friar), but it may give some idea of the sheer excitement of its wide sweep. It produces the 'effect like music' that someone once described as the effect of *War and Peace*.

The *Odyssey* is Kazantzakis' most important work; eventually, his reputation must stand or fall by it. It is hard to believe that such a work could be written in the twentieth century, when Eliot has talked so convincingly about the difficulty of finding an 'objective correlative' for the artist. Kazantzakis has ignored all the objections – particularly the objection that he comes too long after Homer, and that he is a member of a self-divided, analytical culture, and therefore *cannot* write a convincing epic.

The lesson is an interesting one. So many modern writers declare that their honesty compels them to write about defeat and futility, and to focus their attention on a pool of tea on a tabletop. 'Modern life being what it is . . .' Kazantzakis makes one aware that it is not a question of modern life, but of the artist himself.

The *Odyssey* was written seven times between 1924 and Christmas 1938, when it finally appeared in Greece in a limited edition. The critics were puzzled. The poem is immense – 33,333 lines long. The spelling was peculiar – Kazantzakis was like Shaw in his desire for a reform of the alphabet, and dispensed with most of the Greek accentuation. The seventeen-syllable lines were not easy to grasp on a first reading. It would be near the truth to say that the poem was a flop. (Kazantzakis was already known as a poet for his translations of *The Divine Comedy* and *Faust*.) Undismayed, Kazantzakis went on to write his series of great novels. *Captain Michalis* (translated as *Freedom and Death* in England and *Freedom or Death* in the US) was begun in 1936, *Zorba the Greek* was written in 1942, *Christ Recrucified* in 1948, *The Last Temptation* in 1951, and *The Poor Man of God* in 1953. There is also an unpublished novel with the curious title: *He says he wants freedom, kill him*, and an early novel about Russia, *Toda Raba*. The 'ascetic exercises', *The Saviours of God*, are also of considerable importance.

It is possible to offer only the briefest comments on these works in the present essay. *Captain Michalis* is important to a full understanding of Kazantzakis. Its original title was *My Father*, and it deals with the unsuccessful rebellion of the Cretans against the Turks in 1889. Kazantzakis was old enough to remember this clearly, as well as the rebellion of 1896, when the Turks were finally expelled. Crete had been oppressed by the Turks for a hundred years, and there had been many bloody uprisings and endless violence. On one occasion, a monastery was besieged by Turks; as they rushed into the courtyard, a young fighter fired his rifle into the open powder barrels in the basement. Six hundred women and children were hiding there. The monastery and everyone in it were blown to atoms. In these risings, both sides were completely merciless; women would be raped and murdered, children bayoneted, the men often tortured to death.

The novel is a huge, leisurely affair that reminds one sometimes of *War and Peace*, sometimes of Dylan Thomas's *Under Milk Wood* in its detailed and amusing descriptions of the private lives of the people of Megalocastro. Its hero is the 'wild beast' Captain Michalis. (Kazantzakis' father was also Captain Michalis, and was also known as 'the wild beast'). He is a typical Kazantzakis figure, of immense physical strength, taciturn, brooding, completely brave. He is obsessed by a beautiful Circassian girl, the wife of his blood-brother Nuri Bey, a Turk; but, being a self-divided man, he never gets around to sleeping with her, although she would be happy enough. The novel is full of sex and slaughter; it would be very easy to parody it in the manner of *Cold Comfort Farm*, with its strong, silent men and sensual women. But one only has to read fifty pages of it to realise that, whatever Kazantzakis' faults as a man (or 'outsider'), he was the greatest European artist since Tolstoy. But in one respect he falls below Tolstoy. He never seems to question whether all this slaughter is worthwhile, or whether his heroic men are only hotheaded fools. His power as a writer is so great that the reader is not aware of this while he actually reads the book. But at the end, when Michalis and his followers allow themselves to be slaughtered merely because they are too proud to surrender, one feels that there was something seriously lacking in Kazantzakis if he did not feel the futility of the whole thing. Shaw said: 'When the shooting starts, I get under the bed'; one wishes Kazantzakis' heroes had half as much sense.

This brings up another point about Kazantzakis. He was all his life ashamed of being a 'pen-pusher', and hankered after the life of action. This again reveals a curious immaturity. In the novel, Michalis's nephew is also a poet and a 'pen-pusher' who lives abroad; he returns to Crete at the end of the novel, and dies with his uncle in the final stupid act of resistance. One suspects that Kazantzakis saw himself as the nephew, and was somehow trying to propitiate his father's ghost.

This same self-division is apparent in the other novels, *Zorba the Greek* is the most amusing of these. It is told in the first person by Kazantzakis, who meets Zorba in a waterfront café in Piraeus, and agrees to take him to Crete. Most of the book is taken up with the adventures of Zorba, a kind of lesser Ulysses, healthy, happy, roguish, loving women, wine and food, completely lacking in self-division, while Kazantzakis struggles with an epic about the Buddha and renunciation. Again Kazantzakis reveals a kind of naïveté, like Whitman's praise of the placidness of cows. He is the unhappy intellectual, who never makes the effort to heal his own self-division and becomes reconciled to the 'original sin' that makes him at once greater and less happy than Zorba. In *Man and Superman*, Shaw makes Don Juan say: 'Were I not possessed with a purpose beyond my own, I had better be a ploughman than a philosopher; for the ploughman lives as long as the philosopher, eats more, sleeps better, and rejoices in the wife of his bosom with less misgiving,' But Shaw had no secret longing to be a ploughman, and the 'purpose: is stated explicitly in the third act of *Man and Superman*. Kazantzakis never reached this stage, although he declared (in *The Saviours of God*) that 'God' is saved by the men who dare to be creative, and wrote in a letter: 'If we are to set a purpose, it is this: to transubstantiate matter and turn it into spirit.' This is certainly Shaw's conception. But there was also a streak of Nietzsche in Kazantzakis. Just as Nietzsche could create his conception of the Superman, and then invalidate it by 'Eternal recurrence', so Kazantzakis expresses his gospel of struggle and creation in *The Saviours of God*, but ends: 'Blessed are all those who free you and become united with you, Lord, and who say: "You and I are one." And thrice blessed be those who bear on their shoulders and do not bend under this great, sublime and terrifying secret: *That even this one does not exist.*' There can hardly be a better example in all philosophy of what the logical positivists call 'nonsense', a statement that invalidates itself by destroying its own meaning.

There is this taint of nonsense about all Kazantzakis'

work; but he is far too big and impressive to be invalidated by it. To some extent, one suspects, he creates his own strife out of a perverse love of strife. But then, the same might be said of Dostoevsky. The 'Outsider' easily becomes the neurotic; the self-disciplinarian easily becomes the masochist. Kazantzakis' dissatisfaction was partly frustrated Messianism and partly ordinary 'itchy feet', a lack of self-discipline.

The Messianism appears strongly in the later novels. *Christ Recrucified* tells how Manolias, a timid young man, is chosen to play Christ in a Passion play. He wants to avoid the burden; but, having accepted it, he becomes steadily more Christlike. Crowds of dispossessed Greeks come to live outside the village, and the villagers hate them. The boy Manolias takes their part. Eventually, Manolias is ritually murdered by his own villagers. The 'dispossessed' villagers have to move on. Manolias is Kazantzakis' version of Prince Myskin. Kazantzakis works out his parallel with Christ in some detail, the Turkish Aga being Pilate, the village 'pope' Caiaphas, and so on. Again, the power of the book lies in the breadth of its canvas, its hundreds of living characters. It caused Kazantzakis some trouble; the Greek Church wanted to excommunicate him. When he died, the Greek archbishop refused to allow his body to lie in a church. He was later given a hero's burial in Crete (although he had irritated the Cretans with *Captain Michalis* which was regarded as a libel on the Cretan character).

Having got into trouble with *Christ Recrucified*, Kazantzakis repeated the offence with *The Last Temptation*, this being an immense novel on the life of Christ. Unlike other novelists who have dealt with Jesus, Kazantzakis was not intent on creating a sinless god-man. He wanted to create Christ in his own image – tormented by everlasting temptation, a Promethean Jesus, learning, step by step, to cast off the fetters of the family, the body, the ego. On the Cross, the devil sends him a final temptation: he imagines that he had chosen the easier road of men, had become a respected and happy old man, with his family about him. He thrusts aside this temptation to approve the human road, and dies with the sense that he has accomplished his mission, taught men that there are greater values than mere 'living'. The novel is an amazing achievement, simply as a piece of historical recreation. Whether Kazantzakis' Christ is convincing is another matter. He is rather like Frank Harris's Jesus – a wish-fulfilment aspect of his creator. Kazantzakis wanted to convince himself that all his own sufferings and temptations had somehow been justified; he may have suspected that, after all, he had made rather heavy weather of being a Promethean god-man, had flagellated himself a little too vigorously. Perhaps his master, Nietzsche, might have dismissed him as another conscience-ridden self-torturer who needed some of Zarathustra's lightness of spirit. One is too aware that his Jesus is a piece of self-defence, an apologia. To be convinced by this Jesus would be to regard Kazantzakis himself as a kind of superman.[1]

Perhaps the nearest literary relative of Kazantzakis in English-speaking countries is, surprisingly enough, W. B. Yeats. Yeats had the same admiration of the 'pen-pusher' for men of action, the same mystique of the wanderer, the same self-division, the same obsession with 'fire and blood' and sex. Yeats also had this idea of the man of genius as a self-consuming flame, and the longing for a mystic vision that would destroy the hunger of the flesh. And Yeats, like Kazantzakis, was no thinker; he expended enormous efforts on feeling at home in the 'realms of intellect', but was never at home there. Kazantzakis had studied under Bergson, but his novels are novels of passion and sensuality, with none of the Dostoevskian dialectic that one might expect from the author of The Saviours of God.

In the years before his death, recognition had begun to come to Kazantzakis. His books were translated into many languages, but were not widely read (although Captain Michalis became something of a best-seller in Holland). Schweitzer, Thomas Mann and Camus hailed him as one of the greatest European writers. In 1952, he narrowly missed the Nobel Prize (which, for some reason, he lost by one vote – a matter reflecting great discredit on the Nobel Prize committee). In 1953 he contracted leukemia, and dictated parts of his St Francis novel when in great suffering. In 1956, he was awarded the Soviet Peace Prize (although most of his books were banned in Russia, and he had never been a Communist). It was his incorrigible need to travel that finally brought about his death at seventy-four. He accepted an invitation to visit China, and was given a smallpox vaccination in Canton, with fatal results. He died in Germany (where Schweitzer came to visit him in the hospital).

The final criticism against Kazantzakis is his defeatism, a kind of ultimate nihilism, 'What Purpose?' he asks, in a letter. 'What do we care? Don't ask, fight on! Let us set ourselves a purpose . . .' 'We must conquer the last, the greatest of temptations – that of hope.' 'We sing even though we know that no ear exists to hear us; we toil though there is no employer to pay us our wages when night falls. We are despairing, serene and free. This is true heroism . . .' At the end of the *Odyssey*, Ulysses' mind makes a last leap from 'its last cage, that of freedom'. Kazantzakis is a nineteenth-century figure, the religious philosopher crucified on the cross of metaphysics. On Kazantzakis' tomb in Crete are engraved the typical words: 'I do not hope for anything. I do not fear anything. I am free.' It is significant that his epitaph should be a Buddhistic expression of nihilism.

NOTE

1. At the time of writing (1961), Kazantzakis' last novel, *The Poor Man of God*, dealing with St Francis of Assisi, has still not been published in English. Kazantzakis had been fascinated by St Francis since the 1920's, when he spent many months in Assisi, following the steps of St Francis.

Appendix Three

Friedrich Dürrenmatt
Heir of the Existential Tradition

Although two of his plays have been performed and two of his novels published in England, the name Friedrich Dürrenmatt is still unfamiliar to many cultured people in this country. This is a pity, for I suspect Dürrenmatt may one day be regarded as the most important writer at present working on the continent of Europe. My estimate of him is based upon nine works that have been translated into English: four novels, four plays, and a short story published by the *London Magazine*. On the evidence of the story, 'The Tunnel', one might assume that Dürrenmatt is merely a late disciple of Kafka. His other works soon dispel that impression. Of the plays,[1] *The Old Lady's Visit* is a macabre fantasy, full of Gogolian humour; *The Marriage of Mr Mississippi* utilises the techniques of Pirandello, yet sounds a distinctly Shavian note; *An Angel Comes to Babylon* is a delightful satirical pantomime that brings to mind the early pages of Flecker's *Hassan*; only his comedy *Romulus the Great* is tedious, an extended joke like those unutterably bad humorous stories of Poe. The novella *Traps* is reminiscent of Mann, Dickens and Kafka. The novel *The Pledge* is a powerful and realistic story of a sexual killer; it would have filled Frank Wedekind with admiration. *Suspicion* and *The Judge and His Hangman* are detective novels with no deep overtones.

Because these works are hardly known in England, I propose to give a short sketch of each before I speak more generally of Dürrenmatt's relation to the tradition of existential writing that extends from Goethe to Sartre.

Begin with 'The Tunnel' (*London Magazine*, June 1959). I would judge this to be an early work, influenced by Kafka. It is about a fat young student who is travelling by train to the university, two hours away. The train enters a tunnel he does not remember, which goes on and on. He begins to worry, but no one else seems to be bothered. He consults the guard, and they make their way to the driver's cabin, to find that it is empty. The train is now plunging down a slope. The guard tries to return to the main part of the train, but this is impossible, since the train is now falling almost vertically. The guard asks the student what they should do. 'Nothing,' the student replies. 'God let us fall, so we are rushing down towards him.'

The meaning of the story becomes clearer when one considers its imagery. The young man always wears two pairs of glasses (one of them dark) and has cotton wool stuffed into his ears 'so that the horror behind the scenes should not come up too close to him'. He has deliberately made himself blind and deaf to avoid facing the fundamental horror of existence. And yet at the end of the story, it is he and not the guard who can face the oncoming catastrophe with resignation and a kind of faith. He views the abyss with eyes 'that were now for the first time opened wide'. He replies to the guard with a 'grim cheerfulness'. He has become strong. The parable is less pessimistic than Kafka; Dürrenmatt recommends facing 'the horror behind the scenes' but also preserving a faith in God. It is not unlike the position of Eliot in *Ash-Wednesday*.

It would not be true, on the evidence of his fiction, to say that Dürrenmatt is a religious writer, although he is obviously more so than Sartre or Camus. But in everything he has written, one is aware of revolt against the makeshift standards of the modern world. His attitude might be intellectual. There is heaven as well as hell, but since it requires a long discipline to become aware of heaven, I am not going to bother you with it. Instead, consider the following . . . In this respect, Dürrenmatt might be compared to Graham Greene, but with the important difference that Greene has no visionary faculty whatever; in him, the necessity for heaven is demonstrated in an abstract kind of way by overwhelming his readers with the hell of human existence. In Dürrenmatt, no matter how pessimistic he seems to be, one never ceases to be aware of his underlying joy in being alive. (He makes a very welcome change from such existentialists as M. Sartre.)

The Old Lady's Visit is Dürrenmatt's best-known work in England to date. (The Lunts made her an attractive middle-aged lady, and so changed the title to *The Visit* to serve as a vehicle for Lynn Fontanne). Claire Zachanassian, a multi-billionairess, is returning to her native town of Güllen. Since she left it as a young woman, Güllen has ceased to be prosperous; now it badly needs the old lady's bounty. A man who is known to have been her lover, Anton Schill, is among the crowd who wait for her at the station; he has been promised the post of mayor of Güllen in exchange for his anticipated help. Claire arrives, an imperious old lady who is carried everywhere in a sedan chair by two bruisers whom she saved from the electric chair. She is accompanied by her future husband, two blind men and a black panther. (In the days when she and Schill were lovers, she called him 'Black Panther'.). Claire is perfectly willing to make the town rich again, but in exchange she wants the life of Anton Schill, her lover who betrayed her. The two blind men were the witnesses whom Schill had once bribed to swear that they had slept with Claire (and that her baby was not Schill's). Claire has hunted them and had them blinded; they are now her servants.

The townspeople naturally reject her offer; but soon Schill notices that everyone is buying expensive goods on credit in anticipation of wealth. The black panther escapes, and everyone hunts it with guns. This symbolism is not lost on Schill, who tries to leave the town by train but is prevented by the crowds. Finally, like the boxer in Hemingway's 'Killers', he knows it is no use running away. At a meeting in the town hall, he consents to his own death; the townspeople close round him.. When they draw back again, he is dead.

The play is a dramatic *tour de force*, but it is hard at present to feel that it plays any central role in Dürrenmatt's Weltanschauung. Its central feeling, as usual, is for a world without values, and for the way in which the world allows a drama of betrayal and revenge to take the place of values. Schill's betrayal of Claire was sordid and immoral, and yet Schill can become a prominent citizen when Claire has been driven to a Hamburg brothel. It was Claire who ruined the town by buying up its factories and then closing them. When she makes her offer of a billion marks, the townspeople justify the murder they contemplate by recalling the betrayal they condoned and deciding that the murder is 'justice'. Moreover, Claire tells Schill at one point that she still loves him, but that she must have his

233

body buried in her garden; her love has become poisonous and morbid. The play is about the betrayal of values, about lack of will and the human tendency to drift. The towns-people do not dare to leap into the immorality of murdering Schill, but they allow themselves to drift into it; in this way, they preserve their illusion of moral values.

The Marriage of Mr Mississippi is another *tour de force*, more experimental in technique than *The Visit*. It is in some ways a confused and confusing play, but there can be no doubt about its artistic power. Florestan Mississippi is public prosecutor in a mythical mid-European country. He is a Calvinistic Bible student whose dream is to restore the Mosaic code to a world without values. He even believes that adultery should be punished by killing the two parties to it. In the opening scene, he visits Olympia, whose husband has recently died, and reveals that he is aware that Olympia has murdered her husband with a poison that resembles lumps of sugar. Olympia defends herself by saying that her husband was unfaithful to her and she loved him. Mississippi then reveals that the partner in the adultery was his own wife, and that he has 'executed' her by dropping the poison lumps into her coffee. He proposes that he and Olympia should marry to 'expiate' their crime, and she finally agrees. The rest of the plot is too complicated to detail here. It ends, like *Hamlet*, with everyone dead on stage; but it is Mississippi, with his simple-minded notion of Mosaic law, who is most completely betrayed. The play is like Pirandello's in technique. Characters often address the audience; the end takes place before the beginning and is repeated again at the end; stage instructions are chatty and informal; some characters discuss the author of the play with the audience. One of them even explains that the author wanted to treat the problem of 'whether the human mind is able to alter a world which *merely exists*'; but, as with Pirandello, the characters got out of hand once they were created. The play seems to contrast the grotesque complexity of the world with Mississippi's single-minded desire for order and morality; it seems to be saying, 'Order and morality are the total meaning that *may* emerge from the totality of experience; it cannot be imposed'. It may be noted in passing that there is some satire on communism in the play, as elsewhere in Dürrenmatt, but the satire is good-natured, in the manner of *Animal Farm*.

I shall deal with the other two plays very briefly. (Dürrenmatt has written seven so far, but I have not read the other three.) *Romulus the Great* is a not-very-funny comedy in the manner of Offenbach (*La Belle Hélène, Orpheus*, etc), poking fun at antiquity. Romulus is the last of the Roman emperors, very broke and rather bored by it all. As the barbarians (Germans) advance on Rome he refuses to do anything about it all. He admits that he had done nothing to save Rome, but denies that he has betrayed Rome. 'Rome has betrayed itself. It knew the truth but chose force; knew humanity but chose tyranny.' But for all his 'incompetence' he is the one who survives best; he gets on excellently with the enemy general, Odo, and is given a house and a pension. Romulus brings to mind Shaw's King Charles, but the play suffers by comparison with Shaw.

An Angel Comes to Babylon is in every way delightful, a fantastic romp with serious overtones. The Angel is instructed to give the beautiful girl Kurrubi to the poorest man on earth. She falls in love with King Nebuchadnezzar who is posing as a beggar. The king is trying to run his empire as a Communist-type welfare state, and has forbidden mendicancy. The comic hero of the play is the beggar Akki, for whom begging is a kind of religion; he throws the gold he begs into the river. At the end of the play, as he and the girl leave Babylon behind them, he states Dürrenmatt's credo: 'I love an earth that exists in spite of everything, a beggar's earth, unique in its happiness ... An earth that I subdue over and over again, intoxicated with its beauty, in love with its image.' One of the apparently insignificant and yet central figures in the play is the Angel who delivers the girl to earth. He is a comic figure, deceived by the king, a conventional absentminded professor. And yet, like Rilke's Angel, he is pure affirmation. He is delighted with the earth and can see nothing wrong with it. He tells the girl that all apparent disorders are only temporary errors in the divine order. He spends most of the play flying round the earth to examine its wonders, reappearing at intervals full of enthusiasm, wholly unable to understand the trivialities that human beings consider as sufferings. He is the symbol of the

235

Nietzschean order of reality and affirmation, beyond good and evil, beyond the indignity of suffering. 'Heaven never lies, my child. Only sometimes it finds it difficult to make itself understood by humans.' And when Kurrubi comments that the poorest beggar on earth must be unhappy, the Angel replies: 'All that is created is good, and all that is good, is happy. In all my travels throughout creation, I have never encountered as much as one grain of unhappiness.' This is a Shavian conception: when men cease to be so trivial and self-preoccupied, they will also cease to suffer.

The most remarkable thing about *An Angel Comes to Babylon* is its breadth and good humour. From the author of 'The Tunnel', it is an amazing work. Here is a man who would only chuckle satirically at Sartre's comment that the reality of life is horror. The spirit might almost be called Chestertonian. And yet Dürrenmatt proves again and again that he possesses to the full the 'terrible insight' of the most pessimistic of existentialists.

This is proved in what I consider to be Dürrenmatt's two most clear and powerful works so far: the novels *The Pledge* and *Traps*. (The other novels, *The Judge and His Hangman* and *Suspicion*, are simply thrillers with philosophical overtones.)

Traps is a mere eighty pages long. It tells how a little commercial traveller, Alfred Traps, has a breakdown on the road and has to stay in a small village overnight. A retired judge offers to put him up. Traps is given an excellent supper, and introduced to three more very old men, a retired hangman and two retired barristers. The four old man are in the habit of playing a game over their epicurean suppers; they have mock trials at which the judge presides, and the two counsels defend and prosecute any guest who can be persuaded to play. The hangman is there purely for effect. Traps agrees to play. But he persists in saying that he has no crime to confess to. (This sounds like Kafka, but the resemblance is only superficial.) So, over a huge meal, with many different wines, they proceed to cross-examine him. He admits that his former boss has died of heart disease, and that he, Traps, has taken his place. The lawyers scent a crime: did Traps not murder his boss, Gygax? No, Traps says, although it is true he wanted to get rid of him. Business is business, and dog eats dog. Finally, he is made to admit that he seduced Gygax's wife, and that when Gygax found out, he had heart failure. But how did Gygax find out? Traps arranged for him to be told, knowing that heart failure would probably be the result.

The lawyers are delighted. Here is a perfect murder! The prosecuting counsel makes a powerful speech in which Traps is depicted as the most Machiavellian criminal of the twentieth century. Traps blushes with pleasure. Then the defence counsel rises. To talk of crime is nonsense, he says. As his client has pointed out, business is business. Traps is no criminal, but an ordinary little man, ambitious, home-loving, not very clever. His worst sins are his infidelities to his wife, but what commercial traveller does not commit these? In fact, our human lives are confused and makeshift; we have to invent our morality as we go along. Traps may have been indirectly responsible for the death of Gygax; but this is a world dominated by chance, and cause and effect are very seldom calculated. Traps is no master criminal; like the rest of us, he has small virtues and petty vices; nothing as romantic as the prosecuting counsel suggests.

This speech infuriates Traps. It is not true, he shouts; he *is* a master criminal. He demands to be sentenced to death. So the judge obligingly sentences him, and the party breaks up in good humour, with everyone on the best of terms. Traps then goes to his bedroom and hangs himself. When the judge finds him, he cries with anguish: 'Alfred . . . you've ruined the best evening we've ever had!'

Here the meaning is very plain. Traps lives the same pointless, futile life as the rest of us. Suddenly he sees himself as a superhuman criminal – not a man whose life is dominated by chance, but one who has guided himself step by step with immense certainty. He prefers this new vision of himself; it frees him from his futility. He is like a lunatic who wants to believe he is Napoleon or Christ. And if believing this involves carrying out on himself the sentence of death, then he prefers to die.

At this point, I wish to abandon for a moment the role of literary expositor and say that the ending of this book strikes me as somehow all wrong. It is contrived, unlike the rest of the tale, which seems realistic enough. In fact, the logical conclusion would surely be that Traps would demand that the retired hangman should execute him. The others would naturally refuse, because it would spoil the game. And Traps would stagger drunkenly off to bed with a deep sense of grievance; there is no justice in the world. Such an ending would surely have made Dürrenmatt's point as clearly as the more 'dramatic' but more contrived suicide. One feels that Dürrenmatt has allowed a stagy sense of drama to dominate the ending instead of the sense of reality that appears so brilliantly throughout the story.

This cannot be said of *The Pledge*, the work that succeeds in suggesting the deepest implications of Dürrenmatt's 'philosophy'. Matthäi is a police officer in Switzerland who has always been known for his mechanical precision. But he is not well liked. He is offered promotion to the police force in Jordan. Just before he goes, a small girl is murdered by a sex maniac. He promises the parents of the child – Grittli Moser – that he will avenge her death. An old peddler is suspected. The police grill him until he confesses. He commits suicide in his cell. But Matthäi is convinced that the peddler was not the killer, and he sets out to investigate the murder himself. His fellow policemen naturally dislike this interference; the case is closed, and Matthäi is due in Jordan. Mattäi decides not to go to Jordan; he will stay and continue to investigate the murder as a private citizen.

He finds a few clues that indicate that the murderer is a big man who drives an American car with the sign of the Swiss cantons on the number plate – an ibex. By now, the case has become Matthäi's obsession. He buys a garage near a main road, and persuades a prostitute to become his housekeeper. The prostitute has a small daughter who looks very much like Grittli Moser – and like two other girls who have been murdered in recent years. The prostitute, of course, is unaware that her daughter is being used as bait for a sex maniac with a razor.

Finally, Matthäi phones the police in excitement; the child Annemarie is seeing a stranger who gives her chocolate truffles. Matthäi is convinced that this is the killer. All the police have to do is lie in wait near the child. They do this, as the child waits unsuspectingly in the woods. But the murderer never comes. The prostitute goes on working for Matthäi, becoming more and more sluttish. Her daughter Annemarie grows up, she too becomes a slut. And Matthäi, going on waiting for the killer beside his gasoline pump, becomes a hopeless drunk.

The police officer who is telling the story to Dürrenmatt finally stumbled on its conclusion. An old lady, dying in a hospital, confessed that she knew the killer. He was a boy, many years her junior, whom she had married. He was on his way to murder his fourth victim, Annemarie, when he was killed in a car by an accident. This is a problem in ends and means. Matthäi was right. If it had not been for the accident, the killer *would* have been caught in the woods. As the police officer points out, Matthäi was the 'genius type'. He had a 'hunch' and he played it. If Hollywood had made a film of his story, the murderer *would* have been caught just as he was about to attack the girl, and it would have been assumed that Matthäi's triumph had justified the means – his use of Annemarie as bait. (Ironically enough, a film *has* been made of the book, and the ending *has* been changed to a spectacular capture of the murderer in the woods.)

Dürrenmatt's ending leaves the problem naked. And it also reveals a profound and typical aspect of human psychology. We are inclined to accept the ending as the meaning of a story. Our lives may be messy and imperfect and meaningless, but we refuse to accept this, and prefer to see films or read books that give an illusion of 'meaning' by ending neatly. This is why we so admire artists who die young, from Keats and Shelley to Rudolph Valentino and James Dean. Their death gives an impression of a life neatly rounded off, like the happy ending of a romantic novel.

The Pledge, like all Dürrenmatt's work, is a demand to face the disorder of our lives, an attack on specious oversimplification, on 'bad faith'. He is writing about the same subjects as Sartre and Camus, but writing of them instinctively, without an intellectual superstructure. In my own book *The Age of Defeat*, I analysed the work of Sartre and Camus and commented on the extraordinary penetration of their intellectual assessment of our disorder, while finding their pessimism wholly depressing and unsatisfactory. Dürrenmatt, it seems to me, has already found a way out of the impasse of Sartre and Camus. He uses all the

239

traditional analyses of existentialism, the concepts of inauthentic existence, human self-deception, etc., yet with the instinctive, mystical optimism of Shaw or Chesterton. If he continues as he has begun, he might, it seems to me, become one of the major figures of twentieth-century writing, an artist who unites in his person some of the greatest currents of his time.

At the time of writing, Dürrenmatt is thirty-nine years old – an age at which Shaw had written only the earliest of his plays. Dürrenmatt is the son of a Swiss pastor, who apparently studied philosophy and theology at Basle and Zurich; he lives at Neuchâtel, and has three children. In *Mr Mississippi*, he describes himself jokingly as 'this pen-pushing Protestant, this strayed visionary, this lover of gruesome fables . . .' I do not know how far Dürrenmatt regards himself as a member of the Protestant Church, but the rest of the description strikes me as wholly apt and accurate.

NOTE

1. I wish to thank Jonathan Cape, the publishers of Dürrenmatt, for allowing me to see four unpublished plays in manuscript.

INDEX

243

245

259

SUPERPSYCH

TIMOTHY HALL AND GUY GRANT

HYPNOSIS – SCIENCE OR MAGIC?

Since time immemorial, Man has believed that it is possible to create a state of mind in which thought and behaviour can be controlled by others. Lacking scientific understanding, he attributed this power to magic or the supernatural: he thought himself bewitched, entranced, mesmerised or, more recently, hypnotised. In the fourth and fifth centuries BC, we have evidence that Greek, Egyptian and Roman cultures were familiar with, and made use of, the practice. But the advent of Christianity tolled the death knell for hypnosis, which was branded 'the work of the devil'.

Although the practice had its proponents – notably Mesmer and Freud – throughout the eighteenth and nineteenth centuries, it wasn't until after World War II that it finally achieved respectability.

This book is the first comprehensive analysis of the fascinating subject of hypnosis: its history, its techniques, its uses. And at last we break away from the superstition and mumbo-jumbo that have surrounded it for so long.

0 349 11626 1   £1.50

SOCIOLOGY/PSYCHOLOGY

A selection of Bestsellers from Sphere Books

TEMPLE DOGS	Robert L. Duncan	95p	☐
THE PASSAGE	Bruce Nicolayson	95p	☐
CHARLIE IS MY DARLING	Mollie Hardwick	£1.25p	☐
RAISE THE TITANIC!	Clive Cussler	95p	☐
KRAMER'S WAR	Derek Robinson	£1.25p	☐
THE CRASH OF '79	Paul Erdman	£1.25p	☐
EMMA AND I	Sheila Hocken	85p	☐
UNTIL THE COLOURS FADE	Tim Jeal	£1.50p	☐
DR. JOLLY'S BOOK OF CHILDCARE			
	Dr. Hugh Jolly	£1.95p	☐
MAJESTY	Robert Lacey	£1.50p	☐
STAR WARS	George Lucas	95p	☐
FALSTAFF	Robert Nye	£1.50p	☐
EXIT SHERLOCK HOLMES	Robert Lee Hall	95p	☐
THE MITTENWALD SYNDICATE			
	Frederick Nolan	95p	☐
CLOSE ENCOUNTERS OF THE THIRD KIND			
	Steven Spielberg	85p	☐
STAR FIRE	Ingo Swann	£1.25p	☐
RUIN FROM THE AIR			
	Gordon Thomas & Max Morgan Witts	£1.50p	☐
EBANO (Now filmed as ASHANTI)			
	Alberto Vazquez-Figueroa	95p	☐
FIREFOX	Craig Thomas	95p	☐

All Sphere books are available at your local bookshop or newsagent, or can be ordered direct from the publisher. Just tick the titles you want and fill in the form below.

Name..

Address...

....

Write to Sphere Books, Cash Sales Department, P.O. Box 11, Falmouth, Cornwall TR10 9EN

Please enclose cheque or postal order to the value of the cover price plus:

UK: 22p for the first book plus 10p per copy for each additional book ordered to a maximum charge of 82p

OVERSEAS: 30p for the first book and 10p for each additional book

BFPO & EIRE: 22p for the first book plus 10p per copy for the next 6 books, thereafter 4p per book

Sphere Books reserve the right to show new retail prices on covers which may differ from those previously advertised in the text or elsewhere, and to increase postal rates in accordance with the GPO.

(12:78)